I CAN'T BELIEVE SHE DID THAT!

I CAN'T
BELIEVE
SHE DID THAT!

WHY WOMEN BETRAY
OTHER WOMEN AT WORK

Nan Mooney

ST. MARTIN'S PRESS ✖ NEW YORK

www.stmartins.com

Library of Congress Cataloging-in-Publication Data

Mooney, Nan, 1970–
    I can't believe she did that! : why women betray other women at work / Nan Mooney.—1st ed.
        p.   cm.
    ISBN 0-312-32206-2
    EAN 978-0-312-32206-9
    1. Women—Employment—United States.   2. Office politics—United States.   3. Interpersonal conflict—United States.   4. Competition (Psychology).   I. Title.

HD6058.M58   2005
158.2'6'082—dc22

                                                    2005047707

First Edition: October 2005

10 9 8 7 6 5 4 3 2 1

Contents

Acknowledgments

This book came to fruition because of the many women who were generous enough to share their time, stories, and insights. My deepest gratitude to all those I interviewed. Thanks also to the many more who informally shared their experiences. Throughout this project I found myself continually amazed by what all of you have accomplished. Your generosity cannot be repaid, all the more so because you didn't expect that it would be.

Thank you to Diane Reverand, who has stuck with me through race horses and office politics and who has consistently provided the sort of careful and caring editorial treatment that's rarer with each passing day. Thanks to Regina Scarpa for fielding questions and schedules and messenger mix-ups and occasionally staying at her desk far too late on my behalf.

A number of people read drafts of the book and provided valuable feedback along the way: Heather Boushey, Claudia Citkovitz, John Radanovich, Rachelle Sussman. Their input was crucial to its development. Special, special (and one more special) thanks to Martha Brockenbrough not only for her reading savvy but also her Web site skills, title savvy, marketing genius, and overall capacity to be an endlessly loyal and giving friend.

To the many others, too many to mention, who have helped me keep mind, body, and soul (reasonably) intact during the creation of this book, thank you and thank God for you.

Thank you, as always, to my parents for their support and for never once asking when I'm going to settle down and get myself a real job.

Finally, gratitude beyond measure goes to my agent and polestar, Tanya McKinnon. I would not be able to write any books without someone in my corner who understands that there are so many things in life that mean so very much more.

Not the Same Old Story

When one woman takes aim at the heart of another, she rarely fails
to find the vulnerable spot, and the wound she inflicts is incurable.
—MADAME DE MERTEUIL IN *LES LIAISONS DANGEREUSES*

I grew up surrounded by strong-minded women. My grandmother was
a fur trapper, horse trainer, and iconoclast of the first order, adventure
a key ingredient in everything she undertook. My mother was one of
the few girls in her small-town high school who went on to graduate
from the state university. Both taught me early on that women were free
to test any boundary they pleased. I attended a women's college, emerging pumped high on the significance of women helping one another up
the success ladder whenever possible. I used a female doctor and a female mechanic. Shortly after graduation, I headed to Los Angeles to
make my woman's way in the entertainment business.

I found a job as an assistant to a successful female executive. Though
the position was on the dirt-level rung of the Hollywood ladder, my boss
espoused promoting from within, and I had hopes of eventually working
my way upward. After about six months, it became clear that our company pipeline was far too clogged for me to get anywhere at all. We were
chock-full of junior executives, none of whom showed any inclination to
leave. I was spending most of my time toasting English muffins and
chasing down elusive brands of Swedish bath salts with no sign of future
reprieve.

My desk was stationed in a small outer office that I shared with two
other assistants. One of them, Hope, was about my age and, in the long

silent afternoon stretches, we took to bemoaning our similar dead-end positions. We fantasized about dream jobs and joked over our limited responsibilities. Occasionally, we would get together for movies or a drink.

When I'd been at the job close to a year, the itch to move on began to take over. I had always wanted to live in New York. My entire persona—from blue-pale skin to freeway aversions to dreams of becoming a novelist—seemed better suited to the Big Apple than the Big Orange. When I confessed my new plan to Hope, who had lived in Manhattan for a few years before heading west, she was all for it and immediately wished me luck. Feeling optimistic for the first time since I'd hit showbiz, I started searching out film jobs that could transport me across the country. I gave Hope daily updates on my employment quest and gratefully accepted her steady flood of queries and encouragement.

After cruising down several dead ends, I finally heard through an industry friend about a New York–based production company planning to open a new division. I called the vice president in charge, who encouraged me to apply for a job. I sent a résumé and evaluated several scripts for them. After a few weeks of back and forth, I learned that the field had been narrowed to three candidates. I had to fly to New Jersey for a wedding and arranged to meet the vice president while I was there. Excitement blooming, I told Hope about every development.

About a week after I returned from New Jersey, Hope took a long weekend for a family function back east. The day after she came back, during a quiet patch of afternoon, she cleared her throat.

"I just wanted to let you know that I applied for that New York job, too."

I tried not to appear as completely flabbergasted as I felt.

"You did?"

She nodded. "A little while ago. I just had an interview while I was in New York."

"Oh." I swallowed. I had no idea what to say.

"I think we should just be really open about this," Hope continued.

"You know, let each other know when we hear anything. So there's no weirdness. How does that sound?"

"Sure," I nodded.

At that point, my boss came in and our conversation snapped shut, but my mind continued reeling. How did that sound? It sounded like I had been incredibly naïve. It sounded like Hope's solicitous checking in had really been a way to pump me for information. I knew that she felt as stuck as I did. I knew that she had friends and family in New York and had considered moving back there. How stupid, stupid, stupid had I been to share those job search details without a second thought.

Beyond such self-recrimination, I was shakier in my convictions. Was Hope out of line? After all, the entertainment business was fiercely competitive. A girl had to do what she had to do to get ahead. It had never occurred to me that Hope, however unhappy, might want what I wanted, too. Had I been shafted or educated or both? And how was I supposed to react now? Should I believe she really wanted to start sharing openly, that this was her way of remedying the guilt she felt about being underhanded? Should I continue coming clean or should I start lying and omitting right back, dosing her with a spoonful of her own medicine?

In the end, I settled on a road of least resistance. I didn't offer up any new news—and I certainly didn't tell Hope when I uncovered further New York job possibilities—but when she asked what I had heard about that first job, I answered truthfully. I have no idea whether she did the same. The job wound up going to a third party, a guy based in New York, and we continued working together, dodging the tension between us and not mentioning the job search again. It all felt too fraught and loaded. We both did everything in our power to continue behaving as if nothing in our relationship had changed.

The entire situation left me confused. I had expected a workplace in which women went out of their way to support other women, not one in which they operated behind each other's backs. In the rosy picture I'd concocted of my professional future, I had somehow skipped over the fact that in a competitive workplace environment, the ambitions of my female friends and colleagues would naturally collide with my own.

Would I have reacted differently, expected competition more readily, had Hope been a man? Either way, the experience would have left me bruised, but the fact that this conflict had arisen with another woman made me feel worse. I had different expectations of the women with whom I worked, regardless of their circumstances. I anticipated a greater degree of empathy, far less looking out for number one. I had been exposed to the stereotypes about female ambition—Sigourney Weaver in *Working Girl,* Joan Collins on *Dynasty*—but had little experience with the subtler shadings of the real thing. I had not considered whether it was possible to pursue my own career goals without ever stepping on another woman's toes, or for other women to avoid stepping on mine.

At the time, I didn't explore these thoughts much further. I certainly didn't ponder what I might have done in Hope's place. Instead, I vowed never to find myself in such a vulnerable position again. From then on, I would take care with just who earned my professional trust.

Several jobs and a year later, I moved to New York and accepted a position as an associate to a woman who owned her own business. Buoyed by the chance for advancement, I arrived on the scene determined to do her and the company proud. I scheduled office meetings and daily lunches and lugged home work to read and evaluate for our clients. At first, my boss seemed nothing but pleased by my initiative. She urged me to get out and network even more. By the time I'd been there several months, clients had started to call me directly, and stacks of envelopes were arriving at the office addressed to me. One afternoon, my boss thumbed through them and only half jokingly observed, "Maybe we should start calling this place Nan Mooney and Associates."

Though I tried to let it roll past, the edge to her voice surprised me. The subtext was clear. Her own encouragement notwithstanding, in putting myself out there I had done something wrong. I returned to my desk with the sensation that I just might want to watch my back.

We were a small office, just two or three of us. All work focused around servicing our clients, and contact with them was a natural, even necessary, aspect of the job. Nevertheless, shortly after her comment, my boss instituted a new rule: Every client under every circumstance must be passed directly to her. Other dictates soon followed. No fax or letter could be sent without her approval. She began listening in on my phone conversations and took to wandering into my office and reading my to-do lists, my calendar, and my mail.

Before long, I felt as if every step I took was monitored, each mistake immediately seized upon and trumpeted. Before accepting the job, I'd heard rumors about the string of unhappy employees who had preceded me—most of them young women, capable but inexperienced, very similar to me. That high turnover rate no longer appeared much of a mystery. It seemed that to feel secure in her position as head of the company, my boss had developed a pattern of undermining every young woman who passed through her door.

The year culminated in a high-stress convention attended by all of our clients, one of whom wound up wooed and possibly won by a key competitor. After our tumultuous week away, I walked into the office on a Friday morning. My boss trudged in a half-hour later.

"Get in here," she ordered, and marched through to her office. I obeyed and she proceeded to erupt.

Her anger about the lost business poured forth, all of it directed at me. Why hadn't I been in closer contact with our clients? I should have known they had a problem. When I objected, she rose from her swivel chair and flung a stack of papers my direction.

"You're a moron," she railed. "How could anyone be so irresponsible? How could you do this to me? You're trying to ruin my business!"

"But I couldn't check in with them!" I finally flung back. "You wouldn't let me."

For a moment she stood stone still, fuming, arms rigid at her sides. Then she charged across the room, cocked her fist, and hit me square in the shoulder. That's when, amid a hail of notebooks and ballpoint pens, I finally walked out the door.

I continued to walk the full fifty-three blocks home, shaking, tears streaming down my face. A few hours later, sitting alone in my apartment, I did something that now seems just short of absurd. I contemplated going back. I called a friend for sympathy. When I told her what I was considering, she said I was flat-out crazy.

"If my boss touched me," she declared, "I'd sue him for everything he owned."

Her comment made something click in me, parting a veil that I had not cared to look through before. If my boss had been a man, if he had undermined me on a regular basis, called me a moron, marched across the room to punch me in the arm, what would I have done? Filed assault charges and sounded off to everyone I knew. So why was I reacting so differently here? Why had I spent more than a year accepting treatment from my female boss that I would not have tolerated for two minutes from a man?

In the months following my dramatic exit, I clung tight to the one thing that seemed 100 percent certain. My problems with my boss had not stemmed solely from the quality of my performance. Our troubles took root because she saw me—and probably all those competent young women who had preceded me—as a threat. Though she was twenty years older, owned her own business, and had experiences and connections it would take me years to acquire, our relationship was dictated by her fear that I would use any power she allotted me to stage an office coup. We never discussed our expectations of the job or of one another. Instead, she seemed to have pegged me as a rival from the day I stepped through the door.

Assuming my professional troubles had been isolated experiences, I began to worry that there was something wrong with me. I feared I possessed a fatal flaw, some personal defect that brought out the worst in the women with whom I worked. I might have mined this vein for years if that job's explosive ending had not proved too explosive to keep to myself. I began telling the story to people—former business acquaintances, college friends, even strangers I met at parties—as if to really know me you had to know how badly I had tanked.

An unexpected thing happened. I began hearing tales from other women who'd had problems with their female colleagues, too—in the film industry, in academia, in medicine, restaurants, high-tech firms—everything from a magazine reporter plagiarized by her boss to an Outward Bound trip leader literally abandoned in the wild by another female river guide. Instead of answers, I found people asking the same questions I had been asking about what had gone wrong. Sometimes the details came out awkwardly, piecemeal, accompanied by embarrassment and even shame. As we talked, laughed, and theorized, it became clear that I had tapped into something significant. Women all over the country were encountering problems with other women in the workplace. Nobody felt comfortable talking about it, and most of us were at a loss over what to do.

While I was tossing these ideas around in my head, I attended a panel discussion—composed of a group of well-known feminist writers, journalists, and academics—about the struggles faced by contemporary women in the workplace. Most of the evening centered around male-female dynamics. When one of the speakers asked for audience feedback, I raised my hand and floated my concerns about how often tensions rose among women themselves.

Despite the stories I had been exchanging with friends, I was nervous about how an entire room full of women might react to my comment. I worried my words might be construed as a gender betrayal. At first no one spoke. Eventually, one of the panelists leaned forward and assured me that if there were women undermining other women in the workplace, they were unfortunate exceptions to the overarching sisterhood rule. Then each panelist in turn voiced her version of the party line: Good women support each other, bad women do not. End of story. The discussion quickly returned to more comfortable subjects: male-female dynamics such as glass ceilings and sexual power plays.

I had been steeling myself against a negative response, but the panel's lack of response stunned me. Of course, the issues they wanted to discuss were significant, but did they have to be the only ones? These speakers represented the front line of feminist thought, yet their vision of women in the workplace seemed drawn from a previous generation—a world cast in black and white, peopled by wicked witches and fairy godmothers, victims and victimizers, with nary a hybrid in sight. I had to wonder where these cutting-edge thinkers had been for the past few decades. Didn't they realize something far more complicated was going on between women on the job today?

As the panel wrapped up, I felt both frustrated and disappointed by the theoretical black hole I had encountered. Then, once again, that spark I had dropped found unexpected fuel. The moment the discussion ended, I found myself engulfed by members of the audience. People stopped me in the bathroom, in the elevator, on the street outside. Over and over they told me that the conflicts in women's professional relationships were something we should and must address. They, too, longed for the discussion our panelists hadn't provided, and they left no question in my mind.

Fantasies about the workplace as a happy bastion of sisterhood are just that: fantasies. Our real-life scripts don't star Cinderellas or evil stepmothers. Instead, they feature real people with shaky self-confidence, thwarted ambitions, buried prejudices, and sexual jealousies. They feature a cutthroat corporate culture in which colleagues, male and female, are pitted against each other for jobs and promotions. They feature tension between conflict and collaboration, ambition and generosity, and uncertainties over how to meld the two. The workplace fosters competition in all its guises, healthy and unhealthy, direct and almost impossible to detect. Only when we recognize this, when we admit the full spectrum of our desires and limitations, can we start building healthy relationships with other women in the working world.

Fracturing the Fairy Tale

In 1971, 32,202,000 women over the age of sixteen were considered members of the civilian workforce. By 2004 that number had more than doubled, with 68,421,000 women either working or looking for work.[1]

For the first time, women are represented in nearly every field, on nearly every level. We have opportunities for positions and salaries unimaginable even twenty years ago. As a result, the role work plays in women's lives has changed dramatically during the past few decades. Increasingly our careers are how we define ourselves, making our professional achievements and relationships far more important than they have ever been. Not only are there more women in the workplace, there are more young, driven, educated women who have been raised with the idea that they can and will support themselves with long-term, fulfilling careers. Ambition and competition play an ever-expanding role in this new game.

But though women may have "arrived," we have yet to arrive fully. We are still subject to pay inequity and job discrimination. We still earn only 76 cents for every dollar a male earns.[2] Women may have found their way into the top companies, but they are still a rarity at the top levels—only eight Fortune 500 corporations have female CEOs.[3] According to a 2002 report on the banking industry, the percentage of female professionals and managers on Wall Street actually dropped in the decade between 1990 and 2000, and those numbers have continued their dip into the new century.[4] For women, a career has become possible, but it comes riddled with pressures and tensions that differ markedly from those experienced by our male counterparts.

Most working women today are aware of the glass ceiling and all its tangents. These are serious problems, certainly worthy of the discussion they have provoked. Yet many of us arrive on the job unprepared, as I was, for the fact that our professional conflicts will not be confined to members of the opposite sex. Though there has been a recent surge of public attention focused on aggression among adolescent girls, we are still uncomfortable exploring how these same tendencies unfold in adulthood. From *CSI* to *Sex in the City,* the professional woman looms large in pop culture, but her relationships with her female colleagues lie largely unexplored. In its inaugural season, Donald Trump's hit reality show *The Apprentice* delivered a handful of ambitious and driven working women, capped off by the unrepentantly bitchy Omarosa. Though Trump himself expressed surprise at the behavior of his sharply competitive female contestants, there was little delving into where such behavior came from or why.

It's as if a simple, politically correct, "don't ask, don't tell" lid has been clamped down on the very complicated truths about women working together. If my own investigation is any indication, women want and need to break this silence. Until we launch a more formal discussion, our individual experiences risk remaining just that: isolated, personal, and raw. In exploring this subject, I hope to create a forum in which women begin to feel comfortable examining and discussing our professional problems. The more we understand our own actions and motivations and those of our colleagues, the easier it will be to tackle the conflict and competition that occurs among women on the job.

A number of circumstances contribute to the fact that problems among working women remain largely underground. Since men still tend to shape professional priorities, we often see our "female troubles" as trivial, minor setbacks we should be able to work out quietly or blindly swallow as we chase after career advancement. A women-centered sexism can come into play, a tendency to write off other women's behavior as shallow or catty when in truth our surface dynamics often mask significant concerns. In addition, shining a spotlight on our difficulties—risking public admission that women are not always supportive and generous—can feel like a betrayal of our entire sex.

The workplace environment challenges many deep-rooted ideas about how women behave. Women on the job have grown more comfortable with ambition, competition, and success, but that has not negated the value we place on communication and relationships, on being liked and being nice. Striking a balance between these two sides of ourselves is a delicate undertaking. Society's definition of what is and is not feminine hasn't helped. Conflict and confrontation have long been the hallmark of masculinity, a clear dividing line between the sexes, and women can be uncertain how to interact in a workplace where that line is regularly being blurred.

Many women harbor understandably ambivalent feelings about how to compete with one another in a professional context. It's not that we don't know how to "go for the jugular," but that we are searching for a more humane alternative to the typical cutthroat corporate template. Contemporary workplace culture tends to promote money and success above all else, even at the expense of compassion, integrity, and social responsibility. Though our cultural rhetoric may espouse decency and respect toward others, the gears that spin the wheel remain all about money and turning a profit. In most cases, it is better to be a good performer than a good person. Workers of both genders struggle with the moral dilemmas presented by such a value system, but for women—raised to be nurturing and focus on relationships—the choices presented can feel particularly stark. They are also unavoidable. This corporate culture drives our economy and in many respects drives our society. Trying to find our place within it can prompt deep-seated insecurities, doubts, and questions that can't help spilling over onto our professional relationships. We are not inadequate, or crazy, when we feel it is impossible to be both a good worker and a good person. It means we have been brought to a dilemma that all professional women, indeed all professionals, eventually face.

Perhaps the biggest obstacle in tackling the problems we encounter with our female colleagues is the impulse I followed with Hope and my New York boss—the impulse not to address such problems at all. Too often, women stop communicating as soon as troubles arise, because we are afraid to confront those contradictions we experience between nurturing relationships and nurturing our careers. It's difficult to step back long enough to process and understand the feelings stirred up by the pressure to succeed at all costs. When women are thrust into situations in which we see men competing with one another, or into situations where we find ourselves competing with our male colleagues, it can be uncomfortable but rarely confusing. We are raised with the idea that men are natural competitors, trained to get ahead by any means necessary, and even if we do not respect such values, we are rarely surprised to witness them in action. But when women enter into competitive professional situations alongside other women, those old rules are upended. Harmony seems impossible, but rising up "by any means necessary" feels heartless and inhuman. Unsure how to address such tensions, we do whatever we can not to have to address them at all.

Despite such enormous pressures and contradictions, women working together have fostered a breathtaking degree of change. We have revamped territory ranging from labor laws to management techniques. Women's networks, political action committees, job cohorts, and casual friendships have placed women in power on nearly every professional level. We have extended bounteous financial and emotional support. We have held each other's hands and watched one another's backs. None of these facts can or should be called into question. But there is another side to the story. This one is about the troubled places, the conflicting messages demanding that we be both caring and cutthroat. It is about openly admitting to the hard realities of the working world in which we operate and to our impulse—our very human impulse—to compete with, challenge, hurt, and even destroy one another to get what we want. This runs deeper than just a business issue. It is an emotional one. Our stories are often raw, full of confusion, hurt, and disillusion, coupled with a sense of isolation and loneliness. It can be humbling to reveal that we have been stung by another woman. It can be positively shameful to confess to doing the damage.

The Real Story

I am not an academic, and this book doesn't focus solely on statistical theories or analysis. Nor is it a business primer with checklists and formulas. It is a book about real life. The heart of the book, its voice, lies in more than a hundred interviews with and stories about professional women—scientists, social workers, waitresses, lawyers, bankers, soldiers, editors, salespeople, athletes, schoolteachers—all of whom shed light on how conflict and competition play out among women on the job. These are real experiences from real women, tales from the front lines. I have supplemented this rich anecdotal material by talking to a variety of experts, including economists, sociologists, and organizational psychologists, who provide further insight into women, competition, and the quest for mutual respect.

The women I interviewed came to me largely by word of mouth. I found them through friends and colleagues, through Internet postings, and ads placed on Web sites and in local newspapers, all requesting stories about conflict and competition between women on the job. The volume of responses was overwhelming. Close to two hundred women contacted me, and that number continued to swell in the course of writing the book. Although those formally interviewed volunteered to be part of the project and do not represent a random sampling, they came from a wide variety of professions, the only criteria being that they worked with other women. Subjects ranged in age from twenty-three to seventy-seven and represented a racial, economic, educational, and geographical spectrum. A more detailed statistical breakdown can be found in the appendix at the back of the book.

My initial intention, one I have largely stuck with, was to look only at American women. That said, as the questionnaires I sent out were forwarded and forwarded again, I found myself hearing from women from all over the world—Turkey, Cairo, Paris, Switzerland. Despite differences in customs and values, the increasing globalization of business and culture means that women everywhere are having similar experiences on the job.

The interviews were a two-part process. Women began by filling out questionnaires about their professional backgrounds, interactions with female colleagues, and thoughts and opinions about women's working relationships. In addition to their experiences on the job, I asked about their own competitive leanings, their backgrounds in sports and games, and the messages about conflict and competition they had received growing up. I welcomed them to write as much or as little as they liked, and the results ranged from one-word answers to eloquent treatises. The full questionnaire is reprinted in the back.

Part two of the process entailed a one-on-one conversation in which we discussed in more detail the themes and experiences raised in the questionnaire. Whenever possible, I met with the women in person— over coffee or drinks or a meal, at offices and bars and kitchen tables. Otherwise, we spoke on the phone. These discussions ranged in length from a half hour to several hours. As long as they wanted to explore, I kept the tape recorder running. Though the majority of women completed both parts of the interview process, there were some who just wrote or just talked.

In the course of my research, I met and spoke to scores of smart, kind, generous, talented, and perceptive women. They were not interested in reinforcing stereotypes, launching attacks on their coworkers, or getting revenge. Most expressed a real desire to understand the underlying causes of the problems they had experienced with their female colleagues. Our conversations also stirred up some significant doubts and fears. As a high school principal in her early fifties put it, "For women, there's always going to be the worry that telling the truth about our imperfect relationships makes us look like we've failed."

Part of the discomfort I encountered was practical—I conducted my interviews in the first half of 2003 at the nadir of an economic slump. Because people felt their jobs could be at risk, some were reluctant to criticize their workplace or their colleagues, even anonymously. A far greater degree of uneasiness emerged on the emotional level. The women with whom I spoke were eager to know if other women struggled over conflict and competition with their female colleagues. Again and again I heard the questions, "Am I crazy?" "Is this just me?" I found myself repeatedly offering comfort and reassurance that their experiences were part of a greater phenomenon, doing in a small way what I hope this book can do in a larger one.

Though these women wanted to understand and explore the conflicts they had encountered, they also felt strongly about not hurting feelings or burning bridges. It was extremely important to them that their stories not be recognizable. Though my hope is that we will reach a point at which we do not feel so frightened about going public with our problems, I have every intention of protecting their privacy and respecting their wishes. Except when quoting the experts cited here, I have changed everyone's name. I have also changed professions, locations, or other telltale descriptive details. But none of these women are composites.

Sociologically, there are said to be flaws inherent to drawing conclusions from self-reported research. There is frequently a gap between what people do and what they say they do. This might hold especially true for women struggling to meet often contradictory codes of professional and social conduct. On a few occasions, I had the opportunity to speak separately with women who worked together, and their perceptions of events did reflect discrepancies. Far from a pitfall, such personal inconsistencies form the heart of our relationships—and our relationship issues. It is through the cracks between my experience and yours that misunderstandings and hurt feelings arise. To the objective observer, the stories related here may be colored and spun by emotions. In my mind, that is what makes them so true.

This is not a book that says women do not support each other, that men are better at competing than women are, or that women should act more like men on the job. I do not believe any of these things to be true. Nor is it meant in any way to belittle or discount the serious workplace problems that unfold between men and women. Our professional relationships with other women differ from those we form with men. The standards to which we hold one another can be higher or less flexible, and cultural pressures pull us in different directions. My intention is to take a closer look at how women negotiate expectations about constant harmony with one another when confronted with the realities of an often contentious professional world.

Upon hearing what I was writing about, some women assumed that I would treat competition as a taboo, that the answer to our problems was to get women to stop competing altogether. I think this reflects a cultural message women have received, in one form or another, for generations. We have been immersed in the notion that conflict is not feminine and that when women do engage in competition, it pulverizes our self-esteem, ruins our friendships, and divides our loyalties. I don't agree. I believe there are ways in which women can negotiate competitive situations without losing sight of our compassion and respect for one another. This is not an anticompetition book. It is not a book about how women should always be nice to each other. In fact, it is about what happens in those spaces where we are not necessarily nice at all.

Alongside tales of frustration, there exist numerous stories of hope. Women spoke to me about their struggles, but they also spoke about coming to understand how conflict and competition factored into their working lives. I encountered women who had figured out how to negotiate the tensions inherent to the workplace and form productive and respectful relationships with their female colleagues, how to communicate and work through their problems rather than skirting around them. These women had discovered that conflict and competition did not have to cancel out compassion and support, and their professional bonds grew stronger because of it. If women are to continue moving forward in our professional lives, the time has come for all of us to follow their lead. We must examine—honestly and unequivocally—how and why women hurt each other on the job, and what we can do to begin cleaning up the mess.

Most importantly, this book does not traffic in blame. I am not an outsider gazing in, ready to criticize or pass judgment. Any professional success I have experienced in my life so far has been due to the enormously supportive and fulfilling relationships I have had with other women. I am extremely grateful for the women's movement of the seventies and eighties that opened doors through which I and countless other women have walked. I recognize that women's entry into the workplace has spawned numerous advances for both sexes, including relationship-oriented management styles, an increased focus on the balance between career and family, and a more diverse and tolerant office environment. But such positive developments do not eclipse the fact that serious problems do exist among working women, problems many of us are afraid to address. This book isn't about questioning women's contributions. It is about enhancing them by bringing such problems out of the shadow and into the light.

Throughout the book, I will always be considering behavioral tendencies, never behavioral rules. No single truth holds true for the broad spectrum of personalities and situations any of us may encounter. Nor am I seeking a blanket solution to the complex problems that arise among women on the job. It would be naïve to assume such a universal panacea even exists. But as I hear the stories of more and more women who have quit jobs, cried themselves to sleep, sharpened their claws in the name of self-protection, or pledged never to work for a woman again, it is clear that we are ready to go public. It is time to pin words to these unspoken tensions, to shake up the set patterns we have stumbled into and, in the process, uncover their origins. It is time to define our relationships not just as women but as women in the workplace.

ONCE UPON A TIME

1

Lessons We Learned in Childhood

**Among all the forms of truly absurd courage,
the recklessness of young girls is outstanding.**

—COLETTE

When I was eight years old I tried to suffocate my best friend, Crispin, with an afghan. She had beaten me at Monopoly—creamed me in fact—and I wanted revenge. Crispin, loaded with older brothers and sisters, fought back. We tussled on the bed until we wore ourselves out. Then we went for a snack. Soon afterward, I chased Crispin down the soccer field—angry that she had stolen the ball and jealous that she was faster—illegally slide-tackled her from behind, and bloodied both her knees so badly it left permanent scars. Several years before, as she and I knelt in her upstairs hallway peering through the banister at our mothers gossiping down below, she turned around and bit my finger. Hard. I still have no idea why.

These were not harmless girlish hijinks. They were aggressive acts. Crispin and I tucked into each other because we were mad, jealous, frustrated, or just seized with a strong emotion we didn't know how to manage. We were what I venture most girls are—what little girls of nursery rhymes are not supposed to be—greedy, ruthless, wild, and pleased as punch to let each other know about it. Our relationship was as honest as they come.

During the past thirty years, a formidable body of research has been amassed on the development of girls in our society.[1] Though I will not rehash this material in its entirety, there are patterns that have come to light, messages girls receive about conflict and competition that lay the groundwork for our personal and professional relationships later on.

The first and strongest female bond most girls experience is with their mother. This one is inevitably loaded. The basic model of early psychological development—Freud's oedipal complex—is predicated on competition, a triangle erected between mother, father, and child. The male child competes against his father for the attention of the mother. For girls, the setup is just the opposite, a rivalry with her mother for the attention of the man. Psychologist Nancy Chodorow has pointed out that a child's eventual split from the nurturing parent, almost always the mother in our society, in order to establish his or her individual identity is critically different for girls than it is for boys.[2] Since gender is one of the key ways in which humans define themselves, total separation is complicated for a girl by the fact that her mother is actually a version of herself. She is splitting off from her primary model of what she will someday become.

As they maneuver through this separation process, girls need to establish ways in which they are not like their mothers. For some future career women, this means rejecting the housewife model. But many girls, especially those raised in the past thirty years, have had mothers who worked outside the home in traditionally male professions like medicine, law, and finance. Even when such mothers serve as role models of ambitious and successful career women, girls will intentionally seek out goals that run counter to their mother's choices. They promise themselves they will find a more fulfilling career, forge a more equal marriage, and spend more or less time with their children. As each young woman struggles to stay connected to her mother without becoming her, a tangled web of emotions arises. From the outset, female conflict is accompanied by a strong chaser of guilt.

———

On a peer level, our earliest and strongest friendships tend to be with members of the same sex. By age five or six, girls are already operating in sex-segregated groups, making a point to identify themselves as girls as opposed to just kids.[3] Such girlhood friendships—like mine and Crispin's—can prove passionate and volatile. Nursery rhyme wisdom notwithstanding, they are rarely sweet and conflict-free.

For many years, social scientists presumed that since girls were less physically confrontational than boys they were also less aggressive. However, recent research on aggression in very young children has revealed no significant distinction between the sexes before the age of three.[4] When it comes to confrontational behavior, everybody, male and female, arrives in the world similarly equipped—grabbing toys, pulling hair, screaming bloody murder when we have been done wrong.

As children grow older, key developmental differences evolve that affect girls' relationships to aggression and to one another. Girls tend to acquire verbal fluency more quickly and at an earlier age than boys do.[5] This, coupled with the fact that our society discourages physical aggression in girls, makes the drop-off rate for direct forms of attack much sharper among the female sex.[6] But those aggressive impulses don't just disappear. While boys are still busy hitting and kicking, girls increasingly use words and social manipulation to communicate negative feelings to their peers.

The prevalence of relational aggression among girls—including acts that harm others "through damage (or threat of damage) to relationships or feelings of acceptance, friendships, or group inclusion"[7]—was first recognized by a group of scientists headed by Finnish researcher Dr. Kaj Bjorkqvist in 1992. Upending the "girls are just nicer" theory, Bjorkqvist's study revealed that when cultural pressures discourage open aggression in girls, they simply learn to strike out in less overt but equally damaging ways. Instead of fists, they turn to the subtler arts of language and relational manipulation.[8]

By middle childhood, ages eight to eleven, girls are developing relationships that are distinctly different from those between boys. Boys typically gather in loose groups of friends, whereas girls form tighter "cliques."[9] Girls tend to focus less on physical dominance and ego display, more upon verbal and relational strategies to get what they want from their friends—and to punish their enemies. At the same time, girls are already absorbing societal messages about how they should relate to each other, about the importance of avoiding the sort of open conflict that flowed between Crispin and me. A fissure opens up between the negative emotions they feel—anger, aggression, jealousy—and the emotions they are allowed to express openly in their relationships with other girls.

The Games Girls Play

Much debate about women and competition has swirled around the premise that girls just never learn how to compete. Boys play competitive games and girls play relational ones—dodgeball versus dollhouses. In the 1930s, renowned child psychologist Jean Piaget cited girls' distaste for rule-based games as evidence of their lack of moral development.[10] Forty years later, in the early seventies, Janet Lever's research on children's play showed girls more likely to engage in noncompetitive pursuits like jump rope and hopscotch in which arguments rarely developed and nobody won or lost.[11] The conclusions were obvious. Men get a grounding in competition and women in intimate relationships, an imbalance that can seriously hurt us once we enter the workplace. For women raised before the 1970s, this skewed competitive education may remain a major stumbling block. Given limited chances to compete with their peers as children, they can feel intimidated by challenging others, both men and women, on the job.

Thanks to the passage of Title IX—the 1972 law prohibiting sex discrimination in federally funded education programs—this theory becomes suspect when applied to younger women. Title IX meant public education institutions from elementary schools to universities had to provide equal opportunities for students in every field, including athletics. As a girl born in 1970, I grew up steeped in competitive play. I took mandatory PE classes from kindergarten through high school. I played soccer, basketball, and tennis, swam, skied, ran track, did gymnastics, occasionally in coed settings but for the most part competing solely against other girls. And my experience is far from unique. In the past thirty years, competition has shifted from something pursued by only the most inveterate girl athlete to a core element of our collective education.

In 1972 only 7 percent of high school and 15 percent of college athletes were women. By 2002 that number had skyrocketed to 41 percent of high school and 42 percent of college athletes.[12] Among the women I interviewed—women of all ages—72 percent reported playing sports of some kind growing up. Of those who did not, a number mentioned participating in activities like music or theater in which teamwork and competition played a significant role. Few girls grow up these days unfamiliar with what it is like to be in an openly competitive situation with other girls. If access to sports was the sole obstacle, then competition between post–Title IX working women should be direct and healthy as it gets. So why isn't this the case?

Exposure to competitive games has provided modern girls with some valuable tools. They have learned to stand head to head with other girls in certain ways, in certain places. For them, the missing messages do not focus so much on how to compete with other girls as on how to distinguish between competition and conflict in the classroom or on the playing field—where rules are clear cut and officially sanctioned—and the competition we encounter in the more ambiguous context of our broader lives. On a social level, girls are still acculturated away from competition. They learn that their relationships with other girls are supposed to be nurturing and free of conflict. It isn't that they are not primed to aspire to greatness, but that they are simultaneously encouraged to be supportive and generous toward one another at all costs.

"I feel like as girls we were weaned on the idea of limitless potential, but without the sense of personal entitlement, that right to take up time and space, that's passed on to boys," Rosie, a thirty-year-old actress, told me. "We're supposed to look out for number one and take care of everybody else at the same time. It's confusing."

It is confusing. Pre–Title IX women face the contradiction of having been schooled to be unobtrusive and now finding themselves in a working world that demands that women stand up for themselves and compete. Girls raised since the 1970s face the contradictions embodied by female action heroes like Charlie's Angels and Buffy the Vampire Slayer, who rule the world without losing their femininity, freedom fighters with hair and makeup perfectly intact.

Adolescence, Self-Confidence, and Relational Aggression

I have another story. This one happened in the seventh grade, when the girl who had grown up next door to me, a friend since kindergarten, joined my middle school class. That fall, she threw a big Halloween party—the talk of the lunchroom for weeks preceding. She invited a clutch of popular girls, plus most of my friends. She did not invite me.

The night of the party I sat alone in my bedroom and listened to my parents downstairs answering the doorbell and handing out candy to the parade of ghosts and pirates and princesses. Late in the evening, I heard familiar voices traveling up our front walk. My classmate and her entire party had decided to come trick-or-treating to our front door. I raced upstairs so I could watch them through a tiny fan-shaped window in our attic, the one spot from which I could see them but knew they could not see me. I sat there until long after they had gone, flooded with shame. I didn't know how I would look any of those girls in the face again.

I never mentioned the party to anyone who attended, never broached it with my parents, never told a soul until years later when I was out of college and had shed the illusion that my classmate's rejection marked me a social pariah. Looking back, I can trace some of the psychological underpinnings of her inclusion-exclusion game. I can guess how intensely she wanted to fit in with the more popular girls and how she feared that maintaining ties to someone like me, who was not a member of that in-crowd, might work to her disadvantage. I can guess that I was threatening, because I had known her too well for too long, known her when she wasn't smooth or well-dressed or cool. She used her party to send me the message that she was no longer interested in maintaining our friendship, because she didn't know how to send such a message in any other way. I see all this now. At the time, it was simply devastating.

In the written survey I sent to the women I interviewed, the final question asked "While growing up, what messages did you absorb about competition and conflict with other girls or women?" Judging from some of the comments I received—"girlfriends will hurt you for no reason," "no matter how much I hate to admit it, girls can be incredibly cruel to each other," "I learned early on that girls can be wonderful, but they can also be manipulative and ruthless. I was on the giving and receiving end of both"—and the recent popularity of books exploring girl aggression, it is clear that I am not the only one to emerge from adolescence knowing the heartbreak of having been betrayed by another girl.

Adolescence is a pivotal time in identity shaping, a period during which both boys and girls feel at their most awkward and insecure. In the transition from child to adult, girls in particular often lose something they never quite get back. In 1990, the American Association of University Women published a report entitled *Shortchanging Girls, Shortchanging America,* based on the widest ever national survey of gender and self-esteem. The study finally put numbers to what numerous women had experienced firsthand: When girls hit adolescence, their self-confidence tends to plummet.[13]

This drop in self-esteem stems, at least in part, from a disconnect that forms between adolescent girls and their feelings, a pervading sense of having to compromise their identities in order to win approval from their peers and from society in general. According to child psychologist Mary Pipher, adolescence is a time "when girls experience social pressure to put aside their authentic selves and to display only a small portion of their gifts."[14]

Girls at this age are hit with heavy messages about what our culture desires in a woman, a value system that hinges on prettiness, kindness, and restraint, on not asserting oneself too boldly or wanting too much. In the effort to gain acceptance, many of those bolder girlhood traits—like relational honesty and open competition—move underground. In any number of ways, our society contributes to this division of self. Confrontation and acting out are expected and even encouraged in boys, but girls tend to be judged and made to feel unfeminine for such behavior. Adolescence ushers in a new level of anxiety over things like weight, clothes, and sexuality, so that even as they're chasing unconditional approval, girls must grapple with an increase in competitive feelings toward their friends. The emotional land mines multiply with no ready outlet for defusing them.

Alongside this plunge in self-confidence, adolescent girls undergo a second, equally telling psychological leap. Relational aggression between girls spikes dramatically between ages eleven and fifteen.[15] Those tight peer relationships are often turned into weapons. Punishment is delivered by excluding another girl socially—the way my classmate did to me—or by means of gossip, rumor spreading, playing favorites, and exploiting emotional ties or personal knowledge to hurt someone close.[16]

Heating up this mix is the fact that acceptance among adolescent girls is frequently determined by popularity rather than more measurable merits like brains, creative talents, or athletic prowess. This road to social success can feel tenuous and subjective, creating fertile soil for jealousy and manipulation. As a result, girls often grow extremely wary about openly making trouble. The fierce social pressure to belong means it makes sense to attack circuitously in order to avoid both counterattack and blame. Girls can be so eager to mend rifts when they do occur, so quick to apologize for hurt feelings, that the roots of problems wind up frosted over and never truly addressed. When relational aggression becomes the paradigm, girls grow uncertain about what it means to be kind and considerate, since even actions perpetrated by our "best friends" may prove hurtful. It gets harder and harder to trust what we feel or where we stand with our female peers.

Girls from diverse ethnic or economic backgrounds often face pressure to cleave to different female expectations than their mainstream white counterparts, many of which prove equally damaging to self-confidence. Cultures that value female submissiveness can push girls even harder in the "good girl" direction, a dynamic illustrated in the 2003 movie *Bend It Like Beckham,* which is about a teenage girl's struggle to hide her modern, athletic, sexually curious self from her traditional Indian parents. For those from cultural backgrounds that encourage outward aggression, voicing anger, or getting into fights, the confusion can run even deeper. A girl's family and immediate community may reward such direct outpourings even as mainstream society and authority figures—like teachers or school principals—reject them.[17] As we grow older, both the workplace and popular culture continue to reflect the values of middle-class white America. Even if we are not directly party to these values, chances are they will play a role in our lives.

Developmentally, as empathy levels catch up to social and verbal intelligence—somewhere around age fifteen—relational aggression between girls is supposed to subside.[18] In talking to adult women, I found that this was not necessarily the case. As girls, women had learned to reward each other for indirectly addressing conflict and to punish one another for dealing with problems openly. The standards set for our relationships early on—to be both selfless and selfish, quiet and outspoken, cooperative and competitive—had not disappeared. Unless women begin consciously cultivating ways to express our opinions and conflicts directly, those adolescent patterns can and will continue to flourish.

2

Ambition, Competition, and Other Four-Letter Words

One is not born a woman, one becomes one.

—SIMONE DE BEAUVOIR

You've come a long way, baby.

—AD FOR VIRGINIA SLIMS CIGARETTES

One of the first messages I remember about competition between adult women arrived by way of 1950s Hollywood, one rainy June Saturday afternoon. Flopped in front of the TV, my cousin and I stumbled across the opening credits of *All About Eve*, starring Anne Baxter as an ambitious and conniving ingenue willing to go to any lengths to destroy the career of theatrical grand dame Bette Davis. Baxter's Eve Harrington was coy, cunning, and ruthless, as black-hearted inside as she was sugar and spice outside. She wielded her youth against Davis's age, usurped her roles onstage and off, even attempted to steal her man, all in an effort to assume the leading lady throne. The lesson about women, work, and competition slid down easily. It was an either/or choice: You could have either your femininity or your ambition. Either you could be a good woman, or you could be the other kind.

All About Eve reflected an era in which a proper man chased rank, access, and influence while a proper woman cooed admiringly and ironed his shirts. Maintaining such roles played a critical part in preserving the economic and social order, an order that did not include women with careers. In the late 1930s, at the employment-starved height of the Depression, as many as twenty-six state legislatures contemplated making it illegal for a married woman to hold a government job.[1] As recently as 1970, a landmark study was published in which professional psychologists were called upon to classify male and female traits. Women were still defined by weak and fragile qualities like "very easily influenced," "very emotional," "very illogical," and "very sneaky." Such straightforwardly ambitious traits as "very direct" and "can make decisions easily" were the sole property of males.[2]

Tucked behind this tightly bound view of women's capabilities rested, and still rests, an intense fear of the forces ambition and competition might awaken in the tender sex. Traits like aggression and independence not only contradict our images of what is feminine, but they also upset a time-honored balance between male reason and female emotion. For centuries, women in Western society have received the message that ambitious and competitive equal destructive, from Medea to Lady Macbeth, Cleopatra to Hedda Gabler. Before we can begin tackling the problems we encounter with other women in the workplace, we must take into account the political, economic, and social factors that influence our relationships to the job and to one another. Conflict and competition among working women may seem an individual problem, but it is one anchored by a vast network of cultural and sociological roots.

What About Sisterhood? Competition and Feminism

Until well into the later half of the twentieth century, society would condone working women if circumstances forced them into such a position, but a career was never seen as a point of pride. Women who did work were expected to take on "softer" professions that could easily be abandoned when family called, entering such fields as nursing, teaching, and social work. The few women who openly chose to pursue careers—either in real life or on the silver screen—were assumed to have abandoned all traces of femininity. Hollywood films from the thirties, forties, and fifties featuring career women like *All About Eve*'s Margo Channing nearly always painted the ambitious heroine into a morality tale, as a woman who deserved to be, and eventually was, taken down. With a few exceptions— most of them starring Katharine Hepburn—professional women in films were ostracized, labeled defective examples of their sex.

Not until nearly two decades after *All About Eve* reigned at the box office did that perspective begin to shift. In the mid-1960s women began coming together in a solidarity-based feminist movement, later labeled "The Second Wave." Their efforts launched a flood of breathtaking social changes, and women's roles in the workplace proved primary among them. In the two decades from 1971 to 1991, the number of women in the workforce nearly doubled from 32 million to 57 million.[3] Not only were more women on the job, but they were increasingly choosing to pursue full-time and career-track professions. Women entered previously male realms—from law to medicine, engineering to the military— in unprecedented numbers. People stopped questioning why women went to work at all and began asking what they wanted to do when they got there.

This revival of the women's movement spawned a tremendously positive and pivotal time in the history of working women, but it also perpetuated some ideological strands that would prove troublesome to our future relationships. In order to draw women together, the Second Wave heavily emphasized the differences—biological and cultural—between men and women. Such concentration on "us versus them" often overlooked differences among the women themselves.

Before the Second Wave, conventional, male-dominated psychological theories had pegged women as underdeveloped versions of men, stuck in a mushy, unformed emotional state that men merely passed through as they continued to evolve into crisp-thinking, rational versions of the species. Starting in the mid-1970s, a handful of female psychologists—including Nancy Chodorow, Jean Baker Miller, and

Carol Gilligan—proposed the revolutionary idea that women's psychological development was not inferior to men's; it simply unfolded differently. These cultural feminists posited that historical, cultural, and economic influences encouraged women to value relationships while men were pushed toward valuing independence—and that neither approach should be read as right or wrong.[4] Gilligan's work in particular struck a chord with the public. In the subsequent popular debate, her ideas about women's behavioral tendencies often shed their cultural context and were treated as biological facts. The media, as well as some feminist scholars, jumped to label women as inherently all relational—tender, connected, collaborative—and men as inherently all autonomous—independent, aggressive, direct.[5]

The Second Wave's emphasis on solidarity and sisterhood, coupled with the work of Gilligan and her peers, gave rise to a feminist-endorsed version of the "good woman," one depicted as morally superior to men by virtue of her unflagging nurturing and relational gifts. The recognition that women tend to focus more on connection led to an assumption that women would automatically build strong, conflict-free bonds under any circumstances. This leap left little room for internal dissension or debate. Subtleties addressed by those same early cultural feminists—most notably Jean Baker Miller's insistence that conflict among women provided a crucial source of relational growth—slid through the cracks.[6] The idea that "because we're women we should make an effort to support each other" too often was interpreted as "because we're women we should always get along."

Competition among women had no place in this newly fashioned sisterhood. Instead of considering the possibility that once women gained a modicum of power they might become more ambitious and competitive—in other words "more male"—the women's movement rejected internal competition in all its forms. A 1972 article in *Ms.* magazine described competition among women as "the old way," a choice that entailed "raising ourselves by standing on the crushed remains of our sisters."[7] As women finally accrued significant privileges in the working world, this all-encompassing anticompetition stance left little room for the intricacies of our new relationships. It failed to recognize that a fair solution will not always be the same as an equal one, to acknowledge the difference between wanting yourself to succeed and wanting another person to fail, or to understand that competitive and collaborative don't have to reside at opposite ends of the scale.

As the revival of the women's movement gathered speed, female psychologists also began to explore the relationship between women, ambition, and competition. In 1968, graduate student Matina Horner conducted an experiment in which students wrote stories about a same-sex student—women wrote about women, men about men—at the top of his or her medical school class. Horner found that far more women than men associated "bizarre and violent imagery" with competitive success. On the heels of Horner's work, the notion of women's "fear of success"— attributed to the societal conflict women experience between achievement and femininity—entered the popular lexicon.[8]

In the early 1980s, Carol Gilligan and fellow psychologist Susan Pollak conducted a similar experiment with a group of college students. They, too, discovered women more likely than men to associate negative results with competition and achievement, with the added corollary that men tended to equate negative results with intimate relationships.[9] When asked to write stories about a series of pictures, men more often invented a violent or negative outcome when the image suggested personal affiliation—a man and a woman sitting together on a bench, for example. Women proved more likely to assign a violent or negative outcome when the picture suggested impersonal achievement—such as women in white coats working in a laboratory.

Instead of generating discussion about why women had mixed feelings about acting on their ambitions or men on their intimate emotions, this work often fueled the popular perception that women simply lacked the ambition-and-competition gene. When applied to the workplace, such beliefs propagated the notion that real women did not have professional power because real women did not want it. These beliefs continue to thrive in the twenty-first century. An October 2003 *New York Times Magazine* article heralded successful, educated women who abandon their careers as members of a growing "Opt-Out Revolution."[10] A 2004 feature story in *Fast Company* magazine claimed that women rarely reach top-level jobs because they simply don't want to work hard enough to get there.[11] Both articles were written by women. The periodic resurrection of such ideas contributes to keeping the glass ceiling permanently affixed.

The gains made by the Second Wave were tremendous, but the right to be ambitious and competitive—especially with regard to other women—was not necessarily among them. Women entering the professional arena often arrived with a utopian vision of how women should work together, one in which we all loved and supported one another at any cost, in which there was little sense that competition and collaboration could coexist. Perhaps most dangerous of all, women who did not accept this vision were often labeled the same way Hawthorne's seventeenth-century New Englanders labeled the scarlet-lettered Hester Prynne—as traitors to their sex. The revival of the women's movement gave us license to enter environments in which ambition, power, and authority reigned. Sisterhood left us little context to discuss the conflicts those environments would inevitably create among women on the job.

The Ambition Paradox

By the late 1980s, the world of the professional female had undergone sweeping change. An ambitious young woman no longer had to play Eve

Harrington, candy-coating her professional desires. She had a new story. She had become Mike Nichols's *Working Girl*, with Melanie Griffith as a spunky secretary whose Wall Street dreams are nearly strangled by her sweet-talking, credit-hogging boss, Sigourney Weaver. On the surface, this was a story of triumph: Griffith's Tess scaled the corporate ladder and stuck it to her boss on the strength of little more than sheer moxie. If *Working Girl* illustrated the many ways in which the professional woman's role had expanded, it also demonstrated how far she had not come. The film was still a fairy tale cast in black and white, about one woman who wins and another who loses. The most powerful woman was still wicked, and though the film tolerated some female success, it still frowned upon female competition. In a world in which women increasingly needed to compete with one another in order to get ahead, popular culture still cemented the message that only good girls were rewarded in the end.

Though organizational and cultural attitudes towards working women were frequently slow to adapt, the attitudes of the women themselves underwent far swifter transformation. They were no longer so willing to be shuttled into dead-end jobs with sketchy pay and privileges. They didn't plan to quit working as soon as they married or had children, nor did the workplace necessarily play second fiddle to maintaining a happy home. As women began to invest more in their careers, they also became more willing to fight for them. Now, at last, there was something worth fighting for.

I would be curious to see Horner and Gilligan's work on women, ambition, and success repeated today. Nearly every woman I interviewed called herself ambitious. Very few voiced any direct fear of success or associated negative side effects with either. Though mine was by no means a scientific polling, it does hint at a notable change from Gilligan's conclusions in the early 1980s. In fact, the women who felt most obliged to apologize for themselves were those who did not have long-term goals or grand career plans. Women who did admit to downsizing their ambitions usually did so not because they feared ambition was inappropriate or unfeminine but because of conflicts over navigating work and family life. Though they harbored uncertainties about how to balance their personal goals and ambitions with their desires to raise children and spend time with their families, they rarely saw those goals and ambitions as undesirable in and of themselves,

At the same time, the idea of women displaying the aggression and power often required to move forward in the workplace still remains a tough pill for our society to swallow. Popular culture has been quick to split this new breed of working woman into a good version and a bad one. The good girl, epitomized by Mary Tyler Moore and later Ally McBeal, is gung-ho but girlish, harmless and even a bit bumbling, competent but not too terribly ambitious. The bad woman, in contrast, is a calculating and humorless career maven. She's the antisister, the dragon lady, an icy version of the old femme fatale. She shows up in the cinematic likes of murderous TV newscaster Nicole Kidman in *To Die For* or Demi Moore's sexually harassing boss in *Disclosure.* Success for such a woman has required isolating herself from other women and from her own humanity in order to get ahead.

Though leadership research has shown that women express even stronger needs for power than men do,[12] there is still a significant disparity in images we receive of male and female ambition. Look at Martin Sheen's role as the president on TV's *The West Wing,* a man who is equal parts ambitious and honorable. Then consider his largely absent doctor wife, or the sharklike and successful Amanda from TV's *Melrose Place,* or the comically inflated ego of Murphy Brown. Consider the 1999 film *Election* about a power-obsessed high school girl who damages everyone she comes in contact with, the seventeen-year-old embodiment of female ambition gone wild. The film would have fallen flat had it revolved around an adolescent boy.

There is a tipping point about how much success and will toward wealth and power women are allowed, as manifested in public reaction to the woman who has become our cultural barometer of female ambition, Hillary Rodham Clinton. During her husband's first run for the presidency, the media and public opinion transformed Clinton's image from that of an opinionated activist and successful career woman to a pastel-clad, cookie-baking wife, mother, and member of the Bill fan club. Early in Clinton's own 2000 senatorial campaign, considerable media hype surrounded her "woman problem." Suburban white women, Hillary's peers, were cutting her down for being too ambitious, too arrogant, too hard. Polls among such women showed her trailing her opponent—the decidedly ambitious, arrogant, and hard New York mayor, Rudy Giuliani—by as many as twenty points.[13] "Who does she think she is?" has seemed a prevailing sentiment throughout Clinton's political career.

Such messages about reining ourselves in don't just come from social mores. Individual women can put considerable pressure on each other not to overstep the boundaries of propriety by flaunting our knowledge or achievements. We are often uncomfortable when women like Clinton display bald ambition through their goals and accomplishments. Journalist Peggy Orenstein and linguist Deborah Tannen have both noted women's tendency to downplay their authority in front of other women, purposely distancing themselves from their own expertise, because they are "more afraid of being perceived as arrogant than unknowledgeable."[14] Cultural emphasis for women has shifted toward success, but not at the expense of relationships or femininity; toward ambition, but not at the expense of stepping on another woman's toes. Despite the massive changes for women in the workplace, one significant arena awaits exploration. We have yet to understand how to deal with direct, confrontational, negative feelings in other women and in ourselves.

Living in the Good-Bad World

On the popular culture front, the working woman has become commonplace. She is a forensic scientist, an inner-city nurse, a Matrix destroyer.

But her relationships with her female colleagues remains territory that largely has been ignored. In a list of the 150 highest grossing films in American history, the closest thing we get to an imperfect working relationship between women is Catherine Zeta-Jones and Renée Zellweger as a pair of murderous nightclub singers who battle for attention and column inches in 1920s Chicago. Men, meanwhile, run the gamut from *Star Wars* to *The Firm,* from *Men in Black* to *Saving Private Ryan.*[15] As men fight it out in the boardroom and on the battlefield, female competition remains wedged into tawdry territory staked out by women like Linda Tripp and Tonya Harding.

When it does recognize problems among women in the workplace, society tends to lump all conflict under an enormous "women who hate other women" umbrella that encompasses female friendships, adolescence, and mother-daughter dynamics. Disagreements among working women are painted as fluffy or silly and trivialized as "catfights" where "the fur is flying."[16] Such generalizations can make women quick to write off their conflicts, agreeing that women are just bitchy, catty, moody, jealous, overemotional, or suffering from a permanent case of PMS. As a result, women themselves begin taking their problems less seriously.

The success of a recent spate of female-authored, "nasty boss" novels, led by *The Nanny Diaries* and *The Devil Wears Prada*, hint that all is not sweet and innocent among working women. Such fictionalized accounts tend to shy away from the real guts of such problems, veering instead toward the *Working Girl* template. They are tales of good girls who are young, polite, nonconfrontational, and ultimately blameless—though their thoughts may be wicked, their actions are pure and bereft of malice—who fall victim to bad women, women with power that they shamelessly use and abuse.

In its inaugural 2003–04 season, Donald Trump's reality TV show *The Apprentice* provided a rare glimpse into the competitive nature of young career women. It also brought forth an arch-villainess, Omarosa Manigault-Stallworth, who took on cartoonlike proportions. Her tagline was, "I'm going to crush my competition, and I'm going to enjoy doing it," and before long that goal seemed to supercede even winning the game. Largely disregarded by the media and the public was the fact that Omarosa neatly fit into a classic racial stereotype, the hypersensitive, black "woman with an attitude." Despite her over-the-top behavior, she also tossed some female stereotypes out the window. Far from seeking out connections and affiliations, she displayed the poorest relational skills of anyone on the program. Though media attention focused on her sheer gall and tactlessness, an interesting side note was that none of her female competitors—the chief targets of her bitchiness—knew how to handle Omarosa except by attacking behind her back the same way she had attacked behind theirs.

Though Omarosa made for good television, the behavior of our female coworkers rarely climbs to such outlandishly witchy heights. In the real world, tackling the tensions that unfold among working women means resisting that polarity encouraged by the media, the notion that women are either good or bad, successes or failures, sisters or betrayers, and that there are set male and female behavioral styles. These neat divisions are popular, because they propose tidy answers to messy questions. Workshops and self-help books based on catchy phrases and "five easy steps" promote a dangerous expectation of one-stop solution shopping for all our professional problems. Such oversimplified approaches discourage seeing the workplace as a society with individual dynamics, patterns, and relationships that require work and time to change.

There were strong competitive feelings among the women with whom I spoke. They are navigating an environment in which time, money, success, and attention can all be in short supply. In contrast to the messages women of earlier generations got—that competition and conflict are unbecoming in a lady—the prevailing attitude today is a sense of "yes, I'm competitive but . . ." Women are uneasy about the implications conflict can have in their relationships with other women. Many people I interviewed made the distinction between being "competitive with myself" and competing against others, wanting to win but not at all costs. We do have worries—legitimate ones—about how conflict might damage our bonds with one another, about just how ambitious it is acceptable to be. Though we want to be successful, we still value the connective and care-taking aspects of our relationships. We are not always sure how to support other women without sacrificing our autonomy, to be ambitious without being destructive.

In the absence of public dialogue, let alone clear working models, it can be difficult to fight the prevailing and often conflicting signals: Women are not naturally competitive or aggressive; women are simultaneously jealous and empathetic, manipulative and nurturing; women—regardless of their race, class, educational and economic backgrounds—"just know" how to get along. If our experiences differ from what we assume to be the main, it can be tempting to believe that there is something wrong with us. There isn't. Women are competitive, we are collaborative, we are greedy, we are generous. We are, in short, full of contradictions. If we are to begin examining our professional interactions, such contradictions provide the ideal, perhaps the only, spot from which to start.

INTO THE WOODS

3

When the Professional Gets Personal

The strongest pressure in the world can be friendly pressure.

—LESTER PEARSON,
FORMER PRIME MINISTER OF CANADA[1]

Julia and Erica work as science teachers at a North Carolina high school, sharing classroom space and team-teaching a ninth-grade biology unit. Though the two went to college together, they had never been more than casual acquaintances. Erica belonged to a sorority and was prominent on the campus social scene. Julia played the viola and wrote for the school newspaper. Even physically they occupy opposite ends of the spectrum. Julia, who took two years off before college to teach English in Southeast Asia, is in her late twenties, petite with olive skin and green-gold eyes behind cat's-eye glasses. Erica is three years younger, nearly six feet tall, with an hourglass figure and masses of curly black hair.

"The year we were hired, Erica and I were the only new teachers," Julia volunteers over cappuccinos in a New York City coffee shop. "We hadn't been drawn to each other in college, but with work I think we both felt like we had much more in common. It made sense that we'd become friends."

Their relationship started out easygoing and comfortable, a pleasant outlet for the stresses of being new and often overworked teachers. Both women were training for a local triathlon, and they regularly saw each other on the jogging trail that ran behind the school. As the miles unfolded, they would discuss their classroom, their weekend plans, or a new movie or restaurant they wanted to check out.

Gradually that even give-and-take began to shift in Erica's direction. Though she proved a talented and creative teacher, Erica's personal life was in constant upheaval. After only a few months on the job, she started an affair with an assistant principal who was married, though Erica assured Julia that he planned to leave his wife as soon as he could. She was coming off another troubled relationship, which had culminated in a broken engagement, and her life seemed a continual flood of crises and turmoil.

As the year progressed, the friendship grew increasingly imbalanced. Julia was a quieter personality with a quieter life, her biggest drama consisting of moving into a new apartment. She also tended to be more private and felt uncomfortable with the depth of Erica's confessions. Most of the time, she just kept her mouth shut and listened.

"It was clear to me that our lives were headed in two very different directions," Julia recalls. "I tried to be supportive, but I admit I was overwhelmed."

That spring, Erica's personal dramas started to seriously affect her work. Her office romance combusted when the assistant principal accepted a job in Oregon and decamped with his wife firmly in tow. Erica was devastated. She became touchy and volatile, prone to melting into tears at the smallest upset, and Julia dreaded having to team up with her on curriculum projects. Julia found herself regularly stepping in to cover for Erica, composing the entire lesson plans for their shared classes and occasionally handling the classes all by herself. Erica, wrapped up in her emotional overload, just assumed that rock-steady Julia would step in at a moment's notice.

"At that point she was so unreliable and her life was such a mess, I honestly didn't want anything more to do with her," Julia admits. "If it had been an ordinary friendship, I would've just pulled out. End of story. But under the circumstances, I was trapped. However I felt about Erica personally, we still had to work together."

At a loss over how to disengage without hurting Erica's feelings, not to mention their professional relationship, Julia simply froze. She started avoiding Erica whenever possible, running in her own neighborhood and working through lunch. Though upset by Erica's behavior, Julia decided just to stomach the fact that Erica continued to take advantage of her professionally. She felt that complaining to the principal would be a betrayal of Erica's confidences, and Julia didn't want to put Erica's job in jeopardy. Julia admits that Erica probably wasn't sure what happened to the relationship. She started jokingly referring to Julia as "the incredible vanishing lady." Even a year later, relations remained strained. Apart from their required work interactions, the two women rarely spoke.

"We're stuck in this awkward place, and I can't see any way out of it," Julia tells me. "We're clearly not friends anymore but, with everything I know about Erica's personal life, it would be impossible to go back to just being colleagues. I have no idea what we are anymore."

Getting to Know All About You

Expectations about women's "personal touch" have played a major role in defining their position in the workplace. In late-nineteenth-century America, as small business concerns morphed into larger conglomerates, organizations such as banks, department stores, and insurance offices began hiring women not just as clerks but as managers and supervisors. They figured women's propensity to trust and understand one another might help woo an increasingly large female clientele. Utility companies sent out special female "home service agents" to demonstrate gas- and electric-powered appliances, and banks set up separate women's departments for female customers too shy or embarrassed to discuss their finances with a man.[2]

During the ensuing decades, as women took a crack at more traditionally male positions, the cultural cachet attached to this talent for female intimacy began to dissipate. By the 1980s, many women had donned power suits and performed a workplace flipflop. Those attempting to infiltrate fields like law, medicine, or finance discovered that it paid to be considered tough, to blend in as one of the guys. The professional benefits attached to being "good at relationships" were suddenly called into question.

Today, that emotional pendulum has started to swing back again, leaving the relationship between women, emotions, and the workplace in a state of considerable flux. The idea of home as the realm of the heart and office as the realm of the head is rapidly disappearing. Work-social crossover crops up everywhere, encompassing corporate retreats, longer hours, more relaxed dress codes, and companies billed as giant families. In many cases, corporations now provide the support and social opportunities, from exercise classes to prayer groups to gardening clubs, that used to stem from neighborhoods and communities.[3] On the other end, those "softer," more relationship-oriented professions that women have traditionally pursued, like teaching and nonprofit work, have acquired a more competitive edge as they are increasingly treated as serious, long-term careers.

Perhaps the most significant development in workplace attitudes toward interpersonal relationships came in the mid-1990s, when science writer Daniel Goleman began spreading the gospel of "emotional intelligence." Goleman claimed that our capacity for recognizing and managing our own feelings and those of others was as significant to professional success as the cognitive intelligence society had traditionally valued.[4]

"I think it's safe to say Dan Goleman helped to change the face of American business in this regard," says Wharton business school professor Sigal Barsade. "He wasn't the first to discuss emotional intelligence, but his book put the concept on the popular map. It used to be that if you went into an organization and even mentioned the word 'emotion' everyone would look at you blankly. These days emotions are a very hot topic, very respected and very considered."[5]

For men, and for the traditionally cognitive-centered workplace culture, this leap into the "hot side" of organizational life was liberating. For women, who have been practicing emotional availability most of our lives, such an office revolution proved a mixed blessing. When it comes to professional relationships, we now encounter even fewer rules about what is emotionally appropriate and greater emphasis on being emotionally tuned to our colleagues. However, it is possible to be overly intimate on the job. Women do need to pay attention to fostering the personal elements of our professional relationships, but we also need to address what happens when—as with Julia and Erica—the personal and professional become too tightly merged.

Confiding in and sharing with other women on the job can be highly gratifying. Our individual experiences often differ from those of our male colleagues—especially when it comes to gender-related issues like glass ceilings, sexual harassment, or balancing work and family. A female sounding board or voice of experience can provide tremendous help. Many of the women I interviewed said their richest workplace ties had been with other women.

"When the relationships are good they're very, very good," said Robin, a restaurant manager in her early thirties who has had several female mentors. "But when they're bad, they're a disaster."

Women can feel enormous freedom and enormous pressure when it comes to forming bonds with other women. The question of how personal our professional relationships should get was a prominent issue among the women with whom I spoke. Many struggled over just how close they should be to their female colleagues. They felt suffocated when the relationships got too intimate, but alienated or guilty when they held themselves too distant. A number of them, like Julia, resented their female colleagues simply assuming it was appropriate to share the details of their personal lives, and to expect an equal degree of sharing in return. They reported that such personal dramas made the workplace feel awkward and unprofessional, taking up time and energy that got in the way of doing the actual job.

"My office mate used to spend half an hour every morning talking about her divorce," one woman, a YMCA program facilitator, explained. "I listened, because I knew how much she needed someone to talk to, but I also wound up late to every staff meeting, because I never had enough time to prepare."

"My boss was trying to get pregnant, and she used to come in every morning and tell me all the details of her fertility treatments," reported another. "How am I supposed to respect her as a boss after knowing something like that?"

Such tensions played a far more significant factor in women's relationships with other women than with their male coworkers. This makes sense. Our female friendships tend to be rooted in the exchange of intimate information. We share more, and we do it earlier in the relationship. This can create a deeper sense of trust and empathy than may be typical of male bonds, but it can also prime us to anticipate instant intimacy with one another and to pursue such intimacy over respect, loyalty, honesty, and all other aspects of our relationships. Such ready sharing of confidences can lead us to trust other women before the groundwork for that trust, in the form of time and shared experiences, has been laid.

Such a priority scale doesn't translate well to the workplace. On the job, we are grouped with colleagues with whom we did not chose to work and who did not choose to work with us. Our interactions contain preordained goals and responsibilities that often supercede the relationships themselves. We find ourselves in directly competitive situations with our coworkers, and status can shift instantly by way of promotions, downsizing, reassignments, and reassessments. We may be working with people whose value systems we do not share or even respect. For women, it can feel awkward not to engage with one another on a deeper personal level, as if we have become insensitive or unfeeling, as if we have lost our more human side. But a degree of professional distance can also make all these other factors more navigable.

"It's too hard to play both manager and counselor," a supervisor with a major manufacturing company told me, explaining why she steps aside whenever employees turn to her with personal problems. "Because I'm one of the higher profile women in the company, women have approached me about everything from an irritating mother-in-law to spousal abuse. Though they may want a shoulder to cry on in the moment, my getting involved can create real trouble later on. It's too difficult to take a boss seriously or judge an employee impartially when you're in on the messy details of their personal lives."

Julia still finds her experience with Erica uncomfortable to discuss. She understands that Erica was under a great deal of emotional stress. She even sees how Erica might have viewed Julia—a woman of a similar age and background, a woman with whom she had a prior relationship, however slight—as a logical life preserver. She tells me she worries that she might have been too abrupt, not sensitive enough to Erica's plight. Overriding all that, I get the sense that Erica's unbidden emotional onslaught left Julia feeling violated.

"The truth is I'm not comfortable with all that emotional stuff," she confesses late in our conversation. "It's never been my thing. It probably sounds cold, but taking care of Erica shouldn't be part of my job."

Women's cultural roles often include tending to other women—be they friends or colleagues, intimates or strangers—in times of emotional travail. From *Little Women* to *Oprah*, we have absorbed the fact that authentic female bonding entails always, but always, being there in a pinch. Though a competitive office environment may discourage too much personal investment, that same investment still earns women high marks from society in general.

It can be tempting to believe that establishing intimacy with our female peers is one skill that women—with our vast experience as caregivers and caretakers—have down pat. By buying into such expectations, we leapfrog over questions that are critical to shaping our workplace relationships. What's the difference between friend and colleague? Where are the boundaries dividing our personal and professional lives? And how do we know when those boundaries have been crossed?

A Little Friendly Competition

"I'm very ambitious," Paula tells me flat out as we seat ourselves on matching, ergonomically correct office chairs in a conference room overlooking the hazy New Jersey skyline. Paula is on the cusp of forty with chin-length sandy brown hair and a round face with crinkles just starting to appear around the eyes. The office park spread out below us houses the pharmaceutical company at which she started working as a drug rep five years ago.

"As soon as I landed with the company, I got a reputation as a mover and a shaker," she continues, explaining her rapid rise to her current position as marketing executive. "I pushed forward a lot of new ideas and scaled the promotional ladder very quickly."

About two years ago, Paula and one of her colleagues, Isabelle, were named co-marketing directors for a new drug launch, the only two women on the team. Though both had been with the company for a number of years, this was their first opportunity to work together, and they hit it off instantly. Paula had heard rumors that her new coworker could be brash and difficult to work with, but she found she appreciated Isabelle's straightforward style. Isabelle came from a strong financial background whereas Paula was more of a creative person, and their sensibilities meshed well.

Midproject, they flew to Switzerland for a conference, and on the way, over miniature bottles of bourbon, they wound up swapping entire family histories. Both women were mothers of toddlers, and during the ensuing months, they spent many travel hours commiserating over the difficulties of balancing work and home, including how often they had no choice but to let work slide. When Paula, who was two years younger, unexpectedly got pregnant, Isabelle was the first person she told, this time through tears in a bar in Cleveland as she agonized over fitting a second child into her chaotic schedule.

A year later, shortly after Paula's second child was born, her husband got an impossible-to-turn-down job offer in Virginia. Paula decided to try telecommuting, flying up to New Jersey for sales meetings every other week. Though she knew it meant slowing her career track, Paula liked the prospect of getting to spend more time with her children. She talked over the decision with Isabelle, who was supportive and encouraged her to push for the schedule she wanted.

Then, just months after Paula's move, Isabelle was promoted to a newly created position as senior manager of the marketing division. Suddenly, she had become Paula's boss. Though Paula knew she had not been considered for the job because of her decision to work remotely, the shift in hierarchy rankled.

"It was hard for me to accept that Isabelle got a promotion just because she was on the scene and I wasn't," Paula says. "There was no difference in our talent or our experience level, but now she was in charge of me. Our relationship changed drastically."

Paula's primary worry was that all those personal revelations she and Isabelle had shared would come back to haunt her. She regretted how honest she had been about how things were going.

"I'd told Isabelle about how I would take afternoons off to go to my son's soccer games and how working from home usually meant I put in fewer hours. Suddenly I was afraid she was going to use stuff like that against me. As a woman, I always felt a lot of pressure to hide my home responsibilities, and I was grateful for the chance to share family trials with an equal. But I never would've done it with a boss."

Given their friendship, Paula expected Isabelle to treat her more as a collaborator than an underling, but Isabelle's promotion seemed to have the opposite affect. Paula felt as if none of her ideas were making it to the higher ups, and she hated that she now had to go through Isabelle to reach those power players with whom she used to communicate directly.

Whenever Paula made suggestions, whether about budgeting a project or boosting promotional efforts, Isabelle always seemed to disagree. A palpable tension developed between them.

"At this point my emotions were very much involved, so I may be wrong about this," Paula admits, "but it felt like she wasn't just rejecting my ideas. She was rejecting me."

Feeling frustrated and shut out of the creative process, Paula started going around Isabelle and directly to the vice president to get her ideas heard. When Isabelle found out, she hit the roof. There were fights, accusations, and plenty of tears.

"In the end, we abandoned the friendship entirely," Paula says. "That shift in the hierarchy ruined it. My pride wouldn't let me answer to Isabelle. We were both just too ambitious to work things out."

In their research on female friendship, psychologists Susie Orbach and Luise Eichenbaum found that close bonds between women frequently depend upon the status of both sides remaining similar—socially, economically, professionally. Women's relationships are easily threatened when one friend accrues more money, a successful romance, a better job, or anything else that throws this synchronicity out of whack.[6] When a close female colleague moves ahead as Isabelle did—or gets a new job or even switches careers—she can leave her friend feeling deserted on that level they used to share. The accompanying jealousy and sense of abandonment are disconcerting. We can feel torn between selflessly wanting the best for our colleague and selfishly worrying what her advancement says about us. Left unaddressed, such negative feelings are capable of destroying the relationship for good.

I heard from a number of women who had experienced difficulty reconciling such shifts in power with the personal relationship they had forged on the job. They worried about how to react when they advanced ahead of a friend or a friend ahead of them, or when both found themselves gunning for the same promotion. A major status shift can be damaging to any workplace relationship, regardless of the gender of those involved. No one wants to feel less smart or talented than his or her peers. Among men it is generally a given that everyone is looking to climb the ladder, but women often had mixed feelings about coming across as more ambitious or successful than their friends. Cultural messages about female generosity and self-sacrifice got tangled up with organizational messages about looking out for number one. It was difficult to locate the point at which success for one party didn't feel like a kick in the face to another.

Like many women's relationships, Paula's connection to Isabelle—based as it was in commiseration over their shared status within the company—depended heavily on maintaining equality. That bond was seriously rattled when Isabelle moved ahead. Paula acknowledged that the personal details the two had shared made her feel as if she had painted a bull's-eye on her own back. She was less comfortable admitting that Isabelle's advancement stirred her insecurities about having abandoned the fast track. Paula's reaction to Isabelle's promotion seemed to have more to do with coming to terms with the life choices she had made than with either woman being "too ambitious" to work together. Seeing Isabelle move ahead raised frustrations for Paula about having had to choose between family and career while Isabelle seemingly got to have both.

Instead of admitting such worries to Isabelle, Paula decided to proceed as if nothing had changed. She even tried to reinstate their equal status by collaborating directly with her superiors and jumping the chain of command. It's no wonder the relationship splintered. By refusing to acknowledge the new hierarchy, Paula compromised her own professional integrity and cast a clear vote of nonfaith in her friend's ability to perform.

The new imbalance in their relationship raised Isabelle's defenses as well. The intimacies she and Paula had swapped probably made her feel equally vulnerable. She may have worried that Paula would use that personal knowledge to undermine her. She may have felt guilty that she had opted for a faster career track and less family time as opposed to Paula's more culturally accepted choices—family first, job and career a distant runner-up. Instead of taking steps to ease Paula's transition from peer to subordinate by including her in decisions, she asserted her newly acquired power by shutting Paula out. Neither woman was willing to sit down and discuss the ways in which not just their job status but the status of their friendship had changed.

"I think both of us could've been more respectful of the other's situation," Paula reflects over a year later. "We could've gone into it with our eyes wide open, saying: 'Hey this is going to be a little weird, what are we going to do if we have a disagreement?' But even that may not have been enough. The situation brought out a competitive streak in both of us and there was no way around that. At this point, I feel like the best plan is just to never work with a friend again."

Paula's idea that ambition and friendship can't mix made me wonder about her definition of friendship. Many women I talked to were still unsure how to reconcile the fact that a personal friend can also be a professional rival. There is often a belief that when another woman befriends us, she will stop competing with us. It can be jarring to realize that, to the contrary, she is still aggressively—even to our eyes selfishly—pursuing her own goals.

When forging friendships with our female colleagues, it is important to factor in the realities of working together. Would you feel comfortable with this level of intimacy if your friend became your boss, if she got promoted over you, or if you got promoted over her? We need to recognize that those intimate details we freely exchange in our private lives can have far more serious consequences when thrown into the professional mix. On-the-job revelations do make us vulnerable. They can give our colleagues leeway to be less respectful professionally—the way Paula was with Isabelle—forcing situations in which we feel compelled to choose between our friendships and our careers.

What Could I Do? She Was a Friend

Georgia was in her midthirties when she was first elected to the district court in her Chicago-area county. Now a presiding judge, she has served on the bench for the past twenty years. When she started, only 5 percent of her fellow judges were female; now that number has risen to almost 40 percent. She has the measured, rational demeanor you would expect of her profession, carefully considering each question before offering a response, but she also has a rich laugh and an irreverent sense of humor.

Part of Georgia's role as presiding judge is to deal with complaints filed about her fellow judges and to mediate when conflicts arise. Not long ago, the supervisor for the county district attorneys' office came to Georgia regarding one of her colleagues, Olivia.

"Olivia and I came up through the ranks together," Georgia tells me. "We were both part of that original 5 percent, and we've been close friends for years."

The supervisor expressed concern over Olivia's habit of inviting young male prosecutors to basketball games or out to dinner. Her advances made the guys uncomfortable. Though they felt Olivia was crossing a professional boundary, they were in no position to turn her down. Alienating a sitting judge could do serious damage to their conviction records and their careers.

Georgia found herself in an awkward position. She felt confident there were no shady ulterior motives behind Olivia's behavior. She was just partaking in some ego stroking, enjoying the prospect of being popular with all those young male attorneys. At the same time, Georgia found her friend's behavior professionally inappropriate.

"As a judge, impartiality is tantamount. You shouldn't be fraternizing or forming friendships with district attorneys, who you may have to rule against in the near future," Georgia explains. "A judge shouldn't want to be popular or even liked. I've always respected Olivia professionally, but I found her behavior very unsettling."

Despite the fact that she felt Olivia was clearly in the wrong, Georgia was hesitant to intercede. She feared it would prove embarrassing, given their friendship. She did not want to jeopardize the relationship by humiliating Olivia or questioning her judgment.

"I couldn't even imagine what to say. 'Hey Olivia, these guys really don't want to go out with you.' How was that going to make her feel?"

Past experience had taught Georgia that women can be hypersensitive to criticism of their performance, especially judges whose work records are regularly subjected to public opinion polls, something Georgia equates to "having your report card published in the newspaper." Once, several years ago, she had pulled aside a friend who had received a low approval rating and tried to offer advice on how to improve things. The woman wound up accusing Georgia of being a lackey to the system and making ethical compromises to get ahead. The accusations hurt, and the friendship was all but over. It was not an experience she cared to repeat.

At the same time, it was Georgia's job to step in. Much as she wanted to, she could not just ignore the complaint. After a week spent reviewing and discarding various options, Georgia finally settled on a stopgap remedy. From then on, only female lawyers were allowed to appear in Olivia's court. Georgia was not pleased with the decision. It felt neither fair, nor unbiased.

"It was more patch job than a solution," she admits. "I probably should've talked to her, but the prospect was just too uncomfortable. What could I do? She was a friend."

I deally, friendships with our female colleagues create a more open and trusting environment, but when issues involving professional judgment or job performance are on the line, those same bonds can become a barrier to honest communication. Many women I spoke to shared Georgia's impression that relationships among women are emotionally fragile, requiring more psychological caretaking than those with our male coworkers.

"I'm terrified to raise problems with the women I work with, because I'm convinced I'm going to hurt their feelings," says Kedra, a twenty-nine-year-old field biologist at an environmental agency. "I know it's ludicrous—God forbid someone not like me—but I'm sensitive to criticism, and I don't anticipate my colleagues being any tougher. It just seems safest to handle every woman like she could potentially fall apart."

As Georgia had already discovered, there are grains of truth in such fears. Women are not necessarily moodier or more emotional than men, but we are encouraged to express our emotions more openly, making others aware of both our pleasure and our resentment. Our still shaky professional status can make women especially sensitive to workplace criticism. Since we often feel more pressured to perform perfectly, with less room for error and more at stake if we mess up, we can come to rely heavily upon outside approval as proof of a job well done.

"Women are very easily upset by feedback," says sociologist and sex therapist Pepper Schwartz. "Men are a bit more likely to think that is part of the deal, or accept smaller slights without even noticing them, while women—attentive to emotional detail—are more easily offended or feel put down and unappreciated."[7]

An isolated critique can come across like a resounding note of overall disapproval. When that criticism originates from a female friend, the stakes climb once again. In women's relationships with one another, conflict and intimacy are oil and water. We are taught to anticipate only positive support and "nice" behavior from other women, even those in a position of authority over us. Georgia had a legitimate fear of being seen as the betrayer if she criticized Olivia. As with Paula and Isabelle, the boundaries separating their interactions as friends and their interactions as colleagues were difficult to define.

Georgia saw herself taking the appropriate steps to preserve her long-standing friendship, but in the process she deserted her professional responsibilities entirely. Her choice to bypass the district attorneys' complaint placed both women in a precarious spot. Georgia chanced subjecting herself to criticism from those male prosecutors no longer permitted to appear in Olivia's court. She also gave Olivia the impression that fraternizing with the district attorneys was acceptable behavior, leaving the door open for someone less compassionate to call her on it down the line. Though the details of the decision were kept between Olivia and the DA supervisor, the fact that men had stopped appearing in Olivia's court was sure to be noticed and commented upon, setting rumor mills abuzz. In acting to protect Olivia's feelings, Georgia risked ruining her friend's judicial reputation.

Two years after "resolving" the complaint, Georgia continues to harbor a long shadow of uncertainty. Though Olivia went on to accept a leadership position in the local judicial association, the ban on male DAs in her courtroom—which lasted roughly a year—did hurt her reputation in the short term, generating a fair amount of courtroom gossip.

"Was it the right decision?" Georgia reflects. "I honestly don't know. As a judge, no, as a friend, yes. In retrospect, I'd say I made a mistake. I should have discussed the problem with Olivia, but I still have doubts about whether our friendship could've survived that conversation."

Georgia's either-or interpretation of the situation—seeing herself as able to act as either a judge or a friend but not both—resulted in a decision that compromised her on all fronts. Though it may have felt like the easiest route, it was neither honest nor judicious. Confronting Olivia directly and attempting to work with her on a viable solution would have given Olivia the opportunity to defend her actions and participate in her own future. If Georgia had been less daunted by the prospect of Olivia's discomfort and her own, their friendship and their professional integrity might have emerged intact.

When we establish friendships with our female colleagues, there may be times when we are tempted to bypass professional duties in order to avoid personal upsets. In such cases, it is wise to weigh carefully the potential damage and ask whether there is a better way to respect and retain our personal ties. "It sounds counterintuitive, but when you're working with friends, you can't be too compassionate," a product engineer in her late fifties told me. "If you're ruled by the impulse to protect everyone's feelings, you'll find yourself in a position where you can no longer trust your professional judgment." Tackling a workplace problem will challenge a friendship. It may require difficult conversations, extra time, and added sensitivity. Most of all, it requires trusting one another enough to communicate openly without assuming the whole relationship will come crashing down.

Tossing It All Out There

Kim had worked as a professional opera and pop singer for twelve years when she met Annabelle, a fellow performer and teacher at a Minneapolis music school. Music, particularly opera, was a highly competitive field, and it was rare that Kim befriended another female singer.

"The music business practically requires that you be self-centered," she explains over tea in an outdoor cafe one cloudy spring afternoon. She is pint-sized and waifish, dressed in sweatpants and a tattered orange T-shirt, the opposite of every opera diva stereotype. "I met Annabelle at a point when I was feeling very disillusioned. I loved singing, but I hated what being a professional singer had turned me into."

Their friendship bloomed quickly. Kim and Annabelle spent hours discussing how much they missed the pleasure they had once found in singing, and fantasized about opening a music school that emphasized process over performance. Several years later, with the talk still going strong, they decided to give their fantasy plan a whirl. They found a small studio space in the city and, four months later, opened a music school catering to children and adults of all levels.

"It was exciting," Kim says. "We had a real mission. Most vocal training is so strict and humorless. We wanted to create something where people could learn without having to sacrifice the fun."

In many ways, Kim and Annabelle complemented one another perfectly. Kim, having run her own opera company, came with all the necessary business and promotional skills. Annabelle, who had studied and sung all over the world, excelled at the musical and creative end of things.

"Everything came together very quickly. We found a space, we found students. Then, that first week, Annabelle and I tried to teach a group class together. It was a disaster."

Both women were accustomed to being the center of attention—what Kim refers to as their shared diva complex—and once in the room together, they continuously interrupted and stepped on each other's toes. Neither wanted to cede control. The students were confused, and the class grew tense and awkward.

"Neither of us was willing to give way," Kim recalls. "There was this power struggle going on between us right in the middle of the classroom."

Both Kim and Annabelle felt blindsided by what would prove a significant problem. They had assumed that, given their close friendship, they would just naturally work well together. For a few weeks, they kept quiet and tried to plow through, but it was clear that if they continued on that path they risked ruining the relaxed atmosphere that was the school's raison d'être. So one afternoon they sat down together and starting talking.

"We communicated as honestly as we could about what was and wasn't working," Kim says. "We didn't try to be nice. There was ego damage on both sides."

That first session was followed by a string of others. "It was challenging. There were points when I was afraid we wouldn't make it through. But in the end, fulfilling our vision for the school was more important than protecting our feelings. The only way to preserve what we had going was to toss it all out there and dig through."

Eventually, they agreed that the best solution entailed dividing the work in a way that would minimize the competition between them. They set up a system in which Annabelle covered the school Mondays, Wednesdays, and Fridays, and Kim taught Tuesdays, Thursdays, and weekends.

"We really wanted to work together fluidly, but it was clear that couldn't happen," Kim explains. She adds that it felt even harder to address such problems with an intimate like Annabelle, because she didn't want to damage the relationship. The whole process required communication, compromise, and a fair degree of self-reflection, none of which came easily but all of which bore results. Three years later, the friendship and the school continue to thrive.

"It's ironic," Kim reflects. "Our relationship became most harmonious when we admitted we couldn't work together. Initially, we just assumed every day would go smoothly, because we were friends. Now, when we have to work together, we discuss it in advance and try to anticipate problems before they happen. We communicate a lot. It works beautifully."

Moving Forward by Stepping Back

Navigating emotional ties with our female colleagues is rarely an either-or proposition. It is far too simplistic to say we need to separate the personal and professional entirely, that our external concerns should not spill over into the workplace, that intimacy doesn't belong on the job. Socialization is a key part of working together and to attempt to cut that out would leave something cold and impersonal behind. Though emotional investment in and of itself certainly is not a bad thing—for Kim and Annabelle, their friendship proved a key component to a dream job—it should arise as a choice and not a compulsion. Julia was right in saying that, as women in the workplace, it is not our job to manage the insecurities and emotional dramas of our female colleagues, nor is it their job to manage ours.

The dangers of getting overly enmeshed in our colleagues' lives are a logical offshoot of today's work-obsessed culture. Professional and financial success often demand that women and men spend inordinate time and energy at the office, meaning many of us have begun to look to the workplace for the emotional fulfillment that earlier generations found in family and community. People often don't have time, or perhaps are just no longer taught, to prioritize friendship for friendship's sake. For women, who tend to draw even more sustenance from social ties than men, there's a natural tendency to try picking up this relational slack by developing closer bonds on the job.

As career continues to play a larger role in women's lives, it is tempting to believe the rewards we glean from our jobs can fix and fill us, providing all the security, acceptance, and peace of mind it is so difficult to find in the broader world. But that is too much pressure to place on our professional ties. When we search for validation and a sense of purpose exclusively from workplace relationships, we are far more likely to feel betrayed when those relationships take an unexpected turn. As Julia, Paula, and Georgia all discovered, it is not always wise to bond with our coworkers as freely and closely as we might with acquaintances outside the office. A number of the most successful women with whom I spoke said they maintained their professional equilibrium by purposely keeping their private lives private—friends and family in one compartment, work and colleagues in another.

"I have cordial relationships with the women I work with," said one high-level food industry executive in her early fifties, "but I make it very clear that we are not buddies. I'm their coworker or their boss, not their best friend."

There is no shame in stepping back. Emotional intelligence in the workplace requires being emotionally tuned and present, but it also requires wisdom and control. A degree of professional distance does not preclude being supportive or generous toward our female colleagues, nor are we being disloyal by tempering our personal investment. With promotions, salaries, and reputations on the line, chances are our most successful professional relationships will be those based less in intimacy than in mutual respect.

4

Looking Clean, Dealing Dirty

Penelope meets me at a coffee shop in downtown Boston clad in a T-shirt and denim skirt, her long brown hair caught up in a haphazard ponytail. She arrives late and apologetic, having squeezed our interview in between a client appointment and her daughter's softball game. In her midforties and a mother of three, Penelope has spent the past ten years working for a children's clothing store just outside the city. The job evolved out of a friendship Penelope struck up with the store's owner, Natalie, who had started the business a year earlier upon emerging from a difficult divorce.

A frequent customer, Penelope had come to admire the company ethic, which emphasized handmade items and environmentally friendly materials. She began doing some volunteer work for the shop, and eventually Natalie hired her part time. Though the pay was low, Natalie made up for it by lavishing Penelope with attention and compliments.

"Natalie seemed so beautiful and gracious and smart," Penelope recalls. "I really admired her and what she stood for, and I so wanted her to like me. The fact that she was paying me at all seemed like an afterthought."

Penelope continued working with Natalie for the next eight years, acquiring a growing understanding of the business and building relationships with clients. She took over much of the daily contact with designers and began to manage other employees. Natalie even graced her with a title, creative director, but her salary stayed exactly the same. Penelope—who had no college degree and whose work experience ran the gamut from cleaning houses to managing a chiropractor's office—felt lucky to be trusted with such responsibility. It was not until her oldest son left for college that financial realities intervened. Penelope flat-out needed to earn more to keep her family afloat.

"I was so embarrassed about having to raise the issue with Natalie," Penelope admits. "I didn't want her to think I was just in it for the money."

When Penelope told Natalie that she would have to quit if she did not get a salary increase, Natalie complied with a slight raise. She also made her colleague legal owner of a small share in the company, roughly 10 percent, in appreciation for her contributions over the years.

Around the same time, with business booming, Natalie decided to open a second store. She offered to place Penelope in charge of the satellite operation, giving her a chance for real autonomy. Excited and flattered, Penelope immersed herself in plans for the new space. At first, Natalie was nothing but encouraging, but when Penelope saw the formal version of the new organizational structure, she was surprised to find her boss had taken back all the responsibilities they had initially discussed. Natalie shrugged off the change, explaining that she felt keeping one person in charge was better for the company.

As they proceeded with coordinating the new store, Natalie continued to block Penelope's contributions. In fact, the more Penelope asserted her knowledge and ideas, the flimsier Natalie's support grew. She vetoed a line of baby items Penelope had chosen, saying they did not fit in with the stock. She began drumming up excuses for Penelope not to contact clients directly and continued to knock down Penelope's suggestions about designs and products.

Soon Natalie began to sabotage Penelope more directly, doing things like setting impossible deadlines then blaming Penelope when she couldn't come through. Penelope learned via a coworker that Natalie had gone to the store's clients and employees and expressed doubts about Penelope's commitment to her job. When Penelope tried to speak up in her own defense, Natalie accused her of being selfish and putting her own needs before those of the business. Any confrontations between them happened behind closed doors or over the phone. In front of others, Natalie continued to wrap Penelope in compliments, acting as if they were the best of friends.

"After a while, it started to feel like she was undermining me just to undermine me," Penelope says. "She was making really stupid decisions that hurt the company. It was so disappointing. The whole setup is based on values like respect and compassion, but when it came down to it, all Natalie cared about was control. She loved me when she didn't have to pay me anything and I did whatever she said. As soon as I started having ideas and opinions, everything changed."

Though the new store opened successfully, the split it wrought between Penelope and Natalie worsened. Natalie still acted as though they were confidantes, but Penelope was afraid to speak up about anything, never knowing whether she'd be coddled or cut off at the knees. She felt both used and betrayed.

"At this point there's an 80 percent chance I'll leave," she tells me, fiddling with the rim of her empty coffee cup. "I've pulled out of our friendship entirely. All the joy of the job, the human connection part, is gone. I feel like Natalie's been deceiving me for the past ten years."

Penelope's experience with Natalie echoes a pattern described by a number of the women I interviewed: looking clean while dealing dirty. When conflict or competition arises in the workplace, some women avoid engaging directly with their female colleagues and opt for what can seem a less troublesome route. Afraid of what might happen if they openly acknowledge tensions with their coworker, they shirk potential problems—often those rooted in discomfort with their own power or ambition—by way of passive-aggressive behaviors, attacking underground while continuing to appear warm and friendly on the surface.

Throughout history, women have had a reputation for using deception to get ahead—just look at *I, Claudius* or Shakespeare's *Antony and Cleopatra*. The less genuine access women have had to power, the more inventive, and often duplicitous, they have had to become in order to secure it. The stereotype of the backstabbing female rival went professional with our old classic *All About Eve*, in an era in which working women possessed few chances to compete anywhere but behind the scenes. Women might have hoped to shed this pattern entirely now that we have swapped ladies' luncheons for the front office, but in talking to professional women, I found that the phenomenon of looking clean while dealing dirty has far from disappeared.

Duplicitous maneuvers are by no means exclusive to women. Studies have shown that adult men gossip, cheat, and employ other modes of "indirect aggression" to veil villainous behaviors as often as women do.[1] So why does the image of woman as saboteur prevail? Maybe we have spent too much time looking through the wrong end of the telescope. Instead of marveling at the underlying treachery that can unfold among women, we might consider the real root of the problem: not our dirty dealing, but our perpetual need to look clean.

Though we tend to hear more about women's efforts to please the men in our lives, our need for approval from other women can become an equally driving force. When I stepped into those jobs alongside my female bosses and colleagues, there is no question I was towing a long line of expectations about what they could and should provide. From the start, those relationships were infused with grains of my past—of my mother, my childhood girlfriends, my feminist education. Friction with my female coworkers made me more uncomfortable than friction with men might have. Pleasing them carried a different sort of reward.

We often ask more of the women in our lives. We ask them to be nicer, gentler, more generous and self-sacrificing than their male counterparts. We assume they will understand us without our having to explain ourselves. We are less willing to forgive them their flaws or contradictions. When these stricter standards flow into the workplace, they create rosy visions for our relationships that prove nearly impossible to fulfil. In order to live up to such expectations, women often perform a personality split—into a "clean" side that wins constant approval and a "dirty" side willing to compete.

Conventional interpretation might peg Penelope as Little Red Riding Hood and Natalie as the Big Bad Wolf of their tale. In looking closer, their problems stem from both sides of the story. Though Natalie wanted to fold Penelope into her company, she was not secure enough to risk sharing her control, her power, or her spoils. She had created a near spotless image for herself—mentor, buddy, font of wisdom—one she discovered she couldn't possibly live up to. So she resolved her conflict by letting those uncomfortable feelings play out beneath a squeaky clean facade. As long as she was acting "for the good of the company," Natalie could convince herself that she was being neither selfish nor competitive. As long as she was nice in small ways, sprinkling everything with compliments, she felt free to take advantage of Penelope in larger ones.

Penelope, too, played her part in the situation. By refusing to stand up to Natalie, she made it far easier for her boss to exploit her. Penelope wanted to see herself as the willing collaborator, the constant support system, the good egg, even at the price of her own self-respect. If she did nothing to confront her problems with Natalie, she could not be blamed for what went wrong in the relationship. Like Penelope, many of us tend to imbue our female conflicts with a strong moral flavor. There is a prevailing myth that we should not express, or even experience, negative feelings toward other women, that if we are only good enough—what one interviewee described as a "peace at any cost" person—we can create relationships that are conflict free.

Even as the women I interviewed worried about coming across as too harsh or critical, one of the most common complaints I heard was that women were not direct enough, that we were unwilling to lay our problems and conflicts on the table. A number of women admitted they preferred working with men, because they felt issues could be addressed openly and honestly without risk of triggering hurt or hidden feelings. Men's emotional reactions were more upfront and predictable, rarely shaped by the expectation of peace at any cost. As one woman put it: "With men, it is what it is. With women, you worry about what it is and about what it could be."

Women's tug of war between looking clean and dealing dirty reflects a point at which our ambitions clash with cultural expectations. In the past, such duplicitous behavior may have stemmed from women's fear of openly displaying their achievements or desires. Today, those fears have evolved into something new. We are not maneuvering to look nice instead of looking successful; we are maneuvering to do both—an emotional version of Superwoman. In order to sustain this split persona, it is no surprise that women often employ the same sort of relational aggression girls develop in adolescence. We find ourselves in a similar position, one in which we worry that exposing strong feelings or competitive impulses might get us into trouble. We are unsure how the ambition and drive demanded of the workplace might affect our relationships with other women, relationships in which qualities like empathy and sacrifice are supposed to prevail. By asserting our darker needs indirectly, we manage to get ahead and retain a reputation that is wholly kind, generous, and noncontroversial. We compete without appearing to compete.

Queen of the Hill

Elena is in her early fifties, fast talking and demonstrative, with titian hair and perfectly manicured purple fingernails. Born and raised in the Dominican Republic, she came to the United States in her early twenties to launch a career as a journalist. She went on to open a photography studio then spent ten years in the retail jewelry business, all the while "raising"—as she puts it—two husbands and four children.

Six years ago, she entered the real estate business, drawn by the money to be made and the fact that success was limited only by how hard you were willing to work. She traffics in high-end residential properties in an affluent Connecticut suburb. Though Elena is the sole Latina, all but one of the brokers in her office are women.

"The atmosphere is very competitive," Elena says. "You have to be a barracuda just to survive."

Elena acknowledges her own robust competitive streak. Since childhood, she has been driven "to set the world on fire." She works constantly and prides herself on her reputation for professionalism and perseverance. For the past two years, she has been top earner in her group.

These days, Elena's most pressing career troubles stem from Hannah, a fellow broker who has been selling in the area for fifteen years and who regularly captured top-earner status until Elena arrived on the scene. As soon as Elena started to register major sales, she heard rumors that Hannah had been undermining her with the other brokers, floating doubts about Elena's abilities and staying power.

Outwardly, Hannah was nothing but kind and generous. She often complimented Elena's hair or car or outfits, and was the first to offer congratulations when Elena made a big sale. Though Elena was just as friendly back, she put little stock in Hannah's warmth.

"When you've had as many careers as I have, you develop very good radar," she tells me. "Hannah may have pretended to love me to death, but underneath I got the feeling she really wanted to break my legs."

Elena's suspicions were borne out recently when a woman who had listed her home for sale with Hannah attended an open house Elena was conducting and fell in love with the property. Elena and the client hit it off beautifully. When the woman made an offer on the house, Elena was surprised she opted to have Hannah handle her half of the sale. Being cut out of the buyer side of things meant Elena lost a significant chunk of commission on the seven-figure deal.

Shortly after closing, the client called Elena and asked if they could speak privately. Over several glasses of wine, she confessed to feeling horribly guilty. She said she had wanted Elena to handle the entire sale, but Hannah had convinced her that Elena could not be trusted to act for both buyer and seller, that the client would get screwed unless Hannah brokered her end of the deal. Elena was livid. If the client opted to go through Hannah because they already had a prior relationship, that was fair game. But Elena considered stealing a sale by impugning her honesty, the cornerstone of any broker's reputation, "a definite stab in the back."

In analyzing the situation, Elena fell back on those old good girl/bad girl stereotypes. She figured the incident with Hannah proved that she should not trust the women with whom she works, no matter how supportive they appeared on the outside. She stopped sharing information with other brokers and admits to getting paranoid about when and where Hannah might strike next. She always locks her office door and is even afraid to take a vacation for fear that Hannah will shanghai her best listings. This obsession, added to an already stressful job, is taking its toll.

"I've been in tears about this job more often than anything else in my life." Elena confesses. "I wish we all could just be open about the fact that the business we're in is dog eat dog. I've tried telling other brokers how weary I am of having to watch my back all the time. They pretend like they don't know what I'm talking about."

Elena gritted her teeth through Hannah's pleasant chitchat about how wonderful it was that they had managed to throw the deal together. She contemplated challenging Hannah about the stolen client, but opted to keep her mouth shut.

"With a man I would've confronted him directly, but women aren't worth the risk. The retribution can be brutal. Men are competitive, but you see it coming. Women can go from saccharine sweet to downright nasty in the time it takes you to turn around. Suddenly you're bleeding, and you never even saw the knife."

W omen can face a considerable challenge when our relationships with one another encounter the sort of direct competition common to the workplace. There is a widespread cultural belief that our female bonds are based on a natural gift, a shared brilliance for caring and communication. This intense relational focus can clash with a corporate culture set up to foster rivalries among its workers, both male and female. As a female attorney quoted in a 1998 study on women lawyers describes it, "There isn't the sense that this is a profession or that we're all in here together. It's economics and numbers, and there's only so much room at the top. . . . Immediately, people are in competition and out for themselves."[2]

In the workplace, the urge to bond with a female colleague will not always trump personal ambition. The business world measures success by rank and earnings, by who has power and who does not. In order to forge our way—male or female—we have to challenge our coworkers in upfront and sometimes not entirely friendly ways.

Though women today regularly find ourselves in highly competitive work environments, we still have few models for how to play professional hardball with our female colleagues. We are told we should value connection; we are told we should value ambition. We are rarely told how to integrate the two. Historically, women have spent centuries prioritizing self-sacrifice and the belief that we can compete on behalf of others—our children, our friends, our charitable causes—but never on behalf of ourselves. Openly ambitious women tended to come up against the harshest of criticism from both sexes. They were labeled deviants who had betrayed their gender in the quest for more knowledge or experience than they deserved.

Looking to the contemporary world offers little more in the way of guidance. As a society, we still come down like the Inquisition on any woman, from Martha Stewart to Hillary Clinton, who lets her hunger for power leak through that external "good girl" guise. Though women today are permitted to desire success, we are still supposed to pursue those desires in a generous and ladylike manner. One woman I interviewed, a communications professor who teaches on gender issues, said her female students' greatest fear about entering the workplace is not balancing work and family or garnering equal pay, but how to be successful without coming across as "the bitch."

Given such limited notions of femininity and power, it is no surprise when ambitious women like Hannah choose to handle a female rival with such backdoor methods as rumor spreading or sabotage. Of course Hannah felt competitive toward Elena. They were both angling for the same listings and clients. Of course she was jealous of this woman who had usurped her position as queen of the hill. But Hannah had no way of negotiating such envy and insecurity while still maintaining her nice-girl guise.

In dealing with Hannah, Elena proved as much a victim of her preconceptions about how women behave as Hannah was of hers. Boxed in by the idea of women going "from saccharine sweet to downright nasty in the time it takes you to turn around," Elena exchanged Hannah the person for Hannah the stereotype. Shedding our ideas about having to form ever-supportive female relationships does not mean leaping to the other extreme, keeping a constant eye peeled for the knife in our backs. Instead, we need to recognize the mutual existence of opposition and affiliation, and learn to strike a balance between the two.

Together, Elena's stereotypical thinking and Hannah's inability to deal openly with their competition formed a solid barrier toward resolution. Both women retreated to a comfort zone from which it was impossible to address what was really going on. Despite Elena's conviction otherwise, the possibility of an honest exchange between two similarly ambitious and successful female colleagues did exist. They could have risked openly acknowledging where things stood. As long as neither woman dared to speak up, their rivalry only threatened to swell, becoming one then two then five elephants in the corner. As Elena's locked doors and mounting stress illustrate, when we feel we cannot trust our colleagues, we wind up diverting far too much time and energy toward covering our backs.

The health of women's professional relationships depends upon allowing direct competition to flourish. When competition is accepted and considered part of the norm in a group or organization it is far less likely to generate tension between individual members.[3] As sociologist Dana Crowley Jack writes, "healthy relationships require mutuality (being with), but they also require positive aggression (being opposed)."[4] By sanitizing our interactions—turning our backs on the murkier, more selfish elements imbedded in disagreement—we may come across as nicer and less threatening, but we also erase any chance for communication, let alone growth, discovery, or debate.

When Looking Clean Is Dealing Dirty

Margaret and I talk parked side by side on the plump couch dominating her San Francisco living room, mostly because every other seating option is covered with paperwork relating to her soon-to-begin training as an airlift nurse. Margaret is a fresh-scrubbed redhead in her late twenties with a sprinkle of freckles covering nose and cheeks. A self-described adventurer, she splits her leisure time between skiing, sailing, and hiking in the mountains with her two chocolate labs. Otherwise, her days are consumed by training shifts and classes. Nights, she works as an Oakland-area emergency medical technician.

Though her nursing colleagues are almost all female, for more than a year Margaret was the only woman on her EMT squad. When Jamie, another nursing student, had joined up the previous spring, the general assumption was that Margaret would take her under her wing. Jamie was soft spoken and mousy, far from typical medic material, but she was also compassionate and expressed a real desire for a long-term stint with the squad. Margaret did everything she could to ease her new colleague into the mix. She gave her special extracurricular training sessions and assigned her the least stressful responsibilities.

"Basically I babysat her," Margaret explains. "I tried to break it to her gently that to succeed at this job you need to be willing to stick your neck out. You can't worry about being sweet and nice."

Then several months ago, during a wicked rainstorm, Margaret, Jamie, two firefighters, and two police units found themselves handling a "car vs. building" collision by themselves. A sedan had plowed headfirst into a brick housing complex on a steep hill. There were three victims, two with no heartbeat and a third with a severe head injury, who had to be extracted from the smashed rear seat of the car.

In EMT parlance, Margaret and Jamie were operating "above their scope of practice." Translation: They were in way over their heads. Since nobody else was available, they had to step up to the job. Margaret didn't have time to hold Jamie's hand. Left on her own, Jamie froze. When Margaret ordered her to help stabilize the accident scene, she objected that she had not been trained to do that. She had never driven the ambulance at night and was too afraid even to back it up so they could load the victims. She refused to ride in back with the head trauma patient, saying he was too sick.

"I was really harsh with her," Margaret recalls. "I was so frustrated. I wanted her to yell back at me or throw things or something, but all she did was sit there and cry."

Finally, Margaret shoved Jamie into the back with the patient and drove the ambulance through the rain-slicked streets herself, keeping the connecting window open the entire time and making Jamie count the patient's breaths out loud to keep her calm and focused.

When they returned to the firehouse in the early hours of the morning, Margaret took Jamie into a supply room, sat her down, and informed her that she was in the wrong career. They spent the next hour perched on boxes of cleaning fluid, with Jamie sobbing and apologizing and begging for another chance.

"I'd been beyond nice," Margaret asserts, a shade defensively. "I'd already given her far more chances than I ever would've given a guy. I sympathized, but I also told her in no uncertain terms that her actions had risked all of our lives. I would not work with her again, and if she didn't quit herself, I'd see that it happened for her."

Margaret knows that Jamie was devastated by their conversation. Months later, she is still grappling with guilt over coming down so hard. "I feel awful about it, but this is a tough job, and not everyone is going to make it. Not everyone should."

I ask her if she wishes things had played out differently, and she pauses before delivering a verdict.

"I feel like there was no right choice. Either desert Jamie or endanger everyone else. It wasn't a pleasant experience. I know Jamie thinks I'm a horrible mean person, but I had a responsibility to the unit. I did what I guess I had to do."

In speaking to women about their relationships with their female colleagues, I noticed an interesting phenomenon. While many of us are getting trapped by too strict a definition of looking clean, we are also falling victim to an excessively broad definition of dealing dirty. We assume that any situation in which we do not go out of our way to soothe and avoid negative feelings is a form of betrayal. Overcompensating as Margaret did, being too nice at the expense of another woman's best interest, can be just as damaging as being too harsh. Though we still look clean on the surface, we wind up doing our colleagues a serious disservice.

The guilt Margaret felt over coming down so hard on Jamie echoed a common sentiment among the women I interviewed, and society in general, that women should unequivocally stand behind one another just by virtue of our sex. Our culture has long glorified women's unity. Good girls bond, bad girls do not. Heroines from Nancy Drew to *Sex and the*

City's Carrie Bradshaw had gal pals. Emma Bovary was corrupted and friendless. Scarlett O'Hara's nastiness found clear expression in her not liking Melanie one bit.

This idea that women should only exert power over each other in nurturing ways can lead to some fancy footwork when we are forced to make authoritative decisions about our female colleagues. It is understandable that Margaret would feel a stronger pull toward her fellow emergency workers, the ones she knew would step up in a crisis, than toward Jamie, who had failed to prove herself. It is understandable that Jamie's meek personality and inability to follow through was frustrating in the extreme. Margaret was so concerned with being appropriately patient, supportive, and "beyond nice" that she lost sight of her professional judgment, misreading the degree of Jamie's inabilities and ultimately putting lives at risk.

Granting Jamie such massive—in fact dangerous—leeway allowed Margaret to sidestep those contradictions ingrained in having simultaneously to evaluate and cheerlead for our female colleagues. As women move upward in the workplace, we are encountering territory that increasingly challenges the old ideals of equality as the cornerstone for feminine interaction. As linguist Deborah Tannen notes in observing gender dynamics at work, "Our expectations for how a person in authority should behave are at odds with our expectations for how a woman should behave."[5] Authority is inherently uneven—it means we can hurt and unsettle each other. Using power, even using it responsibly, often entails using it in ways that do not please those women feeling its effects.

Though most jobs will not leave us in life-threatening circumstances, Margaret's situation illustrates what can happen when we are too frightened to adopt the full mantle of our authority. Her uneasiness with flexing her professional clout echoes Georgia's struggle over how to balance her roles as a judge and a friend. But Margaret, like a number of women I talked to, was not acting to preserve a friendship. She was not interested in a long-term relationship with Jamie; she didn't even particularly respect her. As a woman wielding power over another woman—any woman—she simply felt an overriding pressure to play the good girl, regardless of the professional cost. Communications researchers Karen Tracy and Eric Eisenberg have found that women in leadership roles actually make greater efforts to avoid hurting the feelings of those who work under them than they do with their superiors.[6]

As Margaret experienced, being an effective leader does not entail coddling those under us, no matter how sweet or fragile they may seem. It requires communicating difficult messages—from pink slips to performance reviews—and accepting that such messages will not always go over well. "Women tend to focus on connections, which can make wielding power difficult," says sociologist Pepper Schwartz. "No matter how powerful a woman is, it often goes against her past training to tell people the truth about their efforts. Like anything else, it's a skill that can and must be learned."[7]

Upon reflection, Margaret admits she was overly concerned with looking clean, waiting until emotions were high and Jamie had thrust them into physical danger before letting rip with the truth. She has decided that the next woman who comes through will weather a far tougher initiation.

"In this job," says Margaret, "trust is nonnegotiable no matter what sex you are. I put people at risk because I chose to nurse Jamie along instead of confronting her lack of job qualifications. I was so afraid of coming off like the bad guy, but the bad guy is exactly who I'm supposed to be."

Embracing Conflict

Perhaps the biggest problem with looking clean while dealing dirty is that in the short term, the approach can seem to work beautifully. It allows us to do battle without ever appearing to engage. For Natalie, Hannah, Margaret, or any woman navigating the conflict-ridden territory of the workplace, operating behind the scenes can seem like the perfect quick fix. Upon viewing the broader picture, it is clear that those difficulties we gloss over do not disappear. When we deny the complexities unfolding in our professional relationships, those relationships get stuck and so do we.

As women have established ourselves in the workplace, our relationships with other women have grown in ways for which the old rules did not prepare us. Instead of merging the nice woman of old with the ambitious one of new, we too often try to fill both roles simultaneously. We believe that the truly successful woman rises above other women graciously, tidily, without ruffling a feather. While she may fight valiantly in the boardroom, she is always nurturing toward her female colleagues. Conflicts are resolved so that nobody's feelings get hurt and everyone comes out ahead. When our coworkers break this mold, when they seem abusive or self-centered or simply unconcerned, we can wind up feeling helpless or betrayed.

This new setup runs the danger of being just as restrictive as the either-or model of old. A successful woman is still allowed only one choice: constant harmony with her female colleagues. In order to be professionally demanding without alienating the women around us, in order to act on our ambitions while still seeming generous, we resort to covert acts like lying and sabotage. If we are to remain so heavily invested in looking clean, we have little choice but to continue dealing dirty.

No matter how we frame or mask our behaviors, conflict with our female colleagues is a fact of professional life. There will always be more applicants than jobs, five ideas for a single project, a flock of smart, eager young women on the rise. It is imperative that we start learning how to confront such situations.

Competition, contention, even aggression in and of themselves are crucial elements in self- and communal development. Psychologists from Jean Piaget to Carol Gilligan have cited conflict as a major harbinger of growth. From such rifts and rumblings, new life forms emerge. These are the roots of creation. Without them, women will be left behind.

5

Sex and Beauty on the Job

There was a little girl
Who had a little curl
Right in the middle of her forehead;
And when she was good
She was very, very good,
But when she was bad she was horrid.
—HENRY WADSWORTH LONGFELLOW

Rachel and I meet just a few days after her thirtieth birthday. She greets me at her door dressed in loose jeans and a tight red T-shirt, her face sprinkled with summer freckles, and her curly red hair temporarily tamed into two long braids. Until the birth of her son six months ago, Rachel was the managing editor of an alternative music magazine in Austin, Texas. She was the only female editor on staff. As she describes it, "Just me and a sea of smart, quirky, funny guys."

She had started with the magazine as an intern and worked hard to earn her coworkers' loyalty and trust. One of the things she grew to love most about the job was the camaraderie, how the group pulled together to get each month's issue out. She has been married to her college sweetheart for five years, so the relationships boded nothing more than flirtation. Nevertheless, she calls being the center of such attention "sheer ecstasy for the ego."

About six months after Rachel was promoted to managing editor, the magazine hired another full-time woman to write reviews on the underground music culture.

"The guys in the office fell in love with Ursula immediately," Rachel recalls. "She was half Filipino, very small and thin and exotic looking. She'd show up at the office wearing motorcycle boots, a miniskirt, and dark purple lipstick. She was totally up on the club scene. She could dance all night. She even looked good hung over."

Ursula was also single, meaning she garnered the sort of hot and bothered attention the married Rachel could not. "Just being around her made me feel stodgy and dumpy and old."

At first Rachel was eager to write Ursula off as the avant-garde version of a bimbo, but Ursula proved talented and smart. She got along well with their editor-in-chief and moved up quickly from reviews to feature pieces to her own monthly column. Her popularity with the guys only seemed to increase. For Rachel, it was disheartening to feel that camaraderie she had worked so hard to foster could be sucked away by the first pretty girl to stride through the door.

"Ursula felt like an intrusion. She was perfectly capable at her job, but I felt like the guys liked her for her image as much as her abilities. She had this tough babe thing going, very jaded and mysterious, and these were a bunch of music geeks. My winning personality just couldn't compete with that."

Rachel had scaled the magazine's promotional ladder almost as quickly as Ursula did and, despite an MFA and a sterling performance record, she admits she harbored doubts about being qualified for her job. Her role as managing editor bore more responsibility but less glamour than Ursula's as a columnist. Suddenly, she noticed staff writers turning to Ursula to ask her opinion on their articles. She worried that having a more exciting and attention-grabbing woman on the scene would somehow expose the fact that she did not belong, that the powers-that-be would choose Ursula over her.

"It was completely irrational," she asserts. "Ursula was even less qualified for my job than I was. I'm embarrassed to admit it, but I desperately wanted that 'it girl' role back. Being the center of male attention made me feel smart and valued."

Rachel was in a position to extend support or camaraderie to Ursula, but she never reached out. Instead, she became obsessed with hoarding credit, making sure her boss knew how much she did and that she did considerably more than her new heat-seeking colleague. Though they worked together for nearly two years, Rachel never managed to shed her distrust of Ursula or the guilt that accompanied it. The situation only resolved itself when Rachel got pregnant and decided to quit and focus on her writing career. Even now, she hesitates to admit how consumed she became with envy.

"It sounds so shallow and petty," she tells me. "I'm totally ashamed. I felt really weird about not wanting Ursula around. I consider myself an enlightened, educated feminist and would like to think I'd be the first to give another talented woman an opportunity to succeed. Ursula did nothing wrong but, to be perfectly honest, I would've done almost anything to push her out the door."

Fair Is Fair?

Like Rachel, many of the women with whom I spoke felt uncomfortable and even silly admitting that they cared about adolescent concerns like who is prettiest and who gets the guys. They feared that revealing their insecurities about how they looked or whose attention they drew would peg them as vain or shallow or self-absorbed. Nevertheless, they felt compelled to care about—and even compete over—such things just the same.

We live in a culture of appearance. Our society encourages women to compete over looks and sexual appeal and bestows power and favor on those who come closest to success. There is a long history tying together women, desirability, and competition. The timeline stretches from the

Judgment of Paris to Snow White to *General Hospital*. It wends through the Bible, Shakespeare, Jane Austen and Jane Eyre, Clare Boothe Luce's *The Women*, Miss America pageants, *Fatal Attraction*, and "reality TV." When I worked in the film industry, rumors abounded about beautiful stars known for only hiring the plainest of female assistants so as not to eclipse their own glamour. Biology adds its bit to the pot as well. Recently, researchers at York University found that women at the peak of their fertility cycles actually make a point of downplaying other women's attractiveness, theoretically giving themselves an edge with a potential mate.[1] Our looks and our sex appeal are key elements in how we define ourselves as women.

In contemporary culture, with its particular reverence for celebrity and all its trappings, how well we maintain ourselves—from who designs our clothes to the size of our rear ends to how many minutes we clock on the StairMaster—can be a major determinant in our status among other women. Unlike men, a woman can rarely exist without making a statement about her beauty, style, and sexual availability. In doing so, she makes a statement about other women's choices, or lack of choices, as well. Our appearance sends instant messages about how we view ourselves in relation to others, messages about class, confidence, personal values. A conservative businesswoman can make her bohemian counterpart feel like a tart. A marathon runner casts the nonexerciser as undisciplined and undesirable. Before even opening our mouths, we can make another woman feel judged.

Given the power and privileges her looks may accord her, a beautiful woman like Ursula can set off alarm bells in those of us less bounteously endowed. The idea that a knockout does not have to work quite as hard or accomplish quite as much has been backed up by hard research. A 1993 National Bureau of Economic Research study on "Beauty and the Labor Market" found that people perceived as good-looking earned salaries at least 5 percent higher than those considered average.[2] Though we may long to be the pretty girl, we also learn to distrust her. On her end, the pretty girl learns to expect both resentment and rewards.

The Beauty Myth

Francesca is twenty-nine, a second-year graduate student, getting her Ph.D. in American studies. She's smart and earnest and full of ideas, but the first thing you notice—the thing you cannot miss—about Francesca is that she is gorgeous. Six feet tall, she has Katharine Hepburn cheekbones, large green eyes, and a confidence that rolls off her and blankets a room.

Francesca loves her Ph.D. work and, until recently, thought she was jelling well with her professors and the small group of students—fifteen in all—who make up her graduate cohort. She especially admired her adviser, Charlotte, an acclaimed researcher in her early forties who taught with a passion and perceptiveness that Francesca longed to emulate. She quickly adopted Charlotte as a role model and felt as if the two of them had developed a special connection.

During her year-end review, Francesca was shocked when Charlotte coolly informed her that she had to work on her social skills. She accused Francesca of monopolizing class time and offering too many ideas and opinions. To cap it off, she intimated that plenty of others in the department felt exactly the same way. Francesca felt blindsided by Charlotte's comments.

"It sounds melodramatic, but I think what she said triggered an identity crisis. Suddenly I felt like I had to reevaluate my whole personality. I so valued Charlotte's opinion, and I was so sure we'd formed this wonderful relationship. How could I possibly have been so far off base?"

In the wake of Charlotte's critique, Francesca did what she could to check her free-flowing confidence. She started monitoring herself in class, swallowing the impulse to speak, and sitting at the back of the room. She began worrying about how the other students viewed her and grew gun-shy about unintentionally stepping on their toes. She tried asking some of her classmates whether they thought she was coming on too strong, but they all sidestepped the question. Then a few weeks into the new semester, a fellow student, a young woman from Australia, approached Francesca in the hallway.

"What's happened?" she demanded. "I want the old you back. Who's broken Francesca's spirit?"

The comment brought Francesca sharply back down to earth.

"Until then I hadn't thought to question Charlotte's motivations for trying to reel me in," she explains. "But if I was truly infringing on everybody's experience, why didn't anyone else speak up? Why did it feel like I got on perfectly well with all the other professors? I finally realized that maybe Charlotte wasn't representative of the entire department. Maybe this was about something between her and me."

Francesca admits that upon reflection, it seemed that Charlotte's out-of-the-blue comments were designed to "break" or diminish her in some way, as if something in their relationship—or in Francesca herself—had stirred up feelings of jealousy or competition.

"I know women see things like my stature and my confidence and make automatic judgments about who I am," she says. "Usually I'll make a special point to come off as goofy or humble so they don't feel threatened. But Charlotte seemed so confident and accomplished in her own right, it didn't occur to me that she might see something in me to envy."

Given the pressure women are under to measure up aesthetically, looks can prove a point of particular vulnerability for even the most successful among us. A 2004 interview with Madeleine Albright in *Ms.* magazine concluded with a few lines on her stint with Weight Watchers.[3] Charlotte, like Rachel, may have felt threatened by a woman who brought too many riches to the table. The student-teacher relationship was supposed to be weighted heavily in Charlotte's favor. Despite the wide gap in knowledge and experience, Francesca did trump her professor in one department. Her appearance and charisma lent her a brand of cultural cachet that no matter how much effort she poured into it, Charlotte couldn't capture. Regardless of how untethered she may feel underneath, Francesca does come across as an intimidating package.

Six months after receiving Charlotte's critique, Francesca continues to tamp herself down in front of her adviser, though with some of the other professors—particularly the more confident male ones—she has started contributing again with her old verve. She says the toughest aspect of the entire experience has been losing the connection and respect she once felt for Charlotte.

"Role models are incredibly hard to find. You hate to lose one over something as silly as how the two of you look."

Before I spoke to Francesca, I had assumed the most frustrating element of dealing with her own looks would be fending off the resentment of other women. As I departed from our interview, I was more struck by how pressured she feels by always having to define herself as beautiful, constantly unsure of how it might factor into her relationships, of where another's reaction to her appearance ends and reaction to her personality begins. It is an integral part of her identity, one from which she is incapable of shaking loose.

"If I could change one thing for women in this world," she told me, "I would take away that hunger so many of us have to be seen as beautiful. We spend so much energy worrying whether we live up to this impossible standard. If women didn't care so much, I think a lot of the divisions between us would start to disappear."

I t is difficult to know how to feel toward a woman who wins attention because of how she looks. It can be hard to respect success that stems, even in part, from what nature arbitrarily endowed. On some level, dismissing an attractive woman also provides us with an easy out. It is simpler to attribute a colleague's achievements to her looks rather than talent, hard work, or other things we could potentially develop in ourselves. I spent three years in college alongside a sultry blonde with pouty lips and hair that always looked as if she'd had mad, passionate sex ten minutes before class. Everyone wrote off her academic achievements as bombshell-related. I readily accepted that until I actually had a conversation with her in which she displayed considerable intellect. It can be hard to let go of that tidy equation, the comfort we draw from the "if she's sexy, then at least I'm smart" package deal.

"I used to have a boss who, whenever I made a mistake, would tell me it was a good thing I was beautiful or no one would put up with me," says Adrienne, a sales executive who worked as a fashion model during college. "At first I was horribly insulted, but over time I realized she had this complete fantasy world built up in her head. She'd convinced herself that all her problems stemmed from the fact that she wasn't attractive enough, that if she were beautiful, she'd suddenly be able to walk on water. She was very smart and successful, but she thought I had it made because I came closer to capturing the beauty ideal."

Our society's disproportionate focus on female attractiveness can easily cause us to overestimate the degree to which being pretty or sexy will benefit other women on the job. Beauty does have power, but only a limited amount. Those who try to ride it too far often wind up less respected and taken less seriously than those who advance on the merits of their job skills alone. Though a male executive might find short skirts and cleavage appealing in his assistant, he is far less likely to value it in a manager who meets face to face with important clients.

Targeting another woman's appearance or sexuality can stand in for larger scale ambivalence about our own feelings of competition, envy, or self-doubt. In Rachel's case, her jealousy toward Ursula was tangled up in a nest of insecurities, to some degree about what she looked like, but even more so about whether she deserved and belonged in her job. Competing over externals provided a comfortable and familiar channel for diverting more complicated and deeply imbedded fears.

Babes in Boyland

Samantha meets me in a divey San Francisco bar sporting hip clothes, a ready smile, and a slew of opinions she's not afraid to voice. She's thirty-three, a San Diego native with the sun-streaked blonde hair to prove it, who migrated north after college and has worked in advertising ever since. We start talking about her previous job as an assistant producer at an advertising agency where she worked under a female creative director, Eliza, a woman highly respected in the industry.

Though Samantha was not a direct report, Eliza essentially held the reins when it came to her future with the company. Eliza worked with the best clients and the top creative talent. If she brought you into her circle, you pretty much had it made.

At first, Samantha was excited to come in under such a powerful and well-respected woman, but it didn't take her long to discover the lay of the land. Eliza surrounded herself with attractive young male employees, some talented and some not particularly so. They jetted up the promotional ladder while even the most gifted women sat idling. Shortly after Samantha arrived, Eliza hired a gorgeous but inexperienced thirty-year-old man to serve as her co-creative director. She doted on him, often deferring to his opinion despite her superior talents. Meanwhile, she regularly cold-shouldered the women in her department.

"The entire promotion pattern was extremely suspect," Samantha reports. "She routinely passed me over for jobs I was more than qualified to work on, and the same was true for the other women in the office. She'd say our work wasn't up to par, but—quite frankly—it was. The department was 60 to 70 percent female. I find it impossible to believe every last one of us couldn't measure up."

At one point, Eliza did bring Samantha in on a print ad for a snack food account. For about five minutes Samantha saw it as an opportunity. Then Eliza began finding fault with everything she did. While nurturing her male coterie, she often turned verbally abusive toward Samantha. The most encouraging days were those when Eliza did not pay attention to her at all.

Samantha gradually figured out the best way to ingratiate herself with Eliza was by making friends with the men around her. On the whole, they were younger, less talented, and inclined to take credit for Samantha's work. She found the entire situation degrading.

"It was all about what being surrounded by her team of men did for Eliza's ego. She was in her early forties, a little matronly looking, not ugly but certainly not the prom queen. I'd guess she didn't get a lot of sexual attention outside the office. So she built herself this harem of employees who were young, good looking, and entirely dependent on her."

Samantha figured Eliza felt threatened by other women who were attractive or outgoing or displayed a sense of self-determination. "I think she was afraid of what might happen if she brought one of us up. She couldn't be the only woman anymore."

Samantha found such behavior particularly disappointing, because Eliza had power and autonomy in the industry. "She was in a position to really help some talented young women get ahead, and I think that—especially in male-run areas like advertising—women are under an obligation to do that if we can."

Eliza's "feminism" became a joke among Samantha and her female coworkers. Eliza routinely spoke to women's organizations about how important she felt it was for women to help other women along.

"The whole thing was just breathtakingly hypocritical. It made me furious on behalf of all the women working there. Her behavior was so unjust, and there was nowhere we could turn. Avoiding her meant avoiding all the most lucrative work."

The straw that broke Samantha's back came when Eliza promoted a twenty-seven-year-old man—new to the company and boasting next to no experience—ahead of her.

"Women who really needed the job clung by their fingertips," she summarizes, pushing at the peanut shells littering our table. "The rest of us read the fine print and got out. I realized that no matter how hard I worked, how politically savvy I got, I was stuck as long as I had to work under her. It's too bad. That agency lost a lot of talent because of Eliza. I left there very disillusioned about the advertising world, but also about working for another woman."

We live in a society that encourages women to seek out male validation. Cinderella's story wasn't complete until she'd won her prince. The same goes for Bridget Jones, The Little Mermaid, and Julia Robert's "Pretty Woman." Nothing spun Ally McBeal into a panic faster than being single at the ripe old age of thirty. Though women on the job are rarely competing over an actual mate, it is impossible simply to abandon such cultural conditioning at the office door. The media fuels feelings of sexual pressure in the workplace by depicting the modern businesswoman as equal parts sultry and successful, with long hair and short skirts, whipping open her suit jacket to reveal lacy lingerie. The fact that we are urged to pursue careers and financial independence, to be economically, professionally, and even sexually liberated, has yet to dislodge the notion that a real woman is one who can attract the attentions of a man.

The women I interviewed frequently mentioned sexual competition as a problem. It arose on all levels from secretaries to executives, arose even if the woman in question did not respect the man himself, even—as with Eliza—when her male colleagues were less powerful than she. They mentioned female colleagues who "flirted incessantly," "ignored every other woman in the room as soon as a man entered," or "had this seductive power over men and used it." This need to measure up on the desirability scale, the idea that it is not enough just to be a crack managing editor or creative director, can give birth to a female sexism. Women feel compelled to cut other women off or cut them down in order to court and impress the men around them.

Our reasons for seeking male approval on the job are both political and emotional. In many cases, men are the ones with the power to confer. It serves us to draw their attention—as conquests, buddies, mentors, or some mix of all three. Cozying up to male colleagues can increase our chances of raises, promotions, and other tangible rewards. Coming across prettier or sexier than the woman next door is a way to get noticed and get ahead.

On a more intimate level, dealing with men delivers an undercurrent of sexual energy that can make us feel desired the way we know a woman is supposed to be desired. It is rewarding, in a primal sense, for a heterosexual woman to be pampered and encouraged by a man, particularly one she admires or feels attracted to. When we become the center of such attention, it takes considerable courage to turn around and share that attention with our female colleagues, especially if those colleagues happen to be younger or more attractive than we are. As Rachel experienced with Ursula, sexual jealousy is perfectly capable of arising even when there is no sex going on at all.

In Eliza's case, amassing a crew of male disciples may have fueled her self-confidence in a way that doing her job well could not. Despite her seniority and professional achievements, it is entirely possible Eliza's career alone did not provide her with a feeling of having "made it."

"Advertising is very youth oriented," Samantha admits. "People tend to rise fast and burn out, and you can find yourself in one day and out the next without knowing why it happened." Advertising also remains a largely male-dominated business, making success and power feel all that much more mercurial for the few women who reach its higher levels.[4]

By ignoring Samantha and her colleagues in favor of their male peers, Eliza bolstered her sense of professional security, forming ties to men who, if not more powerful than she was at the moment, could very well be so in the near future. She also fed a fragile side of her own ego. For men, professional accomplishments and sexual confidence often travel hand in hand. The more power and money a man amasses, the more attractive he feels to the opposite sex. For women, success can have the opposite effect. As a woman climbs the job ladder, that increase in authority can clash with perceptions of what makes a woman feminine and lovable. Society frequently equates highly successful women—from television's Murphy Brown to real-life examples like Madeleine Albright and Janet Reno—with being hardened, emasculating, or asexual. A powerful but not particularly feminine woman can compensate by using her professional influence to surround herself with men who need and look up to her. Winning male attention in the workplace reassures us that we are still desirable, that we are still women, even as we rocket ahead.

Dangerous Liaisons

Five years ago, Bridget was a forty-year-old single mother of two who had been mommy-tracked by her old-fashioned Manhattan law firm. Fed up with the corporate grind and corporate priorities, she was on the lookout for a more promising job opportunity. When Adam, an old friend and fellow attorney, approached her about setting up shop with him, she agreed on the spot. Within months, the two of them had hired a support staff, taken over the ground floor of Adam's Brooklyn brownstone, and opened a firm specializing in immigration issues.

"We set out to create a legal environment that valued teamwork," Bridget explains from the sunny front room of her apartment, a home office where she works one to two days a week. "Someplace where family ranked above the bottom line."

Bridget and Adam proved a natural match. He played the rainmaker, drawing in clients hand over fist, and she provided the organizational force that saw the cases through. They began recruiting other attorneys willing to forego big bucks for a more humane working environment. Eventually they took on a third partner, Lucia. Business was good.

Then several years in, Adam suggested inviting Grace, a former colleague of his, to join the firm. Bridget knew Grace casually and was not impressed. Though a solid attorney, she was cold and hard-nosed, and Bridget doubted she would fit with the rest of the firm. Adam continued to push and Bridget finally gave in.

"Neither Lucia nor I particularly jibed with Grace's style," she recalls, "but she and Adam got into a groove right away. He raked in more work than he could handle, and wound up passing quite a few plum jobs over to her."

Some unspoken competition arose between Grace and Bridget. Both women were single mothers, Grace on the heels of a messy divorce, and both needed the revenue generated by big clients.

"I felt more like I was reacting to something Grace initiated than starting it myself." Bridget offers, almost by way of apology. "She had an Ivy League degree and I think she felt pressure to be a superstar. Here I was, state university material, bringing in far more work than she did."

That fall, Adam landed a major client whose immigration concerns fell squarely under Bridget's area of expertise. Instead of approaching her to work with him, Adam asked Grace to back him up. Bridget was angry enough to confront Adam, but he said the client already knew and liked Grace, so he thought it easiest to maintain the existing affiliation. Though not happy about the decision, Bridget decided to let things lie in the name of office harmony.

Then a few weeks later, Bridget bumped into Adam's new client at a business luncheon and was surprised when he expressed regret at not having Bridget on his team. She discovered that Adam had lied to both of them, telling the client that Bridget was overextended and they were better off sticking with Grace. Suspicions piqued, Bridget began paying closer attention to the late nights, light banter, and tight working relationship that had arisen between Grace and Adam. A week later, she found direct evidence the two of them were having an affair.

"I confronted them, and they admitted it," Bridget recalls. "It was a nightmare. Grace was extremely apologetic, but a serious ethical line had been crossed."

Bridget was so floored she did not know how to react.

"In Adam's case, though I love him like a brother, I can't say it came as much of a surprise. He's a married man, but he does have a seamy side to him. But with Grace the whole thing was entirely unexpected. I felt betrayed on so many levels. I couldn't imagine how she and I could ever work together again."

Sex in the workplace is hardly a new phenomenon, but these days consensual office relationships may be more common and inevitable than ever. We work longer hours in increasingly casual atmospheres. We shoot for careers earlier, marry later, and divorce with more frequency, meaning there are more single and available women and men on the job. Sex therapist Pepper Schwartz describes the office as the newest dating and mating market, a fact that can create an ongoing sexual circle. Office liaisons give rise to sexual gossip and seeing one another in a sexual context, which give rise to more office liaisons.[5]

Research conducted by Southern Oregon University business professor Dennis Powers indicates that roughly eight million American workers a year embark on some sort of office romance half of which result in marriage or long-term commitments.[6] Women meet their lifemates in the workplace, they have secret flings, commit adultery, embark on longstanding secretive or open relationships, and they are hardly limited to the passive role in such dramas. They bring their own desires, tensions, and ambivalence to the table. They can and do take the initiative, and they reap a wide variety of rewards.

For Grace, an affair with Adam provided comfort at a time when she was feeling particularly vulnerable. Their relationship may have eased the self-doubt lingering from an unhappy marriage and soothed her insecurities about underperforming on the job. Though it probably wasn't her primary motivation for engaging in the affair, Grace's position as Adam's lover did work to her professional advantage. Bridget was a daunting force, and I would guess that she made it clear that she did not care for Grace. A private relationship with Adam allowed Grace to amass her share of casework while sidestepping that woman-on-woman competition that made her and Bridget both so uneasy. For women who dread competing openly with their colleagues, a sexual relationship can provide a convenient avenue for sating ambitions while still playing the typically cooperative feminine role.

Blending our personal and professional lives in such a way can have far-reaching implications. An affair on the job may awaken resentments among female coworkers, especially when issues of money or work allocation are affected, especially when there is an accompanying breech of trust. Bridget claims there is no question in her mind that Adam was the one who initiated the relationship with Grace. Nevertheless, she admits that from the moment the truth first came out she had a far easier time forgiving him. Though quick to write Adam off as an incorrigible womanizer, Bridget could find no such ready excuse for Grace. She acknowledges the double standard but is at a loss to explain it. "I guess I just expected more of her."

This sexual double standard, the feeling that women can and should exert superior self-control, echoes longstanding stereotypes of men as lusters and women as lovers. But "just expecting more" can also be a way of sidestepping those uncomfortable emotions sex in the workplace can evoke. Chances are Grace's actions fueled Bridget's resentment in a number of ways that Adam's did not. Grace had forged an intimacy with Bridget's valued friend and partner, gleaned professional privileges through personal channels, stirred Bridget's own competitive feelings, and perhaps even awakened a note of envy that Adam saw Grace as more desirable than she.

After much thought, Bridget agreed to let Grace stay with the firm. She empathized too closely with Grace's personal situation to turn her out without any source of income. For six months they tried to proceed with business as usual, but the tensions proved too great. Though she had found a way to forgive if not forget Adam's role in things, Bridget could not find it within herself to do the same for Grace. "I was just so angry with her. I couldn't get past what she'd done."

So Bridget gave Grace a choice: Either quit, or she and Bridget could visit a counselor who specialized in resolving professional conflicts. Grace opted to stay.

"I won't say the counseling fixed things entirely," Bridget concluded. "But it was helpful. It gave us a safe environment in which to raise our problems. We emerged with a workable relationship, which I think was all we could ask for under the circumstances."

While Bridget agrees that working with a counselor was the best possible remedy to a difficult situation, she also wonders whether there weren't some preventative measures she might have taken as well. At the end of our conversation, she mentions that in the two years since all this unfolded, she has thought some about the fact that Grace felt shut out by the other women in the firm. Bridget knows Grace made the choice to hook up with Adam of her own free will, but she also ponders the string of what-ifs that arise. What if she and Lucia been more receptive? What if Grace had felt less isolated?

She shrugs. "I just wonder whether she would have felt quite so compelled to turn to Adam for whatever she hoped their relationship could provide."

Working It

Sex and sexual jealousy have always been entwined in women's working lives. The modern workplace, even if not overtly sexual, still finds women surrounded by men with power and attention to confer. It is easy to say just do not compete, that sexual jockeying does not belong here, just as it is easy to say do not drink or smoke or eat chocolate-chip ice cream. The rewards are still too rewarding, the personal and cultural forces at play too vast to level them in one "good girl" swoop.

I have a friend whose mother grew up in Georgia in the early 1960s and later became a women's studies professor. For years, my friend marveled that her mother could go to class every day and lecture about the fight for equality, then return home to a domineering southern husband who expected her to cook supper, wash the clothes, and tend to all three children. Then one day, she came to me on the wings of a maternal epiphany. She had finally realized the degree to which change is an incremental process. The things we want in our heads are not always the things we can embody in our life choices, at least not right away. Such shifts can take years, even generations. As anthropologist Patricia McBroom says, "every generation of new women is a transitional one."[7]

I think of this maternal epiphany in conjunction with the role sex plays in a working world changing as swiftly as women's has in recent decades. It is fully possible to desire both exclusive male attention and close bonds with our female colleagues. Like Rachel and Eliza, we can embrace the idea of supporting our female colleagues but, when the time comes to act, discover our fear of losing that "it girl" status too much to overcome. This paradox—needing women, needing men—can pull at us until we feel ready to split. The real woman is the one all the men love. The real woman is the nurturing, self-sacrificing, and never sexually threatening professional sister. Somehow, somewhere, something is going to have to give.

"Professional competition over who was skinnier or dressed better, or who was sleeping with whom used to really upset me," says Sally, a film industry executive in her late forties. "These days I find it a lot less intimidating. Maybe it's just because I can no longer kid myself about being the sexiest woman on the block, but I think it goes deeper than that. There's something about experience, having gone through the wringer and come out the other side, that makes you realize all this stuff really isn't that important. If I had a daughter, I'd tell her to stop worrying over surface stuff, but my guess is she wouldn't listen. I think you have to live it for yourself to truly understand."

We cannot divorce sex from the workplace, but as we examine our relationships with one another, we can begin to put it into perspective as a single loop on our vast genetic chain. There will always be someone thinner, prettier, more desirable than we are, and there will always be someone who is working those assets for all she is worth. Though we may not be in a position to confront the situation as directly as Bridget did, if sexual competition is infringing on our ability to do our job, we do need to come to terms in whatever way we can. Sometimes that will entail calling our peers on their behavior. Sometimes it will entail leaving the job. And sometimes it will entail simply curbing that impulse to pass judgment, cutting each other some personal and some sexual slack.

6

The Work-Family Divide

There's one career we all have in common: being a woman.

—MARGO CHANNING, *ALL ABOUT EVE*

Sylvia and I meet for coffee at a sandwich shop just down the street from New York's Grand Central Station. Fresh from a business meeting, she's dressed in a slate-colored suit accented with a gold chain and matching earrings, her short brown hair tucked neatly behind her ears. Sylvia's impressive life résumé includes a brown belt in karate and a graduate degree in economics. Now, at thirty-seven, she's also a single mother with three small children, recently emerged from a messy divorce.

For the past two years, Sylvia has worked in product placement for a soft drink company. Though she has her children in a day-care center she is happy with, her recent lifestyle change was a tough adjustment and she admits she has been under considerable emotional pressure. So Sylvia was relieved when, about nine months ago, she was transferred to work under a new product manager, Teresa, who had two young kids of her own. Sylvia hoped another mother might better understand the tight schedule and occasional emergencies inherent in juggling a career and single parenthood.

"From the start, Teresa talked the support talk," Sylvia tells me. "She said she understood what it's like to have competing priorities and that she'd do all she could to help me out. But, to be honest, I felt like she undermined me just as often. She's not interested in cutting me any, and I mean any, slack."

In their first weeks working together, Teresa agreed to arrange things so Sylvia could leave by six every night to pick up her kids. She then proceeded to regularly schedule late meetings with one of their biggest clients, usually at the client's office half an hour away in New Jersey. Sylvia rarely got more than twenty-four hours' notice that such meetings were happening, at which point she would have to choose between bowing out—an option reserved for emergencies only, given the potential damage to her reputation with both the client and her company—or scrambling for last-ditch child care.

Sylvia's job requires that she spend three or four days a month traveling, and she had arranged to have her ex-husband take care of their kids when she was away.

"I've asked Teresa for as much advance notice as possible when I need to travel, but somehow she sees to it that I'm never quite sure of my schedule. I know clients can be fickle, but I feel like Teresa doesn't even try to forewarn me. She acts like I'm twenty-three and single and can leave town at the drop of the hat."

Earlier that month, after specifically requesting a travel-free weekend, Sylvia had agreed to drive her son and some of his teammates to a basketball tournament. When Sylvia came into the office that Wednesday, Teresa informed her she was scheduled to fly to Denver on Friday morning. Not for the first time, Sylvia had to call on her ex-husband at the last minute, adding stress to their already frazzled relationship.

Sylvia had hoped that because Teresa had two kids she would be more empathetic, but her boss also has a husband and a full-time nanny to help with the care.

"I don't think she realizes or is really even interested that our circumstances are different. She's worked for the company since before her kids were born, and there's an element of 'I figured out how to do this so why can't you?'"

Teresa's lack of empathy even made it into Sylvia's most recent performance evaluation, in which Sylvia was criticized for not keeping her priorities in line with the company's and for having trouble "putting the job first." Sylvia considers the critique unfair, but acknowledges a grain of truth in Teresa's words.

"The fact is I can't be overly ambitious at work and still have time for my children. If it's a choice between the office and my kids, it will always be kids first." Whereas a male boss might simply be oblivious to this fact, Sylvia feels Teresa recognizes this dilemma and makes Sylvia pay for it. "It's not like I don't expect to pull my own weight. I work hard. I have a lot of marketing experience and I think I'm an asset to the department. But balancing both sides of my life is difficult, and Teresa extends no extra sympathy when I run into child-related issues. She knows how to hit me where it hurts."

Sylvia has little recourse for help through company channels. Teresa embodies the organization's "family" ethic—not that they value family so much as that they want to be a large happy one—and she is big on company loyalty. She works long hours, and their department consistently performs at a high level.

"Besides," Sylvia ventures, "I don't even know what I would file a complaint about. It's not like Teresa's throwing things at me. She just refuses to make an effort to accommodate my schedule or priorities. She's turned out to be much less supportive than the male manager I worked under before. He never had a complaint about the quality of my work. The negative reviews I got from Teresa could have a long-term effect on my career."

Without her boss's support, Sylvia has little chance of landing a promotion. She figures her best bet is a lateral move that could get her out from under Teresa, and she is on the lookout for opportunities within her division. She also applied to the company's corporate mentoring program. Though she is more experienced than the usual candidate, she hopes such a relationship might inject some fresh blood into her career. It is likely she will be matched with an older male mentor, someone typically less sensitive to child-related problems, so she doesn't hold out much hope for help in the work-family department. Beyond that, Sylvia feels both frustrated and scared. Her ex-husband pays some child support, but Sylvia's financial and emotional responsibilities have increased since her divorce, and she cannot afford to quit or lose her job.

"I went to college in the mideighties, when the effects of women's lib and the push for the ERA were still very fresh," she says. "I entered the working world really believing that women can and should go out of their way to support each other. I'm not saying that kind of support doesn't happen. But it's been tough to discover that, unfortunately, you can't always count on that being the case."

Family Matters

As a woman who is single and childless, I underestimated the deeply entrenched conflicts that work-family tensions can create among women on the job. The subject elicits strong emotions, vastly polarized opinions, and knots of guilt, anger, and frustration. Popular culture has made much of the battle between working and stay-at-home moms, with scores of opinions—expert or otherwise—regularly hung out to dry. Little attention has been focused on the equally prevalent and equally volatile family-related issues that can erupt among women on the job.

There is no longer one culturally condoned choice for women when it comes to career and family. Among the working women I interviewed, I encountered a wide range of domestic situations. I spoke to women who were single, married, in domestic partnerships, divorced, widowed, with children and without. I talked to young women who dreaded remaining single and childless well into their thirties or beyond, and to older women who had done just that. I heard from mothers who had changed or curtailed their careers to raise families, and from mothers who had opted to stick with demanding full-time jobs. I spoke to women in the throes of juggling career and family, and to women from previous generations who had worked and raised children at a time when there were far fewer channels of support.

The common thread to all these stories was the fact that women, in large part, experience work-home issues very differently from men. The age of equal rights notwithstanding, we still tend to be the primary caregivers—toward mates, toward children, toward aging parents and relatives. The resultant tensions and emotions bind us together whether we like it or not. We do not just desire support from our female coworkers, we often urgently need it in order to keep afloat. The fact that there is not one "right" way to intertwine our personal and professional lives can play on our insecurities, causing us to compare ourselves to the women around us for assurance that the path we have selected is an acceptable one. When their opinions or experiences differ, we can be quick to cry betrayal and those betrayals can feel like the deepest and most personal sort.

Working mothers are the rule in America today—as of 2003, 71 percent of mothers with children under eighteen were in the labor force.[1] These women are dealing with rising demands on the job front. Office hours have gotten longer, vacations fewer, and overnight business trips and take-home work are on the rise, making it increasingly difficult for women to squeeze in competing professional and personal responsibilities.[2] Upswings in everything from divorce to single motherhood to jobless rates have collided to produce more and more women like Sylvia—unmarried parents or those whose partners are under- or unemployed—who rely upon their own salaries and job benefits as a primary means of family support: 77.7 percent of single mothers, as opposed to 68.6 percent of married mothers, are in the labor force.[3] A November 2003 congressional report also revealed that while men with kids earn 2 percent more than men without them, women who have children earn roughly 2.5 percent less than their unencumbered peers.[4]

On the home front, women still absorb the bulk of the responsibilities. In the late 1980s, sociologist Arlie Hochschild revealed the phenomenon of "the second shift"—working women taking on the equivalent of an additional job in the form of child care and housework. Hochschild found that women on average spent fifteen hours more a week on domestic labor than men did.[5] Though subsequent studies show the gap slowly narrowing, they also indicate that women continue to pick up roughly two-thirds of all at-home duties.[6] A 2003 Time Use survey conducted by the U.S. Department of Labor showed the average working woman spends an hour more per day on household activities such as cleaning, cooking, and child care than the average working man.[7]

All these statistics boil down to one troubling reality: The majority of working women are trying to stuff a twelve-foot-long scarf into a two-inch-square pocket, and even Houdini had an assistant. There are gaps, enormous gaps, between what women can accomplish and what they are being asked to do. When I asked Sylvia how she manages a four-year-old, a six-year-old, an eight-year-old, and a full-time job, her immediate response was, "You learn to ask for help." Given the level at which family concerns usually rank on the organizational value scale, chances are we're going to look for that help through informal channels—often from the women around us. That same value scale will play a key role in how much support our female colleagues can and are willing to offer.

In Sylvia's case, only a portion of her problems stemmed from Teresa's personal feelings. The rest lay with company policies and priorities, something over which Teresa had no control. Sometimes, for reasons of survival, a working woman's smartest choice is to back the status quo. As a middle manager, Teresa lacked the autonomy to make "women friendly" decisions. She was rewarded for accommodating her clients and her superiors, not for accommodating Sylvia. Asking to reschedule an evening meeting or shuffling dates for a business trip could very well sully her own professional reputation. Women who find themselves in such positions may want to help—even "talk the support talk"—but feel it is too risky to take actual steps.

Though most of Teresa and Sylvia's department is female, according to Sylvia there are limited managerial roles available for women within the company. If Teresa hopes to ascend to that level, she may not want to be identified with those women who leave early, push for flexible hours, or sacrifice promotions to stay home one day a week. If the higher-ups group her with them, she may wind up reaping the consequences of their choices. Though not particularly fair, this can be a very legitimate fear.

The women to whom I spoke also raised the fact that it is tough to consider putting their own livelihoods at risk to help another woman negotiate family issues when there are real doubts about what they will get in return. Changes in our personal lives can shift our professional priorities, occasionally leaving supportive colleagues high and dry.

"I really stood up for one of my reports when she got pregnant with her first child," says Ruth, a married but childless corporate accountant in her early thirties. "I convinced our boss to grant her four months extra maternity leave. I made sure she was up to date with what was happening on all her accounts. Then, when those four months were up, she decided not to come back after all. The whole incident really undercut my reputation. I understand why she changed her mind, but it was a rough blow. I don't think I'd risk it again."

Ruth's experience plays up the fact that just because we are women does not mean we can predict or understand each other's needs. As Sylvia discovered, even an employer or colleague with children of her own—or an ex-husband or elderly parents—will not automatically prove more sympathetic. Teresa had her family tucked into a tidy corner, with nanny and husband to pick up the slack. Chances are she handled those responsibilities without leaning on her workmates, and she expected Sylvia to do the same. The fact that Sylvia's support system and financial status were not in the same bracket as Teresa's was not necessarily enough to sway her otherwise. Teresa's attitude may not be overly compassionate, but it reflects the ethos of her company and the broader organizational culture. Work is work. It is up to each individual to figure out how to get the job done.

As an employment agency recruiter with two teenage sons explained it to me, "Every project must be completed whether your kids have to get to the dentist or not. If you don't do it, someone else has to stay late or work weekends to cover for you. And that's not fair. If you can't perform your job, then you shouldn't be there. That's just the way it is."

The Parent Trap

Annette and Carmen are development officers for a Colorado-based environmental foundation, having started as interns and worked their way up the ranks together. They are the same age, thirty-three, and until recently their lives had followed similar tracks—office hours, after-work drinks, skiing or hiking on the weekends. Though never bosom buddies, they forged a friendship sustained by their mutual love of the outdoors and their struggle to make it in the hard-strapped nonprofit world. When Annette got married two years ago, Carmen even helped her pick out the wedding dress. Occasionally professional tension arose over a donor both women wanted to pursue, but they communicated openly and problems tended to blow over quickly.

Then Annette got pregnant. When her son was born nine months ago, she took the foundation's allotted twelve weeks of maternity leave then returned full time, leaving her son with a nanny she shares with another family in her neighborhood.

"Ever since I came back, I feel like there's been a shift in how people view me," explains Annette, round-faced and freckled with long dark hair twisted into a haphazard knot at the base of her neck. "The organization is over 50 percent women and very family friendly, so I don't worry that my job is at risk. But I do feel like everybody takes me a little less seriously. It's subtle, but I get the sense they don't expect me to really care about my career anymore."

The most troubling shift Annette noticed was in her relationship to Carmen. The foundation's internal structure underwent some changes while Annette was gone, and shortly after her return, a senior development position opened up. The foundation has been slow to name anyone to the post, but they do have a history of promoting internally.

"Carmen and I are the two naturals to fill that job," Annette explains. "If I hadn't just had the baby, I feel like we would have handled the situation pretty healthily—may the best woman win, that kind of thing. But now, in terms of job flexibility, Carmen's in the stronger position, and I'm in the weaker one. And I feel like she's going all out to exploit her advantage."

Annette describes how Carmen has started taking on job duties that Annette, with baby at home, cannot. Carmen used to be protective of her weekends, only coming into the office for genuine emergencies, but now she shows up almost every Saturday morning. She makes a point of letting their boss know when she works late—dropping comments about being alone in the building or telling a funny story about trying to order in dinner. Carmen and Annette used to split all the governmental reading that came their way, but now Carmen volunteers to take home any new environmental studies and read them overnight, "even when there's not necessarily any hurry." She has also made it known she is available for last-minute business travel.

"I feel like Carmen's doing everything in her power to prove that she's more dedicated and more available than I am," Annette says. "She's making it look like I'm not particularly invested anymore. And that's not true. I feel very passionate about my job. There was never a question of my not coming back. Yes, I miss seeing my son, but I want and need to work. My husband is an architect, and his career isn't stable. He was laid off for six months last year. We depend on my income now more than ever."

Annette is confused about how to react to Carmen's taking her childless edge and running with it. She acknowledges that it is not Carmen's fault if the workplace environment makes it difficult for a woman to be both a mother and a professional world-beater, but she also suspects Carmen's actions are rooted, at least in part, in more personal motivations.

"I feel like this is about something deeper than just two women competing for the same job. Carmen and I have talked about how tough it is to be single and in your thirties. I think she's jealous of how my life's playing out. This is her way of saying you can't have everything. You may have the husband and the child, but you can be damn sure I'm going to get the job."

Annette admits that her competitive side longs to beat Carmen at her own game, to start staying late, piling on the work, proving that just because she is a mother she hasn't lost her edge, but she concedes such retaliation is not much of a reality. The price it would extract—hours away from her family—is too steep.

"The truth is her strategy is working. She probably will get the position. I don't know how to fight back. Yes, I'm out of the office at six every day. No, I'm not available to come in on weekends. But when I'm here I work hard, and my ideas are just as sharp as they ever were."

Annette has responded the only way she knows how, by trying to push her own work front and center and prove that her job performance hasn't suffered. The tension between the two women grows increasingly uncomfortable.

"Our friendship feels like it's falling apart," Annette concedes. "I'm angry at her. I can't help it. She's doing her best to personally mommy track me. How can I not resent that? I think she's jealous of me, but to be honest I'm also jealous of her. She's fancy free. She can stay late or not, go full guns after this job or not. And that's no longer an option for me."

Figuring out how to remain a serious workplace contender once you have had children is one of the trickiest puzzles working women face today, and most of them receive scant societal or organizational support.

Female executives who take as little as 8.8 months in combined maternity leaves, designated in the 1993 Family and Medical Leave Act—for three children that is less than the twelve weeks per child—have been shown to suffer permanent setbacks in career advancement and earning potential.[8] The majority of businesses provide neither on-site child-care facilities nor help in covering expenses.[9]

"We're the only Western country that doesn't have a paid family medical leave," says Heather Boushey, an economist at the Center for Economic and Policy Research. "We don't have any sort of universal child care, which means that all these responsibilities fall on individual women. It makes them more economically vulnerable because it lowers their wages and adds stress to their lives. It makes them angry. They wind up juggling so much that they can't perform on the job."[10]

Women like Annette, who are laden with family responsibilities, can envy those with the freedom to devote themselves entirely to work, earning quicker raises and promotions and accumulating buckets full of brownie points. It is easy to start feeling out of the loop when you are working shorter hours and not taking as active a part in the office social scene. Since personal connections often form a more significant part of the professional fabric for women than for men, this experience of being shut out can be particularly disconcerting.

Working mothers can also resent the assumption Annette encountered even in her "women friendly" office that work will matter less once they have children, that priorities will be reshuffled, and career will drop to the bottom of the deck. To the contrary, a 2002 study showed that working women display no increase in such typically feminine traits as compassion, sympathy, and understanding, and no decrease in qualities like ambition, independence, and assertiveness after the birth of a child.[11] As a number of women pointed out to me, the added financial pressure brought on by life changes—marriage, divorce, motherhood—can make professional success more crucial than ever before.

On the flip side, childless women like Carmen can chafe at having to cover for mothers working shorter hours or disappearing at a moment's notice to handle a sick kid—and 83 percent of the parents taking time off work for day-to-day child-related responsibilities are still mothers.[12] Carmen also might not appreciate Annette's taking three months' maternity leave then expecting to return, logging shorter hours, and pick up as if she had never been gone. Such negative feelings can come coupled with guilt for not providing the selfless support, the sacrifice with a smile, so often anticipated in female relationships.

Despite our broader range of opportunities, society still tends to devalue women who opt out of or delay having children. Unlike men, for whom aspiring to CEO-dom seems as genetically preordained as hunting mastodons, women are not expected to prioritize work over home. Much of a woman's societal value is still attached to her relationship and family successes, and many of us are made to feel incomplete when we are lacking in those departments. The idea that remaining single will help a woman's career has also lost some of its luster in recent years. The "success gap" between married and single women is shrinking and is expected to disappear entirely by 2010. In addition, married white women earn 4 percent more and married black women 10 percent more than their single counterparts.[13] The single or childless woman's sense of having to justify her life choices can make her less inclined to form connections with and provide support for those women who have followed a more conventional path.

"My office mate went to a four-day week after she had her second baby," says Katerina, an event planner in her midthirties. "Now all the work she doesn't finish by Thursday night gets passed on to me. I feel torn. I know it's not easy to be a working mother and I want to support her. But it also pisses me off that just because I'm single, I'm expected to pick up her slack."

The fantasy of "having it all" is very much a fantasy, but it can raise real problems. Contemporary women experience significant pressure to play both the domestic goddess—hand-sewing Halloween costumes and pureeing homemade organic baby food—and the consummate professional—landing clients and publishing articles in our spare time. Making compromises on either front can feel as though we have screwed up all around.

For someone like Annette, priorities have changed. She can't do it all. Having an infant, particularly when you are the primary caretaker, may very well preclude pushing forward on the career front, at least temporarily. The hard truth is that all those things Carmen does not have in her personal life do give her a professional edge. At the end of our interview, I asked Annette how she would behave if she were in Carmen's position.

"Would I do the same thing if I were her?" she replied. "I guess I probably would. I suppose I'm just blaming her for being a realist. In the end, it's not Carmen's fault I can't have my work-home cake and eat it, too."

The Balanced Life

Rita is outgoing, articulate, and brimming with energy, whipping through the corridors of her New York office at a pace perfectly in tune with the city around her, though her brown eyes are rimmed by the dark circles typical of new motherhood.

Rita's own parents emigrated from Cuba before she was born, and from childhood there was no question that she and her two sisters would take advantage of every educational and professional opportunity afforded them. She grew up in Miami, went to college in New York, and graduated with honors and a degree in art history. She and her husband met at school, and when they married four years later, both agreed that the rest of their twenties would be devoted to building their careers.

Since graduation, Rita has done curatorial work with an array of museums and art galleries. Her current job entails orchestrating shows that draw from collections all over the world. She manages five women, all of whom she hand-selected, and loves her job, particularly the opportunities for international travel. Her husband, who runs his own import/export company, has an equally demanding professional schedule. He and Rita purposely waited to have children, because they knew it would change the role Rita's career played in her life. It wasn't until she actually got pregnant at thirty-one that she realized how much having a child would also affect her relationships with her colleagues.

"I'm the first woman in my department to have a child," she explains. "So when the issue of maternity leave came up, I was very much forging new ground. As a team, we were all used to a priority scale where work comes first, no question. But I'd heard stories about women doing conference calls from the delivery room, and I didn't want to be that woman."

Rita and her boss decided that instead of bringing in an outsider, it made practical and financial sense to have the existing team take over during her six-month maternity leave. Though Rita agreed with the decision, she admits it felt strange orchestrating things so that the group could operate without her.

She laughs. "I basically spent nine months proving I was expendable."

It was scary to leave, scary to hear that her second in command, Maya, was managing fine without her, and scariest of all to come back. Rita was fortunate in that she could afford a nanny for her daughter so her child-care worries were minimal, but work anxieties had been building for months.

"From a professional standpoint, the transition was seamless. The team didn't skip a beat. And that was unsettling. I wished—still wish—they'd missed me more. It's not easy coming to the realization that you can be replaced."

A lot can happen in six months. New shows were conceived, new projects executed. Despite the trust she held in Maya and the rest of her colleagues, Rita feared that in taking so much time away she may have permanently nudged herself out of a central role. When she returned to the office, Rita tried to reestablish herself and her authority as quickly as possible, picking up as if she had never been gone. Though Maya said nothing to Rita directly, it was clear she did not relish playing second fiddle on projects that weeks earlier she had been running herself. Rita tried talking to Maya about the problem, but Maya just responded by filling Rita in on more details she had missed while away.

"I realized Maya was trying to tell me something," Rita says. "Our relationship had changed. If I didn't want her to resent having to step back down, I had to let some of my old responsibilities go." So Rita sat down with Maya again, and this time they discussed redistributing the workload, allowing Maya to hang on to some of what she had taken over while Rita was on leave.

"It would be a lie to say sharing what used to be all mine doesn't bother me. It's a demotion. Last month, Maya went to Spain to help set up a show, and I stayed home with the baby. I let her hang on to one of the larger projects she'd taken over, and she's maintained direct contact with our director."

Rita also made a point to let Maya know how brilliantly she had done during the past six months, even telling Maya she would promote her to peer level if she could. "I think showing that level of respect is a worthwhile investment. I can feel sure that Maya knows how much she's valued. And we have a deal that when her baby time comes, it'll be my turn to cover her back."

Rita acknowledges that motherhood has changed her outlook. She values family and family time more than she used to. Her job matters less, which makes it easier—though not easy—to share responsibilities and credit. She used to be a twelve-hour-day workhorse, contacting people on weekends and taking meetings at six or seven at night. Now there's a clear line between work and family.

"I work hard while I'm here, but otherwise—unless it's an emergency—it can wait until tomorrow."

Rita says she doesn't think her work has suffered, but some things have clearly changed. She is not as in control of everything as she used to be, and she depends more upon the others, particularly Maya, to keep things running. She feels obliged to be as flexible as possible about her team's personal choices so they don't resent hers. She also feels added pressure to prove herself to them. Though she is more proactive about shaping her schedule—lunch meetings versus after hours, no weekend calls—she purposely chose not to discuss such changes with her team.

"I don't manage by democracy," Rita explains. "And they don't get to determine my schedule. I'm very aware of not appearing to slack off now that I've become a mother. I think you return from maternity leave and that's the first thing people start to look for. There are times when I feel vulnerable, because I'm not working with the kind of nonstop intensity I had before. This is still a bottom-line business, and I still have to perform."

Rita says that early on she grappled with and rejected the idea that women are expected to juggle work and family all on our own. Professional women do need help. As often as possible, she turns to an external support system for that help, calling on her family and her nonwork friends. She does not want her colleagues to think she is supermother, an unrealistic image that helps nobody, but she does not want them to harbor any doubts that she is still capable of getting the job done.

"I think what made the transition easiest was the fact that, in the end, the baby was more important, and if it didn't work out, it didn't work out," Rita reflects. "Motherhood and age have altered my ambitions. Previously, I was highly motivated by money, titles, and responsibility. Now I'm highly motivated by balance in my personal life. That's not to say I'm not ambitious, but I'm more willing to let Maya step in and carry some of the weight. I trust her enough to take that risk. Work still comes first for Maya, and I can't pretend that's not threatening. But I also feel strongly that you can't operate on the scarcity model. I choose to believe that the pie is big enough for everyone to get a piece."

Bringing It Home

There is no simple answer to the question of what women on the job "owe" other women, but when it comes to the work-family dance, we do owe one another something. On a personal level, the workplace experience is different and in many cases more difficult for women than it is for men. We need extra help. We need to foster empathy for one another. Women who do not have children have to take that additional step or two or ten to understand the life intricacies of women who do and vice versa. Single women do not want to feel worthless on the personal front, nor do women with families want to feel worthless professionally.

Since balancing work and home is one of the areas in which professional women feel most vulnerable, when our female colleagues do come through with their generosity and support, it can make the bonds between us that much stronger.

"Maya and I now have this amazing symbiotic relationship," Rita tells me. "We trust each other and know we can count on each other. It benefits us, and it benefits the museum, too. What I've sacrificed in control has been paid back a hundredfold."

Other women to whom I spoke echoed Rita's sentiments. "She has my loyalty for life," said a doctor whose surgeon boss went to bat for her when she was confined to six months bed rest during a difficult pregnancy. "She got my practice covered, she arranged it so I could talk to my patients on the phone, and she let me know that whenever I was ready to come back I was welcome. I never once doubted that she was more concerned about me than my missing patients. I couldn't have asked for more."

As individuals we are part of a female collective, and the compassion we extend on a person-to-person basis can shape policies that affect women as a whole. Providing support does not mean championing someone beyond her merits or sacrificing ourselves in the name of sisterhood. As Rita said, business is about the bottom line and you still have to perform. Providing support means being sensitive to our employees and coworkers' personal situations, communicating openly, and looking for opportunities to help one another when we can. A study of female lawyers published in 2001 found that women experience markedly less work-family conflict when they have a female colleague or mentor to consult.[14]

The blame for how work-family conflicts damage our relationships often lies more with organizational and governmental policies than with our individual decisions. Flexible scheduling, available child care, or generous parental-leave policies could have helped both Sylvia and Annette balance their children and their jobs more easily. Chances are slim that the men around us will be the first to initiate large-scale or even small-scale change. This is a women's issue, and it is women's responsibility to keep that issue front and center, to start giving without worrying so much about what we will get in return.

7

The New Tokenism

I am alarmed by the violence that women do to each other:
professional violence, competitive violence, emotional
violence. . . . I am alarmed by a growing absence of
decency on the killing floor of professional women's worlds.

—TONI MORRISON, MAY 1979 COMMENCEMENT ADDRESS
AT BARNARD COLLEGE

Leslie greets me at the door of her Manhattan apartment on a spring Sunday afternoon wearing a pink T-shirt and glitter-flecked flipflop sandals. In her midtwenties, she's petite and energetic, a second-generation American of Japanese ancestry. For the past two years, Leslie worked as a junior analyst for a Wall Street investment firm, her second job out of college. Three months ago she quit. Though it was bittersweet to leave the sort of high-profile company at which she had always hoped to make her mark, all that was overshadowed by the prospect of finally getting out from under her boss.

Leslie knew going in that banking was a cutthroat environment, especially for a woman. "I'm no hothouse flower," she informs me early on. "I'd heard all the stories, and I thought I could handle whatever the business could dish out."

She had braced herself for the hundred-hour weeks, the relentless hazing and ruthless competition, the hard-drinking, strip-club-visiting macho-ness that could confront a woman new to the game. She knew her first few years served as a test, the time during which all but the steeliest players were weeded out. What she did not expect was that the hazing would be aimed so specifically at her, or that it would stem from the only other woman in her division.

Leslie's boss, Bella, was one of the department's star performers. She lived and breathed investment banking, seeming to thrive on endless strings of eighteen-hour days. Her commitment was one of the key reasons she had climbed so high in the company. Still in her early thirties, she was among just a handful of female vice presidents. She had proven herself the hard way, by grinding out the bottom line, month after month, year after year.

Any excitement Leslie felt about having a woman in her corner vanished almost as soon as it materialized. From day one, Bella let it be known Leslie could expect nothing in the way of autonomy. She micromanaged every detail of Leslie's performance, down to looking over her shoulder while she was typing and calling out corrections before there was time to hit the delete key. She gave Leslie near impossible deadlines then tagged her as slow and stupid when she missed them by even a few hours. Late nights were par for the course for everyone in the department, and Leslie put in her fair share, but whenever she asked to leave half an hour early for a doctor's appointment or even for a break to order in dinner, Bella accused her of challenging authority and questioned her dedication to the job.

"She basically seized every chance she could to let me know I was screwing up."

Had this behavior been the same sort of heavy handling the other new recruits experienced, Leslie could have stomached it, but Bella's bruising treatment seemed reserved just for her. "With the guys it was different," Leslie observes. "She was more playful and flirty. She could be a stickler, but she didn't act like she was doing everything in her power to drive them away."

Leslie had been right about banking. It was a brutal place for women. She fielded harassment from her male colleagues, from sitting at conference tables as they discussed the anatomical specifics of various secretaries to being "accidentally" left out of meetings she was supposed to attend. She appreciated that Bella, or any woman, required suitable armor in order to prosper in such a climate.

"Bella's tough because of her environment," Leslie offers, "but she doesn't know when to stop." She describes Bella's workplace persona as "one of the guys and then some"—tossing around crass language and dirty jokes and distancing herself from other women in the office by doing things like badmouthing their decisions to have kids. "She's a he-male. Everyone thinks it's ridiculous. She's so inappropriate, you get embarrassed every time she opens her mouth."

Bella was decidedly awkward when it came to social graces, perhaps the one thing stalemating her career. Leslie is more outgoing, friendly, and laid-back. Her clients and coworkers liked her, and she suspects her gift with people got under Bella's skin.

Before long, Leslie found herself near paralyzed by Bella's onslaught. She was afraid to ask questions, since she didn't know what might be construed as challenging authority. She could not focus on the job for worrying about what Bella was saying or thinking about her.

"She made me feel guilty no matter what I did. There was no way I could ever be as dedicated as she was. I felt like she was judging me every time I chose to have a life."

Leslie's misery peaked this past Christmas. Bella's ironclad work ethic meant she almost never took vacations. When Leslie asked for two extra days to visit Japan with her family, Bella was livid. With most of their clients closed for the holidays, she grudgingly agreed to the added vacation time. Then she rode Leslie into the ground in the days leading up to her departure, overloading her with so much work that she had to stay at the office deep into every night to clear her desk. To cap it off, Bella phoned Leslie just as she was departing for the airport and screamed at her for being irresponsible and leaving work undone.

"She ruined my entire vacation. For two weeks all I could think was, I hate her, I hate her. I couldn't stop imagining her back at the office cutting me down."

Early in the new year, Leslie became so undone she finally went over Bella's head to complain to her male managing director. In tears, she told him that she was dedicated to the job, but she could not work with Bella anymore. He spoke to Bella, and she backed off temporarily, but it did not last. Management was unwilling to take any more aggressive action. Bella was far too valuable a worker for them to go out on a limb.

Beyond this, Leslie felt helpless. Bella's rancor had already done serious damage. Leslie heard through the investment-banking grapevine that Bella had complained about her unreliability to colleagues in other firms. Even worse, Bella's criticism showed up on Leslie's performance reviews, saying she needed to show more initiative and giving her low marks for company loyalty. Leslie was afraid any further attempts to rock the boat would affect not only her standing with the bank but her whole future in the industry. Bella had, quite effectively, succeeded in shutting Leslie down.

Tokenism: Old and New

The year 1968 was a pivotal one for women in the workforce. It was the year Lyndon Johnson's executive order mandating "affirmative action" to prevent discrimination on the job expanded to include women. Scores of entirely male bastions—any companies that met certain size requirements and held government contracts—were forced to introduce a percentage of women into their ranks. Concrete goals and timetables added to the law in 1971 provided the leverage necessary to pry open many jobs long closed to the female half of the population.[1]

Though the numbers of women changed, traditional old-boy environments rarely shifted to accommodate or even acknowledge their new arrivals. Regardless of their qualifications, these "token" female hires suffered under the assumption that their advancement had much to do with fulfilling the law and little to do with talent. In order to prove their worth, women had to produce double what was demanded of their male colleagues. They faced fierce prejudices, verbal abuse, and unchecked sexual harassment. They often worked with few, if any, other women. In order to survive, many developed thick skins and "roaring bitch" reputations.

I interviewed a handful of women who had landed those very early token positions, including Beatrice, who in the early 1970s was hired as an aeronautical engineer for a major defense contractor, the first female engineer they had ever taken on. The only other women in her company held clerical positions, quite a few rungs down the ladder. Interactions were cursory when they occurred at all.

"I truly felt like a token," Beatrice recalls thirty years later as we sit across from one another in her sun-streaked Maryland living room. "I consistently had to prove to the men I worked with, and also to myself, that I was being promoted according to ability and not gender or looks or anything else. At one point I was appointed to a Defense Department advisory board. The group was very high profile, nine men—all about twenty years older than I was—and me. The men treated me like I was invisible. After the meetings, they'd all go off to lunch together and just leave me standing there."

In such an old-school, corporate atmosphere, there were no mixed messages about how to operate. Beatrice learned quickly to be very direct, very goal oriented, very much a team player. Proving herself required excelling on the male playing field, because there was no other way.

"This was a very strange point in our history," Beatrice reflects. "Many women were accepted into management positions just to make quotas if their company had government contracts. Often women felt like they had been promoted beyond their skill level, so they were desperately trying to hang on. Either you didn't feel qualified, or you knew other people didn't feel you were qualified. Tokenism created a great deal of insecurity."

A round the time Beatrice was struggling to register on the Defense Department radar, Harvard professor and management consultant Rosabeth Moss Kanter published her organizational classic *Men and Women of the Corporation,* in which she examined the dangers faced by women who filled token positions. She identified three key variables that contribute to an individual's success in an organization: degree of power, degree of opportunity, and relative numbers. In all three departments, token women came up short. Kanter also noted the ways in which corporations kept token women isolated by actively discouraging ties among female coworkers. Token women were often rewarded, directly or indirectly, by their male colleagues for distancing themselves from their female peers, limiting the potential for communication or alliances. Moss Kanter was one of the first to propose that women's professional behaviors—including the damage they could inflict on other women— were not rooted in genetic tendencies, an offshoot of the "way women are." Their workplace environments had an enormous impact on how their relationships took shape.[2]

"Women in the ranks did whatever was asked of them," says Chloe, who in the late 1970s was one of the first female product analysts for a major manufacturing firm. "You couldn't afford to go on record as being different. You didn't even think about calling attention to yourself by bucking the system. All your energy was spent trying to gain acceptance and fit in."

T okenism has not vanished from the workplace in the ensuing decades, but it has shifted. It has morphed into "new tokenism," something subtler and more layered than it was in Beatrice's day. Quota systems have relaxed, if they exist at all. In 1985 President Reagan, responding to complaints that hiring quotas were discriminatory toward

white men, put an end to affirmative action with regard to federal con-
tractors. Women today rarely find themselves in situations where they
are literally the only woman on the scene, but we are far from achieving
full parity.

Women continue to serve as the exception when it comes to police officers, firefighters, mechanics, stockbrokers, investment bankers, computer programmers, and chemists; and the list stretches on. Women
represent just 11.2 percent of all sworn law enforcement personnel in the
United States,[3] 19.4 percent of dentists, 4.2 percent of airplane pilots, and
10.8 percent of engineers.[4] Frequently, even those industries with high
percentages of women on the lower levels grow increasingly polarized as
they move up the ladder. Despite the fact that women make up nearly
half of law school classes, only 16.8 percent of partners in the nation's law
firms are women.[5] And women represent just 15 percent of executive
leaders and 12 percent of board members in top communications companies, a category that includes the telecom, publishing, entertainment,
and advertising fields.[6]

When women populate the workplace in such unequal proportions,
they can experience just as much, if not more, job tension and dissatisfaction than a single token woman does. One woman may be seen as an
exception to the old rules, rules that are still very much intact. When minority numbers start to swell, the majority often feels threatened,
prompting backlash and an even more restrictive atmosphere.[7] Research
has shown that until women represent 15 to 25 percent of a professional
population, colleagues still tend to view them as an isolated and disrup-
tive presence.[8]

New tokenism unfolds in environments like Leslie's and Bella's, in
which influential women still comprise a minority and the traditional
male ethos or corporate structure still prevails. It appears when there are
too many women for too few slots provided, when power and resources
are limited, and when questions about whether women can hack it in the
upper levels have yet to disappear. New tokenism exists in organizations

in which, in their effort to appear diverse, women occupy positions of high visibility but relatively low power, so that while they may appear to have "made it" to the outside world, internally they are still scrambling for a sense of security. It can promote rivalries between women, even in situations in which direct competition does not exist.

In 1994, Harvard professor Robin Ely built on Rosabeth Moss Kanter's research by comparing relationships between female employees in companies with a high percentage of senior women to those in firms where women at the top were rare. She found that in environments with fewer women, female colleagues were "less likely to experience common gender as a positive basis for identification with women, less likely to perceive senior women as role models with legitimate authority, more likely to perceive competition in relationships with women peers and less likely to find support in these relationships."[9] Women in male-dominated firms more frequently reported that their relationships with female coworkers were competitive in ways that inhibited their ability to work together. Collaborating with other women was considered a highly questionable route to success.

Women like Bella, who have acquired a modicum of power but not too much, form the heart of new tokenism. Though they have increased in sheer numbers, many still exist on footings just as uncertain as Beatrice's thirty years ago. As one thirty-year-old electrical engineer put it, "We're all just women in a man's world, and we do whatever we have to do to fit in."

A Woman in a Man's World

Leslie's story is not a pleasant one. Bella regularly reduced her to her rawest elements, made her miserable, made her cry, ruined her evenings, her vacations, and her self-respect. Though Leslie saw herself solely as Bella's whipping girl, the two women's positions were far more similar than it may have seemed. Both were coping with the highly demanding and competitive atmosphere set in motion by the bank that employed them. Both were young, without the confidence, security, or distance some life and work experience can provide. Their positions were mercurial, their futures dependent on catering to the often unfair whims of those above them. On an institutional level, their bank was far from "women friendly." In fact, one of the few powerful women there, a managing director openly committed to helping other female employees, had been fired three weeks after Leslie started work. She sued the bank for gender discrimination and won.

In *Men and Women of the Corporation,* Rosabeth Moss Kanter reprinted a 1942 management survey that questioned 521 young working women about whether they would prefer a male or female boss: 99.81 percent picked a man. Among the reasons listed: Women were too controlling, too focused on petty details, too critical, too jealous, and too unwilling to delegate. Though the list echoed stereotypical characteristics often attributed to women bosses, Moss Kanter pointed out that such qualities are also representative of another group: people with limited power.[10] When employees of either gender feel they have little power in a work situation, they do what they can to hold on to that power, often becoming critical and overcontrolling. If they do not have organizational influence or resources to call upon, they use the tools at their disposal—for example, behaving dictatorially or holding down talented subordinates— to maintain what control they have.

Those same 1940s preconceptions about women bosses exist today. In fact we see every last one of them echoed in Leslie's complaints about Bella. One might say that this is because women are still women, but it seems far more likely that it is because Moss Kanter's premise continues to hold true. Women who reflect these characteristics are often those in positions of limited power. They are women operating in a man's world.

The financial industry is a tough, often exclusionary atmosphere for women. In a 2001 survey of women in finance by the business research firm Catalyst, more than half the respondents reported that women are paid less than men for doing similar work, a third said they had been subjected to some form of sexual harassment, and only 18 percent felt opportunities for women to advance to senior leadership had increased in the past five years.[11] Bella was one of only two female vice presidents in her division. Her counterpart had three children and no eye toward promotion, having abandoned high-flying career ambitions in favor of a well-balanced family life. Bella, in contrast, built her reputation on being tough and aggressive, the die-hard workaholic who could always be counted on in a pinch. She made it clear that she wanted one of those few spots the bank meted out to women at the senior level and that she was willing to make the sacrifices and embrace the values necessary to advance.

In investment banking—or in any industry from commercial real estate to law enforcement in which power still resides mainly in the hands of men—such institutional values rarely encompass the nurturing or compassionate aspects of forging relationships. Women can fear that by emphasizing those softer elements of their personalities they will appear weak, threatening their chances to get ahead. Instead, like Bella, they may travel the opposite direction, lighting upon a forced macho-ness—some elements of which are rewarded and others that garner snickers behind their backs.

Bella's position reflects a common double bind for new-token women. For every woman I interviewed who told me you still have to act like a man to get ahead, there was an equal and opposite voice expressing deep distrust of female colleagues who did just that. Though we may fully embrace the idea that women should be packing the boardrooms in equal numbers, women can be quick to condemn those who openly chase the type of power and resources traditionally required to get there. In addition, when so few women rise to higher levels within a given field, one successful woman's behavioral choices can legitimately feel as if they affect not just her individual career but the prospects of all women in her given profession or organization.

The contradiction between corporate values and feminine values is sharp and can grow sharper as women move up the institutional ladder. Such conflicts are not exclusive to traditional male bastions like the banking industry. Veronica, a twenty-eight-year-old computer programmer, works for a cutting-edge high-tech company in the Pacific Northwest. She has been promoted six times in six years, and her business acumen, organizational skills, and job performance receive consistently high ratings. So Veronica was disturbed when her manager said, in her most recent performance review, that she had trouble with communication skills. While Veronica's "overly direct," style was described as "fine for senior management," it tended to alienate those not as direct as she was, including most women. Veronica does not feel that her manager's complaint is inaccurate, but she does question its importance in the grander scheme of things.

"I'm blunt, and I occasionally offend people," she admits, "but the quality of my work more than makes up for it."

Though Veronica reports to another woman, at its highest levels her company is entirely male and she is well aware that autonomous, performance-based skills are the ones it pays to master. In an environment fueled by individual ambition and a willingness to work until you drop, she sees developing too much sensitivity as "a weakness," one in which a woman in particular can't afford to indulge.

Given her current role within the company, a midlevel position of limited power, she feels that she needs to focus on fostering the traits most likely to help her get ahead. She has learned to negotiate for higher pay—she now makes four times her starting salary—and to call attention to her accomplishments instead of waiting around to get noticed. Her future goals include establishing a solid enough track record that she can relieve her workload somewhat and devote more time to her boyfriend and eventually to kids and a family. She feels she has to make choices about where to direct her energies: either to attain a secure enough professional position to allow her to make space for a personal life, or to tend to her relationships with the women under her.

"I did consider my review carefully," Veronica explains, "but in the broader picture, I don't think the communication issue is all that important. As I move up, it will be less of a problem not to be nice. I'll be communicating solely with men and a few powerful women who won't feel threatened by me."

Though Veronica's decision to ignore her relational skills may be shortsighted, she has focused on an important point. High-ranking executives are far more likely to reward those with whom they feel comfortable and who share similar values. Despite the recent buzz about feminine work styles, employees who exhibit typically masculine-identified traits—like independence, assertiveness, and willingness to take a stand—are more often favored with raises and promotions.[12] In a survey of women in finance, 75 percent of respondents considered developing a workplace style that pleased male managers and partners a key strategy for getting ahead.[13] When it came to a choice between acting like a typical woman or acting like a typical corporate executive, both Veronica and Bella knew their career goals made it fully apparent which side to come down upon.

In Bella's case, my guess is that even acting like a man did not protect her from being treated like a woman. A series of harassment lawsuits filed against various Wall Street firms in the 1990s revealed horrifying levels of discrimination in the financial industry—women who were heckled, flashed, fondled, and raped; who were denied jobs, accounts, and promotions; and whose complaints were blatantly ignored.[14] In her five-plus years at the bank, Bella must have experienced the same sexism that Leslie did. The higher she advanced, taking positions closer to the top and therefore constituting even more of a threat to the established order, the more critical it became for her to come across as "one of the guys." By questioning Leslie's loyalty to the organization, accusing her of challenging authority, and labeling her not a team player, Bella was able to highlight her own support of company values. It would have been risky for her to release her job frustrations on the young men under her. They were potentially future equals or—for those on the fastest track— even superiors. With Leslie, that possibility was far less likely. Given the bank's spotty female promotion record, Bella may have figured Leslie to either replace her or disappear.

For Leslie, there was no feasible in-house escape from Bella's treatment. If she complained too vociferously, she risked being labeled a troublemaker in an industry in which it does not pay for women to do anything that makes them stick out. Upper management had already proved unhelpful and, given Bella's lack of support, Leslie did not foresee much of a future for herself with the company. Ultimately, she dealt with the situation the only way she could—by leaving. She accepted a position with one of the bank's clients, working in a small office where "it's just me and two other men." When Leslie delivered her two-weeks notice, Bella immediately voiced how sorry she was to see Leslie go.

"The amazing thing," Leslie reports, "was she sounded like she actually meant it. It was like she didn't want to have me there, but she also didn't want to be alone."

Leslie and I spoke only a few months after she had quit. Nevertheless, she felt that small degree of distance gave her a better understanding of Bella's motivations.

"Working under Bella was hell. I'd never go back, and I wouldn't wish it on anybody," she tells me. "But looking back, I can also see her as someone reacting to a difficult situation. She was an ambitious woman in a tough environment, and she did what she felt she had to do to protect her career. For me, the most upsetting thing isn't how Bella treated me.

It's the compromises she had to make if she had any hopes of getting ahead."

Room Enough for Two

Jocelyn is tall, purposeful, and athletic, with close-cropped dark hair and the sort of practical, cut-the-crap personality you would imagine could sweep just about any problem out of the way. She is an achiever extraordinaire, sporting degrees from two Ivy League universities and a just-completed cardiology fellowship at a leading Washington, D.C. hospital. Over coffee on one of her rare weekends off, we discuss the intricacies of negotiating a new doctor's schedule. She describes how she has taken to wearing dresses under her lab coat, not because they are more feminine or comfortable but because they take two seconds to drop over her head in the morning, saving valuable time.

Cardiac surgery is still a male-dominated field, and Jocelyn's first experience working under a female attending physician had arrived with the beginning of her fellowship the previous fall.

"Cate and I got off to a bad start before things even started," she explains. "So I guess you could say I had fair warning."

The yearlong fellowship was divided into three four-month rotations, giving each resident the opportunity to work under attending physicians in varying areas of expertise. A month before their rotation together, Jocelyn took care of one of Cate's patients when he came into the emergency room with an infection and Cate couldn't be reached. Instead of thanking Jocelyn, a furious Cate phoned her at home and accused her of trying to take over. Such an unexpected, and in her mind uncalled for, flare-up made Jocelyn nervous about the approaching rotation, but she had dealt with difficult personalities before and figured she was even-tempered enough to make things work.

After her first day in the operating room with Cate, Jocelyn didn't know if she was going to survive the full rotation. "It was miserable," she recalls, drawing out the final word like the endlessness of those coming months. "She did everything in her power to make me feel completely incompetent."

From day one, Cate exhibited disdain for Jocelyn's surgical talents. She would sigh and roll her eyes when Jocelyn did anything from suturing a patient to filling out a chart, stopping to dress her down in front of the entire operating room. Questions were greeted with sarcasm, and she rarely offered praise for work well done. Occasionally, Cate would make as if it were a generous step and "give" Jocelyn part of a case—though sharing surgical duties was ostensibly part of Cate's responsibility as an attending—then stand aside eyeing every move and shaking her head.

"It was very stressful," Jocelyn says. "I couldn't do anything well enough to please her. I've operated with over forty surgeons and had no complaints. All of a sudden, I couldn't even put on a clamp right. I had no idea what was going on."

Despite her past stellar reviews, Jocelyn began to have doubts about her abilities. She started secretly double-checking her choices with other surgeons, just to make sure her skills had not inexplicably taken flight. With their assurances, her anxiety grew more diffuse. She worried that she was doing something unprofessional, unintentionally crossing a boundary that pissed Cate off. Finally, she shared her problems with a few other members of the staff. The verdict came back unanimous: Cate saw Jocelyn as a threat.

"What was there to be threatened by?" Jocelyn says, still sounding amazed at the possibility. "I'm ten years younger, and I'm only here to learn."

At this point in Jocelyn's story, we could go down one of two paths. The first we know well. It is paved with good girls and bad girls, Cinderella and her stepsisters, Snow White and that wicked, wicked queen. The second path, the less familiar one, requires tipping the power

structure on its head. From this angle, we can catch a glimpse of what fueled Cate's fears about being eclipsed by a younger and talented woman.
We can see how it might seem that allowing a potential star like Jocelyn
to run with her abilities risked an Emperor's New Clothes effect—
stripping away Cate's power and making her look less skilled, less successful than she did before. We can see how, in a certain relational light,
Jocelyn has everything to gain here and Cate everything to lose.

Cardiac surgery, like investment banking, is one of those fields in
which women still occupy that "some but not too many" stage ripe for
new tokenism. Though the number of female doctors has increased
overall, the top-earning fields—cardiology, gastroenterology, and ortho-
pedic surgery—are still 93.4 percent male.[15] Before Jocelyn's arrival, Cate
had staked out professional turf that was hers alone, encompassing
everything from her relationships to the senior physicians to how she
presented herself on the job. There was one other female surgeon in the
department, but the two women rarely crossed paths, since her colleague
spent the bulk of her time doing academic research while Cate concentrated on the operating room.

As the senior figure, Cate must have felt pressure to outperform Jocelyn in every category, to be savvier, more poised, faster on her feet. There
is no direct competition between a resident and her attending. Jocelyn's
role is still that of an apprentice—to ask questions, absorb, and gradually
take on responsibilities—but competition can arise over numerous
things beyond salary and job title, things like influence, praise, and attention. Though Jocelyn may have trouble envisaging herself as threatening
in those departments, I certainly do not. Here is just the short list: Jocelyn is confident and personable, a talented surgeon coming off a residency at a top hospital. Her résumé runs the gamut from nationally
ranked college rower to sterling medical student. One of her colleagues
told me that from the moment Jocelyn's application first whirred
through their fax machine, the entire surgical department was wild to

land her. In the ensuing months, she excelled on nearly every front, winning accolades that used to be all Cate's.

As with Bella, Cate's most significant professional relationships revolved around the men surrounding her. Instead of becoming one of Leslie's "he-males," she had opted for a more feminine role. Her blonde hair was salon-tinted, and her wardrobe featured short skirts and pearl chokers, even in the operating room. She was married with two children, both under four years old. Becoming a mother, including working while pregnant and taking maternity leave, had marked Cate as different in a way the young and single Jocelyn had not been marked.

Jocelyn describes Cate as "political," very tuned to her relationships with the senior surgical staff and taking considerable time and effort to maintain them. Though Jocelyn considered such concentration on the hierarchy rather than the work suspect, given their environment I would say it made all kinds of sense. Being a token woman, even of the newer breed, means your success largely depends upon the acceptance and approval of the men above you. Cate had spent her entire medical career at that hospital, at one time even holding the same fellowship Jocelyn does now. In ten years on the job, she had forged strong connections with the senior surgeons. In this area, perhaps most of all, Jocelyn's arrival struck at Cate's professional foundation. Not only did Jocelyn win universal praise, but she also developed a close relationship with the head of the department, a man who had been Cate's mentor since her residency.

Odds are this mentoring relationship had proved critical for Cate. Studies suggest that mentors can be especially important for women's careers, because women tend to face greater organizational, interpersonal and individual barriers to advancement than their male counterparts.[16] As with any businesswoman, Cate's success hinged upon building enough of a reputation to draw in paying patients. She needed a high-profile man in her corner for connections, for entrées, for any situation that might demand a voice of actual power. It is no wonder she felt jealous and threatened by Jocelyn's arrival. Jocelyn's place in their mentor's affections brought home the fact that Cate's role had changed. She was no longer the lone, up-and-coming woman on the scene.

For new-token women, advancing to the next career level often means confronting a fresh batch of stumbling blocks and prejudices. It can entail laying claim to responsibilities that both colleagues and outsiders still do not associate with women. Though our old relationships do not disappear when we move up, they will change. As a full-fledged attending physician, Cate could not turn to her mentor for help and advice as often as Jocelyn could. Though she still occupied a position of limited power, she was expected to manifest a higher level of confidence and ability. In giving up the comfort of her old position for the unknown of the new, it is not surprising that her sense of competence and security would be shaken, or that she might feel jealous of the hypercompetent Jocelyn inheriting that ingenue role. Cate could have easily felt that she still had to fight too hard for her own rights and privileges to behave magnanimously toward a younger woman on the rise.

"Due to the legacy of gender discrimination, I think that many women, myself included, often feel there is a limit to the help or support—to the depth of the relationships—women can offer other women on the job," a thirty-eight-year-old Internet project manager in Atlanta told me. "Sometimes I think we feel we might be accused of being 'unprofessional' by forming close ties, and at other times I think that women who are high achievers get used to being 'onlys' and as a result become more critical and less supportive of other women, for fear of appearing less unique."

Traditional organizations are rarely, if ever, designed on the loaves-and-fishes principle. They do not automatically inflate to accommodate a female influx, and there can be a considerable lag between the increase in women present and the increase in acceptance and opportunities provided them. For new-token women, often there truly are not enough resources and rewards to go around. Like their predecessors, they face challenges unique to defining new roles for women rather than filling roles that have already been created.

"It took time to build up my confidence," Beatrice says of adjusting into her position as a woman in the defense industry. "But the good news is that it happened. As I moved higher up within the company, both the structure and I started to feel more secure. The more successful decisions I made, the more I realized I deserved to be there because I really was good at my job."

Women in Transition

Taken as isolated incidents, stories like Leslie's and Jocelyn's can seem disheartening, an indication that women breaking into traditionally male fields are destined to be forever at one another's throats. But when such tales are strung together, we can start to see new tokenism as one spot on a continuum, part of the grander cycle of absorbing more women into all aspects of the workplace. With this in mind, we can begin to make informed choices about which direction we want our relationships to travel from here.

"When I first entered the military," says Rosalind, an armed forces pioneer and one of the earliest women to undergo combat training, "I encountered two types of women. The ones who cut other women off and tried to play the maverick wound up losing everyone's respect. The ones who supported each other rose to the top. We realized that the better all of us did individually the better things would be for women in general. When we helped each other out, the women coming in under us saw that and helped each other, too. We showed the guys we could be team players, and that opened a lot of doors for a lot of women down the line."

In conducting interviews, I came across a handful of women like Rosalind who had seen their professions travel the full continuum, from almost exclusively male to liberally gender-mixed, within the life span of their individual careers. From a district court judge to a sports medicine doctor, a tobacco company executive to a television newsanchor, their experiences proved remarkably similar.

These women described a three-phase cycle. In the first phase, those initial few women entered the hallowed male halls and united to support each other against a highly unreceptive climate. Some met for monthly lunches, others swapped professional contacts, still others organized to address issues from pay equity to work-family concerns.

Phase two evolved as the doors opened a little farther, wide enough to admit a steady trickle of women but nothing nearing equality. Opportunities were still limited, but now divisions began to appear. The "we're all in this together" chorus succumbed to women seemingly less concerned with collective victories than hoarding their individual spoils.

"Once women didn't have to use all their energy to break down doors, there was a lot less cooperation and a lot more selfishness and backstabbing," Gretchen, an athletic trainer, recalls. "People grabbed whatever they could and hung on to it. As a pioneer in the profession, I found the whole thing very disheartening."

In the ensuing years, as the number of powerful women continued to climb and the sense of limited resources faded, relationships moved forward into a third phase. That below-the-belt competition cooled and a note of generosity resurfaced. Women began forging connections, creating professional networks, and taking a chance on collaborating with their female colleagues. The ugly behavior did not disappear entirely, an unrealistic expectation given our high-pressure, high-stress work environments, but with more opportunity came a more equitable balance between competition and cooperation.

For new-token women, life is still unfurling in that second, highly transitional phase. The rifts developing are not there because we are women. They are there because we are tokens. As long as being female feels like a potential career liability, women will be more likely to peg themselves as different or disconnected from other women in their profession or organization. The insecurities wrought by negotiating a male-dominated environment can trigger a strong self-protective impulse, erasing any inclination to share resources or knowledge with our female colleagues. When there are still relatively few women on the scene, those present can earn a disproportionate amount of ire from their female coworkers for appearing too hard, too deferential, too generous, too greedy, too anything, because of fears that their male colleagues might assume that all women will behave the same way. In addition, there can be an understandable resentment toward a younger woman who is benefiting from any openness accrued because the senior women were there first, breaking in the old boys and making the link between women and success seem palatable.

In many ways, organizational culture still works against women. Subtle and not so subtle forms of sexism and gender discrimination continue to proliferate, as in those meetings from which Leslie was "accidentally" excluded. As of December 2004, there were gender discrimination lawsuits either pending or recently settled with a number of major corporations including, among others, Wal-Mart, Costco, Boeing, Home Depot, and the brokerage firm Morgan Stanley.[17] Such discrimination can quickly cap the amount of support, or even the depth of the relationships, we feel comfortable offering other women on the job. Most new-token women experience a very real shortfall of materials and resources, both practical and emotional. Severing ourselves from and belittling our female colleagues may seem a necessary step, a corporate spin on survival of the fittest. It is easier and more immediately rewarding to take out our frustrations on those who are even less powerful than it is to confront our own precarious place within the system.

In the long run, any choice to isolate ourselves from and diminish other women only perpetuates the damage. No lesser authority than the American Psychological Association has found that both men and women are more likely to be stereotyped or discounted as outsiders when they are solo players.[18] Twenty-five years ago, Rosabeth Moss Kanter predicted that the most potent cure for problems among token women would be the simple presence of more women at all levels of power, and her prescription seems to have largely held true.[19] Professional environments in which it is not disadvantageous to be female—where women figure prominently and where support and communication between them are prioritized—create more productive working relationships, increasing everyone's comfort level from CEO on down. More women equals more opportunity. However safe it might feel, isolation diminishes the possibility of change.

8

Negotiating Race and Class

**We have only been taught three ways to handle difference;
three ways only. If we think it is dominant, we want to become it.
If we think it is inferior, we want to kill it. And if we're not
really sure which it is, we want to ignore it.**

—AUDRE LORD, "WOMEN'S VOICE," 1983

Sasha is thirty-one years old, a dark-skinned black woman with a headful of braids framing her round face and two deep dimples every time she smiles. She holds a Ph.D. in international relations and has traveled extensively through East Africa and South America.

After spending the first year of their marriage globetrotting, she and her husband settled in Boston so he could attend law school. At the height of the technology boom, Sasha quickly found a job as a product manager at a global communications company. Though her technical skills were not quite up to par, she convinced them that her educational background and personal strengths were more than enough to compensate. Everyone at Sasha's level in the company had a Ph.D. She was one of only two black women in the entire organization, the other worked out of a satellite office in Virginia.

Sasha soon befriended one of her fellow product managers, Camille, a white woman in her early thirties who had grown up in a nearby upper-middle-class suburb. There were not many highly placed women in the company, and Sasha and Camille bonded over their struggles against the old-boy network. They occasionally socialized on weekends, and Sasha and her husband spent Thanksgiving with Camille's family.

"We had a very pleasant relationship both on and off the job," says Sasha. "Though we weren't best friends, we did share that feeling of being in the trenches together. We worked at the same job and the same level, but the relationship never felt competitive in the least."

Though Sasha liked the product manager position and felt she was good at it, being the only black woman in a largely white male corporation did take its toll. She felt the men under her more readily challenged her authority. Clients and colleagues were consistently surprised or overly impressed by her abilities and suitability for the work she did.

"The pressure was subtle, but it was there. It was obvious that no matter how well I did, I'd never quite belong."

When Sasha had been with the company just over two years, a Hong Kong–based conglomerate bought them without warning. Word came down that 80 percent of the existing employees would be laid off. New management set up interviews at a conference center outside the city, and Camille and Sasha drove out together. Both women felt tense and worried. Camille had been considering getting pregnant and was counting on her income to cover the needs of an expanded family. With Sasha's husband still in school, her salary supported them both.

"We were talking about how unnerving the whole situation was," Sasha recalls. "Then halfway through the conversation, Camille turned to me and said, 'Of course, you're lucky. They won't fire you, because you're black.'"

Camille went on to explain how the new owners would not dare let the only black woman go for fear she would sue for discrimination. Sasha sat and listened, completely taken aback.

"Two weeks earlier, Camille had been telling me I was too smart to be working at this company. Now, suddenly I only deserved to keep my job because I was black? It was insulting, not to mention absurd. Why would a company from Hong Kong care about holding on to black employees? They're not under any affirmative action pressure. My feelings were really hurt."

Sasha knew Camille had legitimate reason to worry about keeping her job. Her boss had given her few responsibilities, and Camille's role as glorified secretary meant she had not worked on nearly as many high-profile projects as Sasha had. But Camille's take on the situation made any sympathy Sasha may have felt quickly evaporate. If Camille felt Sasha would only keep her job because she was black, did that mean she thought Sasha had been hired for the same reason? Was it so impossible to believe that Sasha's talents and abilities would be enough to recommend and sustain her?

"Camille considered herself very liberal, but she still wanted her share of white privilege. The assumption that I was only there because I was black was so automatic, and she never questioned it. When it came down to it, she didn't think she should have to fight for her job."

The more Sasha thought about their conversation, the angrier she grew. It opened a vein of ill feelings she realized she had been sitting upon for some time. She resented that her being black only struck Camille as significant when she saw it as giving Sasha an unfair advantage.

"Up until then, Camille had been completely oblivious to the fact that I was having a different workplace experience than she was. She never once asked me how it felt to be the only black woman in the entire building. She never asked what I struggled with or how people saw me. I don't think it even occurred to her that things might have been quite a bit tougher for me than they were for her."

White-Girl Privilege

It can be extremely difficult for women to own up to our preconceptions about race and class and to how feelings of guilt, superiority, or victimization play into our working relationships. The women I interviewed frequently added almost after the fact that a coworker was black or did not have a college degree, as if to indicate such factors could not really be part of the problem. We like to believe in tolerance and togetherness. We like to believe we have put our socioeconomic clashes behind us. The tug of sisterhood is powerful, and women who fit the mainstream—white, college-educated, middle-class—often do not know how to sit with the idea of having unfair advantages. They can resent that race or class loyalties may come before gender, resent being depicted as other instead of as us. The thought that "white-girl privilege" exists makes privileged white girls squirm.

Sasha is right. Though the workplace can be tough for all women, it is even tougher for a black woman. On the whole, women of color make less money—in 2002 white women's earnings were roughly 14 percent higher than black women's and 28 percent more than their Latina counterparts.[1] They also hold fewer positions of power. Women in general are still underrepresented in corporate management, but of the 2.9 million women occupying private-sector managerial positions, 86 percent are white, 7 percent African American, 5 percent Hispanic, and 3 percent Asian or "other." Minority women who do hold managerial positions are heavily concentrated in the three lowest paying industries—retail trade, professional-related services, and FIRE (finance, insurance, real estate), with black women particularly heavily clustered on one of the lowest rungs of retail trade, the food service industry. On average, women of color are more likely to report a lack of corporate support and mentoring as a barrier to advancement.[2]

On a personal level, being nonwhite in largely white organizations can be an isolating experience. Traditional corporate culture is not just defined by gender, it is also defined by race. Women of color face the same conflicts as white women regarding whether they should act more or less masculine or feminine in order to be taken seriously, but they are also confronting questions over whether to act more or less "white." Forming alliances can feel like choosing among loyalty to race, loyalty to gender, and loyalty to number one. Was Sasha wisest to bond with Camille, with a black male coworker, or with the white man who was her boss?

In addition, women who enter the workplace from diverse ethnic and cultural backgrounds have often absorbed very different messages about the relationship between women and work. Those from more traditional value systems may face family or community pressures about whether to pursue career-track positions, mix work and family, or even take a job at all, choices far different from those confronted by most mainstream white women.

"Culturally, many women from gender-traditional families are struggling with what we see as old issues," says sociologist Jane Prather. "Outwardly, these women can appear very worldly and sophisticated, so it comes as a surprise when we realize they're facing decisions we consider antiquated. Depending on your background, the benefits of women's movement arrive at different rates."[3]

Women often feel more comfortable in the role of the victim. The part is familiar, one we have been cast in for generations. Rather than acknowledging our own degree of privilege, we can tend to frame our working relationships to play up the fact that we, too, are suffering. In a 2003 *Essence* magazine article about problems between white and black women on the job, one interviewee told the story of a company in which five hundred white women organized a petition claiming their CEO had not done enough for them compared with incentive programs he had set up for black and Latina women. The footnote to the story provides a moral in the dangers of engaging in what African American theorist Barbara Christian has termed "the Oppression Derby." In order to pacify those white petitioners, the company canceled its incentive programs for women across the board.[4]

On some level, I would venture that most of us know racial tensions exist among women. In 1992, a *Ms.* magazine survey of readers representing a wide variety of backgrounds—the sort of open-minded, politically sensitive women we would least expect to hold racial grudges—revealed that a quarter of all participants considered themselves "quite" or "somewhat" prejudiced. A third of white respondents felt uncomfortable discussing racial issues with people of color.[5] I doubt so many women would have gone to the trouble of telling me that their work problems were not race or class motivated if they believed it "wasn't an issue." Like those white men who brush off continuing evidence of sexism, many privileged white women just don't want to talk about race and class tensions. We don't like what they might say about us. Camille's off-the-cuff comment reveals a trail of false assumptions that lead to some very real fears.

Since President Johnson signed the 1967 Executive Order including sex in federal antidiscrimination legislation, affirmative action has added a particular wrinkle to relationships among working women. Corporations often wound up filling their diversity quotas by hiring white women, and many women of color came to resent what they considered minority spots going to women who were not minorities. In contrast, many white women felt that jobs were being rewarded to unqualified women of color "just because they're black."

Statistically, the white women's fears were not borne out. The women of color's fears were. Affirmative action has helped white women, both middle and working class, considerably more than it has helped black women.[6] There is no evidence that those hired under its auspices are less skilled or equipped for their jobs. In fact, a 1997 Michigan State study indicated workers hired under affirmative action actually garnered higher performance ratings than their white male colleagues.[7] Even when it came to policies expressly designed to increase diversity, white-girl privilege won out.

Today, corporations remain under formal and informal pressure to appear diverse. As more and more women of all racial backgrounds push into traditionally male work environments, the competition for those diversity slots threatens to grow fiercer. At the same time, an increasing number of minority women are stepping ahead of their white colleagues on the job. Though white women still earn more in management positions, a 1998 census survey indicated that in such fields as sales and administrative support, black women were beginning to pull ahead of their white counterparts.[8]

For a middle-class, college-educated white woman like Camille, it can be disconcerting when a female colleague with fewer outward advantages succeeds beyond her. Not only does it upset the prescribed order, but it also prompts self-doubt about why she has achieved less while ostensibly having so much more. Rather than turning the mirror inward, she can look to blame external forces—like the idea that Sasha would keep her job because she fit the racial profile—for her own failure to make the cut.

On the surface, Camille's instincts proved right. The new company did hold on to Sasha and Camille lost her job. Sasha tried to be supportive, even helping Camille in her job search, but the relationship quickly disintegrated.

"It became harder and harder to empathize with her situation, because she had no empathy for mine," Sasha explains. "In order to be her friend, I had to buy her version of events. I wish we could've figured out a way to acknowledge our different experiences without it having to split us apart like it did."

When things fall apart, the onus is on both parties to address the rift in the relationship. Instead of silently fuming, Sasha had the option of discussing her bruised feelings with Camille. Perhaps they could have patched things up and perhaps not, but she had little to lose save a relationship already on the skids. There is no way around the fact that white women and women of color experience the workplace differently. Camille probably could not have supplied Sasha with all the support she needed as a black woman in a corporate setting. Sasha may have benefited more by turning to other black female professionals, whether personal friends or members of a networking group or organization, for help navigating race-related issues. Unless she also initiated a dialogue with Camille, chances are her coworker would not develop a deeper understanding of the specific issues Sasha, as a woman and a minority, confronted on the job.

The most common complaint I heard from white women who had experienced racial tensions in the workplace was that women of color could be hypersensitive, overly quick to blame race for every stumbling block they encountered. In their study of corporate relations between black and white women, researchers Ella Edmondson Bell and Stella Nkomo found that white women frequently described their black counterparts as "wearing their blackness on their sleeve."[9] In some cases the white women were probably right about their colleagues being overly sensitive. In others, they just may not have seen what their coworker saw. Though her comment felt like a slap in the face to Sasha, chances are Camille did not realize its full impact or implications. Though Sasha took Camille's words to mean she felt Sasha only got her job because she was black, that may not have been what Camille intended. In a competitive work environment, as outside pressures increase, it becomes easier to make snap judgments, harder to step back and consider another's point of view.

Traditional corporate atmospheres, in which there are few positions open to either women or minorities, understandably heighten race and class tensions. The women I interviewed also made clear that no sector of the working world is immune. I heard from people who had faced race and class conflicts in universities, in women's organizations, in nonprofits and other "politically correct" environments in which differences are allegedly acknowledged and celebrated, in which white-girl privilege was supposedly long banished. In such situations, women of color related the particular difficulties of having to maneuver around that rose-colored, "all for one" stance in order to make their problems heard.

Crista, a thirty-five-year-old black woman, was teaching undergraduate classes and pursuing her master's degree in women's studies at a Chicago university when she heard about a group of fellow students—a mix of white and minority women—who had formed to critique a department curriculum they felt was "too white-oriented." Curious, Crista showed up for the meeting at which they planned to present their case to the faculty. Though the department head, a white woman in her early fifties, professed herself open to all viewpoints and experiences, she cracked like a thundercloud upon hearing their criticism.

"The intensity of her reaction was shocking," Crista recalls, "totally out of line with the issue at hand. I think she saw it as a personal attack. She'd created this identity for herself as the good, liberal feminist, and our challenging her threatened that."

Though the group had no formal hierarchy, Crista—outspoken, articulate, and black—soon found herself labeled the ringleader. The department head accused her of trying to bring down the entire department. Not only did she reduce the number of classes Crista taught, she also began questioning the soundness of Crista's scholarship. What had originated as a simple classroom issue turned into a rift deep enough to imperil Crista's career.

"It got pretty ugly," she admits. "Up until then I'd really respected this woman. I'd even considered asking her to be my thesis adviser. But when it came down to examining her own beliefs, she just couldn't take the heat. The irony of the whole situation was that in trying to silence us, she created what she feared. The department turned into a world of us versus them."

Though eventually the fuss around Crista died down, she and the department head never returned to what Crista would consider a respectful relationship. The tension only ended when Crista left to pursue her Ph.D. at another university.

"I found the whole experience very revealing," she says. "I don't care what sort of environment you're working in or how 'correct' your politics. If you reach a point where you don't think any of your behaviors or viewpoints can be reexamined, you've reached the point where you stop growing."

Between Sisters

"I was the fourth of five sisters," explains Graciella, a round-faced, copper-skinned Latina woman in her late thirties, as we sit across from each other in a crowded beachside cafe. "We were all very supportive of each other. I also learned early on to deal directly when I had a problem with another woman, and to expect other women to deal directly with me."

Graciella's parents came to California from Mexico the year after she was born, and she grew up in a mostly Spanish-speaking section of Los Angeles. After graduating from UCLA with a degree in communications, she set her sights on the television business. For the past six years, she has worked as a producer for an afternoon talk show in the Los Angeles area, carving out a niche doing segments on women's and minority issues.

Ana, a fellow producer and the only other Latina woman on the show, arrived on the job about a year after Graciella did, and the two hit it off immediately. They spent many long lunches and weekend shopping excursions discussing the television industry and life in general, including plans for someday producing their own Latina lifestyle show. Graciella was four years older and, having worked in TV for nearly a decade, had numerous contacts in the business. She made a point of bringing Ana to networking functions and introducing her around.

"I've been around long enough to know it's tough for a Latina woman to get attention and respect in the workplace," she explains. "I feel strongly that we should make a point of sticking together and helping one another out."

Last spring, Graciella took four months off after the birth of her daughter. While on maternity leave, she decided that she wanted to shift from full-time producer to a consultant role. The job switch would involve saner hours, and she liked the prospect of becoming an idea person who could bypass much of the everyday humdrum and politics.

As Graciella worked with the show's executives to hammer out her new role, she and Ana spent hours on the phone talking over details, right down to the intricacies of Graciella's salary negotiations. Ana was nothing but supportive, offering to help smooth Graciella's transition in any way she could.

Then one afternoon, as her negotiations neared completion, Graciella got a call from her boss. Apparently Ana had requested a meeting with him that morning in which she had pitched herself for Graciella's new position at three-quarters of Graciella's new salary. "I'm not interested in her offer," he told her, "but I do think you should be a little more careful about who you trust."

"When I found out what Ana had done," Graciella recalls, "I went through the entire range of emotions from wanting to do what they used to do in the neighborhood—take her out on the street and kick her ass—to wanting to sabotage her right back. Her betrayal was very, very painful. I'd done so much to help her. I just couldn't understand."

Ultimately, Graciella decided revenge of any kind would require stooping to Ana's level. Instead, she opted for the high road, did her best to let the emotions go, and settled into her consultant role. Shortly after Graciella's return, Ana accepted a job with a fledgling Latino film company. Though the two women no longer work together, the Latina production community is small enough that their paths occasionally cross. When they do, things remain civil but purely business. All plans for future collaboration have been dropped.

A few months after her boss's phone call, one of Graciella's coworkers told her that Ana had always been suspicious of Graciella, viewing her as the competition from the day she arrived.

"TV is all about being popular with your boss and colleagues, and I guess she saw another Latina woman as a threat to that. It's sad. We're both passionate, smart, dynamic women. We could've done great things together. It still pains me that we wound up enemies instead."

Women bound together by race can conjure up particularly romantic expectations about unconditional support. When you are an outsider on two counts, it can feel doubly important to find a peer who is willing to include you in her circle and who can understand your particular goals and struggles. Lured by the prospect of a sister in arms, it is easy to forget that the same sort of competition for money, attention, and success that occurs between women in general can unfold within racial groups as well. Given the scarcer resources and heightened sense of isolation she encounters, a woman disenfranchised by both race and gender may feel even more inclined to sacrifice a principle or two in order to get ahead.

For a woman of color entering the predominantly white workplace, professional relationships can feel like an either/or decision—either hang with your own people or forge connections with those in power. It may seem wisest to secure your own position by pushing those too similar to you away.

"Groups tend to want to link with the group above them," says joint black and women's studies professor Toni King. "For opportunities, for resources, for mentoring, you try to ally yourself with those who have power. The more competitive the setting, the more likely you'll lose consciousness of your own group, because you're trying to maintain those ties above."[10]

Graciella's idealized view of relationships between Latina women was severely tested by the environment within which she and Ana operated. Because of their shared race, she assumed their relationship would not experience the pressures those between the other producers did. But in many ways, those pressures became even more intense. TV is a highly competitive business, with producers regularly trying to beat one another out for the plum stories. Though in most organizational hierarchies it is conceivable for every talented, hardworking white man to rise like cream, that possibility shrinks for women and shrinks again for women of color. Imagine the odds of George W. Bush having two black women in his cabinet. Though our overall social structure provides multiple reasons for Ana's white and male colleagues to out-succeed her, getting beat out by the Latina girl next door is just getting beat.

Graciella's open-book willingness to trust made it easy for Ana to take advantage. Graciella admits she was quicker to forge an alliance with Ana than she would have been with a non-Latina colleague. She did not look for signs of jealousy or unhealthy competition, nor did she acknowledge that the competitive nature of their job could play into their relationship. As King puts it, "the my-group-is-all-good lie can be just as damaging as the my-group-is-all-bad lie." Women of same race may have very different insecurities and desires and be willing to make very different sacrifices in order to succeed.

For someone like Graciella, the heightened anticipation of loyalty, empathy, and unfaltering support can lead to a deeper sense of loss when a woman of the same race does let you down. "If another woman of color betrays you, it's bigger than just you and your career," says King. "You look at this other woman and you think: she knows what it's like to be dismissed, she knows what it's like to be invalidated, she knows acutely what it's like when those experiences are based on race and gender combined. She even knows the small things that wear on me, my troubles in my community, the grit in my day-to-day life. There's this increased sense of, how could she, of all people, betray the trust I had in her?"

Negotiating relationships with other women of color requires maneuvering in a way that is separate from and often contradictory to the battle required to scale the organizational ladder. Choices women make to get ahead in one department can find them castigated in another. Even as women of color struggle to position themselves strategically within their organization's framework, they risk punishment from other minority women for getting too close to their white colleagues. Issues like class and skin color, with roots outside the office, can erupt inside as well.

Miranda, who is biracial, was teaching English at a small New England college when she landed a juicy deal from a major New York publisher for her first novel. She had formed what she considered a close and supportive relationship with another black female professor, a poet who had published one book with a very small, independent press.

"When she heard about my book, she said she'd never consider going with a mainstream publisher, because it wasn't staying true to the black experience," Miranda recalls. "Implying that I'd gone and deserted the entire race. Another colleague, also black, told me how tired she was of listening to all these light-skinned women writers whine about how tough they had it. We were discussing another book, but again the implication was clear. Both comments were very hurtful and, honestly, I think they were meant to be. Among black women, you're never allowed to out-perform a sister. Anyone who does pull ahead clearly did something wrong."

Though constrictions against appearing ambitious at the expense of personal relationships exist among all women, the pressure toward maintaining sisterhood is often even stronger among women of color. Minority women are doubly bonded by virtue of being outsiders on the race and gender fronts, further stressing the need to maintain internal loyalties. The sense that no one is looking out for them but themselves can make it seem that much more of a betrayal, the ultimate in selling out, if individual members of the group pursue success in the mainstream white man's world.

"Of course black women should support one another whenever possible," Miranda agrees, "but a degree of autonomy is also necessary.

When something good happens to you, you're punished unless you bring anyone and everyone along with you regardless of their talents, abilities, or personality. But one woman can't carry the entire sisterhood on her shoulders. It would break every last one of us to try."

Though painful, her colleagues' reaction to her success became a pivotal growth experience for Miranda. It prompted her to more closely examine the sorts of professional ties she wanted to foster—particularly with other women of color—and what she herself hoped to bring to them.

"What happened around that first book prompted a real sea change in how I see my relationships with other black women," she explains. "It's helped me to become more conscious of my own jealous and competitive feelings and to transform them into challenges to myself instead of negative feelings about others. I do my best to seek out women who allow for difference, and who don't feel threatened by another's success. I worry less about what everyone thinks about me and more about the kind of professional relationships that can make me a richer person all around. I still work with the same mix of people, but I'm more willing to make room for both their priorities and mine."

Mixed messages still abound about what it means to be loyal to other women of color, about the levels of autonomy and support expected and even allowed. One woman's beliefs will not necessarily be shared all around. As Miranda discovered, there's often more room than we might realize for opposing experiences and points of view. Though limited professional opportunities for women of color are very much a reality, it is a reality minority women can begin working to change by being as honest and upfront about the competitive aspects of their relationships as they possibly can.

When I asked Graciella what she'd learned from her experience with Ana, she told me that most of all, it made her question how trusting she should be in the future.

"I feel like I rushed in too quickly with Ana. I didn't take the time to feel out what she wanted from me. I just assumed it was the same thing I wanted from her. That's a dangerous thing to do."

Though the prospect of plunging passionately and idealistically into our working relationships may be appealing, it's a valuable lesson Graciella took away. Competition does alter the stakes of women's professional ties, no matter how much we may have in common underneath. Proceeding with caution does not mean an end to strong professional bonds among women of color. It just means there are too many other personal and political factors at play to presume race alone, like gender alone, will be enough to join two women at the hip.

A Question of Class

Four years ago, Delia left her home and two children in the Philippines to come to the United States. She moved in to an apartment next door to her cousin in Queens and, through a friend, found a job with a cleaning agency. She works five or six days a week, mostly in Manhattan, juggling almost forty clients a month, spending three to four hours per apartment and often covering three to four apartments a day. Though most of her earnings go toward living expenses and the money she sends home, she hopes to save enough to start college classes soon. In the meantime, she's taking a local business course that meets every Saturday afternoon.

"I like New York," she tells me over the phone early one weekday morning as she readies herself for the hour long commute to her first client on Manhattan's Upper West Side. "There's opportunity here. But if I can't bring my children to join me soon, I'll go back to the Philippines. It's too hard not to be with them."

Delia quickly developed a reputation within the agency for being hardworking, reliable, and easy to get along with. Clients recommended her to their friends, and by now she has enough special requests to fill seven days a week, twelve hours a day.

Two years ago, Delia started cleaning for Lauren, one of the agency's longtime clients. Every week, she spent at least four hours in the three-bedroom apartment Lauren and her husband, a prominent surgeon, shared in downtown Manhattan. Lauren was in her late forties, about five years older than Delia, with one son in college. She worked as an architect and was usually gone when Delia arrived, which on the whole Delia prefers. It is easier to make herself comfortable in the apartment when no one is looking over her shoulder, and she works faster with no distractions.

"I don't like clients watching me," she explains. "It always feels like they're looking out for mistakes."

When they did overlap, Lauren always seemed genuinely friendly. She asked about Delia's children or her weekend, and made a point to tell her what a wonderful job she did. But almost every week, Delia would arrive at the apartment to find a stack of notes telling her what to do. At first, they just requested extra work, things like washing windows or scrubbing the refrigerator that could easily tack another half hour onto the regular cleaning routine. Then, gradually, Lauren began leaving instructions for Delia to do the jobs she did anyway. Though Lauren was still just as pleasant in person, the notes grew increasingly demanding. Phrases like "take extra time to dust today" or "don't skip the bathroom floor" seemed a roundabout way of accusing Delia of getting lazy. On top of that, Lauren did not always pay the right amount and, except for at Christmas, she never left Delia a tip.

At one point, Delia tried talking to Lauren, explaining how much time it required to do all those added jobs. Lauren reddened and apologized profusely, telling Delia she felt horrible about being so demanding. They agreed to compromise on the amount of side work, and for the next few weeks Lauren's written missives all but disappeared. Eventually, the notes started up again, "reminding" Delia what to do and asking for extra services.

"I got so tired of those notes," Delia tells me. "I've been cleaning that apartment for two years. I understand how to do it. Does she think I'm dumb?"

One sleet-ridden February morning, after arriving at Lauren's apartment to find multiple pages of scribbled instruction, Delia hit her limit.

"I figured the least she owed me was enough respect to raise a problem face to face. So I wrote a note back saying I was tired of wasting my time. I told her, 'I work my ass off keeping your apartment clean. If that's not good enough for you, find somebody else.' Then I walked out without touching a thing."

Delia called her boss from her next job and told her she was not going back. Lauren was livid. She took her complaints straight to the head of the agency, pushing to get Delia fired.

"My boss wasn't so happy with me," Delia says, laughing, "but she's good about respecting when we're not comfortable. She knows I'm a good worker. I make a lot of money for that agency, and I never have any complaints."

I asked Delia why she thinks Lauren behaved as she did.

"I can't see any good reason. I've got kids, I've got a job, I'm not so different from her. She knows that. If she's got issues with me, she can talk to me about it. We'll work things out."

A number of feminist women of color have critiqued society in general and the feminist movement in particular over the fact that when they referred to "women" they usually meant privileged white women. Eliminated from the equation were all those who resided in the margins of society for reasons of race and class. "Theories advanced as being universally applicable to women as a group on closer examination appear greatly limited by the white, middle-class origins of their proponents," writes black feminist scholar Patricia Hill Collins.[11]

Poor women and women of color sport a very different work history and experience than white middle-class women do, one that rarely includes a sense of glamour or privilege attached to being on the job. They have worked as maids, nannies, prostitutes, waitresses, sales clerks, and factory labor. Though most women are quick to empathize with the sepia-tinted version of such inequality—the sweatshop workers or servant girls of old—they can feel far more uncomfortable addressing the caste systems based on ethnicity, wealth, and education that remain in place today. Women are used to being in the less powerful position. We know all about male privilege, sexual harassment, and the old-boy network, but when attention turns to questions of class, it can feel as if someone switched scripts without warning. Suddenly we are playing the oppressor as well as the oppressed.

Moral quandaries erupt when the ideals of feminine equality meet the realities of paying other women to do our dirty work. Women make up the bulk of today's service industry—97.6 percent of child-care workers and 93.7 percent of cleaners and servants are female.[12] They scrub our houses, cook our food, and tend to our children. As more and more middle- and upper-class women have moved into the workplace—employing more and more working-class women to pick up the domestic slack—these quandaries have become increasingly prevalent in all our lives. "Even better wages and working conditions won't erase the hierarchy between employer and domestic help," writes social critic Barbara Ehrenreich, "since the help is usually there only because the employer has 'something better' to do with her time."[13]

Lauren and Delia's relationship could not help being colored by domestic work and its long tradition of the advantaged benefiting from the disadvantaged. Since the earliest days of this country, slaves and immigrant workers have catered to the privileged classes. As late as the 1930s and '40s, black women gathered on a street corner in the Bronx to parade before white housewives interested in buying their strength and service for the day, a phenomenon black journalists referred to as "The Bronx Slave Market."[14] Such weighty backstory cannot be erased no matter how pleasant and polite one is. As a society, we have flocked to a *Nanny*

Diaries–like image of whom we employ to serve us—the nanny in question being white, middle class, and educated—one that is free of messy race-class divisions and the accompanying whisperings of guilt or exploitation. The realities of the service industry rarely come so tidily packaged.

Delia is difficult to categorize. She's a confident and well-spoken contemporary mother juggling job, school, and family, her life filled with many of the same ingredients as Lauren's. At the same time, Lauren and Delia are nothing close to peers. Casual chitchat about their children is shadowed by the fact that Delia cannot be with hers. If they share a cup of coffee, they will drink out of mugs that Lauren purchased and Delia scrubs. There is no modern template for such a relationship. In a culture whose rhetoric espouses that all women should be on equal footing, these two are engaged in a professional relationship that highlights the level of inequality that very much still exists.

"The biggest trouble I have with the women I work for is that they don't know how to match up what they see with what I do," says Polly, a Caribbean woman in her early forties who does secretarial work for the charity arm of a local church. "I'm tall and I wear bright colors. I talk with a lot of confidence. I used to own my own business when I lived in Barbados. That's not how a secretary, especially a black secretary, is supposed to be."

Like Delia, Lauren also did not fit the stereotypes. She was not a cold and insensitive upper-crust white employer. There was a level of genuine connection between her and Delia, and she regularly expressed an interest in the details of Delia's life. The fact that she only felt comfortable criticizing Delia via written notes indicates that she probably felt a degree of guilt about making such demands. Lauren's passive-aggressive behavior freed her from having to confront the fact that she may have both empathized with Delia as a mother and woman of similar age and harbored feelings of superiority toward her. Leaving notes meant she did not have to face the contradiction of being too embarrassed to make demands in person, but feeling entitled to make them all the same. She could retain her sense of entitlement without erasing the premise that their shared gender gave her and Delia a "common bond."

Women who employ other women in a service capacity frequently assuage their uneasiness about class inequities by intentionally blurring lines of professionalism. They may take a personal interest in an employee's outside life—her family, her background—or refer to nannies, housekeepers, and other domestic help as "part of the family." They may give gifts like food or clothing in lieu of more professional perks like vacation time, raises, and benefits.[15] This behavior is not confined to the homefront. One corporate secretary with whom I spoke worked for a woman who would present her with an "apology gift," frequently a powder blue box housing jewelry from Tiffany's, every time they had an altercation. In the three years they worked together, her employer never once gave her a raise. "I always wished she could have given me a little less," the secretary told me, "and respected me a little more." Even when well intentioned, such treatment obscures the fact that women in the service sector are employees—in the same way as architects, television producers, or product managers are—with all the rights and privileges that entails.

Delia's rebellion gave Lauren a reality check, a clear message that her "you're my friend, but I still feel entitled to exploit you" version of the relationship was not going to fly. Lauren and Delia had a professional relationship—one between client and service provider—bound by the same work-for-pay agreement and the same laws of respect as any other. Lauren did overstep her bounds by treating Delia inconsiderately and not paying her enough. In extricating herself from a professional situation in which she was consistently treated poorly, Delia responded as any legitimate employee might and should respond.

The Corporate Caste System

The women I interviewed discussed difficulties in dealing across class lines within an organizational culture as well as without. In any corporate environment caste systems can develop, separating managers, executives, and others on the career track from secretaries and clerical staff, who have little or no job growth inherent to their positions. As in most service sectors, the majority of these support workers are female—women fill 78.5 percent of all administrative support positions.[16] In the past few decades, as the number of women in executive and managerial posts has increased, so have conflicts between women occupying these two camps.

Women in higher level jobs spoke about resenting the fact that their secretaries often expected them to be friendlier, more nurturing, and less demanding than their male colleagues. Some felt as if their assistants resisted taking orders from another woman or wanted an undue amount of influence in how things were run.

"When I'm dealing with any of the female secretaries, I have to go out of my way to be 'nice' to get what I need," explains Meredith, a labor relations attorney. "There's definitely a double standard. A male attorney can call up office services and say, 'I need you to make this delivery right now. Get up here!' and no one thinks twice about it. A woman has to be much gentler, with effusive thanks and a grateful e-mail cc'd to the secretary's boss. Otherwise, she gets a reputation for being abusive."

On the other side, I heard from secretaries and clerical workers who felt their female bosses made a particular point of disassociating from them, as if pink-collar status was something that could rub off and stain their own careers. Instead of providing support or mentorship to the women working under them, they seemed to intentionally take steps to cement the notion of an "us" and a "them."

Luanne had worked as a secretary in the fashion business for three years when she landed a position under Nina, one of the company's two female senior vice presidents. Luanne was good at her job—well organized, quick thinking, and personable—and she let Nina know she hoped to advance beyond her secretary role. Nina assured Luanne that the company favored promoting from within and pointed out several former assistants who had risen in the company. But instead of finding the mentor she desired, Luanne spent the next two years watching others climb the company ladder as she stayed put. Nina even brought in outside people to fill several jobs for which Luanne might have been perfect.

"Nina had real power in the company," Luanne says. "She could've helped me anytime she wanted to, but for her there was a very clean line between office people and cubicle people. From the start, she treated me like a second-class citizen. She didn't even acknowledge me when we got in the elevator together. When it came down to it, she saw me as a secretary and nothing more."

When it addresses them at all, our culture tends to depict class tensions between professional women as falling along good girl/bad girl lines. Usually the working-class woman plays the heroine, her more gentrified colleague the bully in need of being taken down a peg. In the movie *Working Girl*, Melanie Griffith literally dons the clothes of her snotty, affluent boss in order to work her way up the corporate ladder. In *Erin Brockovich*, the titular brassy office assistant, despite cheap talk and cheap clothes, rides roughshod over an uptight corporate lawyer.

In reality, corporate life lends far more complexity to both the good-girl and the bad-girl roles. Given Nina's position as one of the few women near the top of the company, their shared gender may have made her less inclined to help Luanne instead of more. Women on the fast track often do not want to risk being identified with those seen as service help. Forming ties with a female secretary—and letting those around her couple them together—could have hurt Nina's status as a player. For someone with her eye on the next rung of the ladder, the connections worth making are not gender-related, but among that successful elite she aspires to join. Though such upward focus is by no means exclusive to women, women often have to transcend more damaging preconceptions about their potential and job commitment than men do. They simply have less room to be generous.

The fact that Luanne was so good at her job may have hurt her more than it helped. Luanne made Nina's stressful office life easier and Nina was probably eager to hold on to a competent assistant for as long as possible, making her even more unlikely to push Luanne for promotion. Even if she fully intended to fulfil her promise of job growth when she first hired Luanne, the disruption threatened by such a move may have seemed far too heavy a sacrifice.

Without Nina's help, Luanne was stuck. Fairy stories in which the working girl transcends her boss are rare. It is extremely difficult to cross socioeconomic lines, especially when those above us do not want them crossed. Class insecurities play on our self-confidence, creating doubts that can be easily exploited.

"I'm sure being skipped over by Nina was related to the fact she had an MBA from Harvard and I had two semesters of community college," Luanne tells me. "And that was partly my fault, too. Because I didn't have a degree, I didn't feel confident enough to stand up to her. I didn't press for all those things I might have pressed for otherwise."

I would give Luanne point number one. The absence of a college degree probably did mean Nina would have to inch a little farther out on a limb in order to help Luanne secure a promotion. As for point number two, Luanne's secretarial position, coupled with her lack of education, meant she lacked the power to apply pressure without the risk of losing her job. In order to move up within the company, she needed someone more influential to go to bat for her. This need led her to expect more from Nina than Nina, who suffered from a power deficit of her own, was willing or perhaps even able to give.

The Reality Check

The issues surrounding race and class are myriad. I could fill a second book with stories—from hotel maids, illegal nannies, and factory workers, from the only black woman, the only Hispanic woman, the only Asian woman on the job. The subject proves just as volatile as it is vast. Wrong notes are easily struck, political correctness annihilated with a single misstep. As a member of the white, college-educated, middle-class mainstream, I have plenty of concerns about balanced reporting. What did I leave out? Who didn't I understand? How do I give full voice to all sides? Such uncertainties rise exponentially when we live these questions day to day. It is tempting to deal with them in the same way Lauren, Graciella, and Sasha all did—by not dealing at all. But denying or smoothing over race and class tensions will not make them disappear. Legitimate diversity, in which all players have a voice, cannot happen without calling forth the very conflicts too many of us try to avoid.

Perhaps the toughest step in addressing these problems involves admitting that women are not blame-free. Whether intentionally or not, we do discount each other. We do take advantage. We do cast decisions, skirt problems, and distribute rewards at least in part because of our preconceptions about where people come from. So do men. It's human nature. Organizational researchers have repeatedly shown that people work best with those who share similar histories and values. We feel most comfortable dealing with those who are most like ourselves.[17] In addition, overt expressions of conflict and competition often carry class connotations of their own. Society uses women's styles of confrontation in order to separate us along the gentility spectrum, labeling those who openly make waves as "low-class." As long as we buy into such preconceptions, we wind up devaluing many of those paths through which we might confront our race and class divisions.

Though mainstream society has largely shied away from admitting to unhealthy competition among women, the phenomenon is widely acknowledged in black and hip-hop culture. There is even a term to describe one woman who takes down another: "player-hater." Riffs on the subject have appeared in publications ranging from *Essence* to *Honey* to the *National Women's Studies Association Journal*.[18] I doubt that woman-on-woman competition is more prevalent within the black community. Perhaps black culture is simply more comfortable with the fact of inequality. They know that hard thoughts and ungenerous behavior always have and always will unfold.

9

Bridging the Generation Gap

Every single inch of ground that a woman stands
upon today has been gained by the hard work
of some little handful of women of the past.

—SUSAN B. ANTHONY

Frankly, I think there's a special place in hell
for women who don't help other women.

—MADELEINE ALBRIGHT[1]

Helen is near fifty, with short graying hair and practical clothes; she is humble and soft-spoken but firm in her convictions. She comes from a working-class southern family, raised by a single mother for whom life was a constant financial struggle. For the past twenty years she has run a series of after-school programs for underprivileged kids that have been imitated nationwide.

Helen recently brought in a new program assistant, April, who is in her midtwenties and just a few years out of college. In their brief interview, April sold herself to Helen by expressing a strong interest in setting up her own youth program somewhere down the line. Though April did not have the experience the job required, Helen was impressed by her keen sense of direction and felt willing to put in the extra effort to train her. But, as they began working together, she was entirely unprepared for April's attitude.

"The most striking thing was her complete absence of respect," Helen offers. "From day one, she behaved as if I was lucky to have her instead of the other way around. When you're dealing with time and budget pressures, maintaining a clear hierarchy is critical. But April would roll her eyes whenever I asked her to do anything. She contradicted me in front of other employees, and offered suggestions when it wasn't her job. Maybe it's just the old school in me, but where I come from you don't treat someone in authority that way."

Helen appreciated that April had been thrust into a high-responsibility job, one for which she was not entirely equipped. She suspects April may have been intimidated by Helen's reputation.

"I think she was terrified of making a mistake. I know I'm not always easy to work with. I tend to move very quickly, and my thoughts jump around a lot. But if she'd spoken up and said 'this is hard for me,' I would've been happy to slow things down."

Helen is quick to point out that April was not unskilled or untalented. She was especially good with organizational aspects like charts and schedules, which are not Helen's strong suit, and Helen tried to praise those things as much as possible. April also had a great deal to learn. She needed to be tougher, more focused, and less emotionally fragile if she was going to continue in social work.

"I spent so much time thanking her and being nice, because I wanted her to relax," Helen recalls. "Meanwhile, I sat there getting more and more pissed off at the way she was behaving." Helen tried her best not to overreact. She didn't yell at April or confront her in front of other people. Instead, she pulled her aside one afternoon for a good, old-fashioned "talking to."

"I sat her down and said, 'Let me tell you what you're doing right and what you should never do again.' Number one on that list was respect the person in charge." Though Helen had hoped to help April by providing advice from her own experience, April interpreted Helen's words as flat-out criticism. "She got tears in her eyes. I asked her if I'd hurt her feelings, and she said yes. I felt awful. I don't think she particularly likes me, but I hope she learned something."

Helen goes on to say that she feels as if April represents a trend she has noticed in the past five or six years. Many of the young women she has worked with come across as rude or cocky, with an inflated sense of entitlement. "They expect to have everything handed to them. No one seems to have explained about paying their dues."

Helen also admits that she can feel intimidated by and even jealous of these same young women, who arrive equipped with a blazing confidence in their abilities and their futures that she never had. Women were not allowed to be so upfront about ambition and direction when she started out in the workplace.

"We would never have dreamed of pulling any attitude," she marvels. "We were just happy to have a job."

A Different World

While researching this book, I attended a workshop for female college students who had joined a mentoring group designed to help them make the transition from school to the corporate world. The speakers were two successful businesswomen in their late sixties, ostensibly there to pass on lessons in how to network. As the women spoke, relaying funny stories laced with carefully polished gems of advice, the main messages that rose to the surface were these:

Focus on meeting and pleasing the men in power, because they are the ones who can get you places.

Feel free, in fact make a point of flattering, flirting, and employing all available feminine wiles.

Watch movies from the 1930s and '40s, particularly anything starring Katharine Hepburn, for lessons in conversation, grace, and manners.

Always be a lady.

Not surprisingly, I questioned how much of this was valuable. Some of it was, but some decidedly was not. The students around me certainly seemed confused about how to separate the useful from the archaic. Though perhaps an exaggerated example, the communication gap I encountered in that lecture hall reflects a problem that is regularly developing among women on the job. Due to the extraordinary changes of the past three decades, women who entered the workplace thirty, twenty, even ten years ago received dramatically different messages, faced different opportunities, and fought different battles from those entering today. The resultant contradictions in values and expectations create ground ripe for hurt feelings and misunderstandings. In talking to women of all ages, I heard a constant refrain. The older/younger generation "just doesn't get it." (In the name of simplicity, throughout this chapter I'll refer to the two sides as older and younger, with no value judgments attached.)

The biggest complaint older women had about the younger generation boiled down to two words: no respect. There was often a feeling that "girls today" don't have proper appreciation for the struggles older women went through to open those doors they are now striding through. Like Helen, they saw the younger generation as too selfish and too hungry, as wanting it all, wanting it now, and having no interest in paying their dues. Some had the impression that young women wanted to use their relationships with older women as shortcuts to success, instant access via the women-support network, rather than as an investment in their long-term professional education.

In contrast, many young women complained that the previous generation could come across as half-dinosaur, refusing to acknowledge the degree to which times have changed. "I get the feeling they think just because they had it hard, we should have it hard, too," a twenty-seven-year-old tax lawyer told me. "But if that's the case, then what was the point of all that struggle?" They felt the older generation could be too rigid about which issues were important, refusing to take the concerns of their younger counterparts seriously. Some added that their senior colleagues had overly narrow guidelines about how to be supportive or that they insisted upon viewing the world as women against men even as the next generation works to blur those lines. There has been a colossal shift in how women are allowed to express their ambitions and what they are allowed to be ambitious for. Roads are more open for women today than they were twenty years ago, and the younger half wants to put the accelerator to the floor.

This is what women of both generations expressed out loud. But beneath the concerns voiced on either side, some more fragile issues were also at play.

Regardless of how long they have been on the job, how prestigious their titles, or high their salaries, older women can feel as though they are on shaky professional footing. For men, professional and societal power tend to rise in tandem, but as women age their cultural cache diminishes, even if they continue to climb the job ladder. As a society, we tend to rate female youth and newness over age and experience, meaning more experienced women can feel disregarded, underappreciated, or shut out. "Once you hit fifty," says a fifty-two-year-old magazine editor, "I don't care how high powered you are, there are certain areas in which a woman just can't compete." Recent jumps in technology and the rapid pace of today's global economy can exacerbate that fear of being eclipsed by someone both sexier and better informed.

In an environment in which attention equals power and power equals respect, older women can understandably resent younger women who siphon off that attention without seeming to put in the commensurate effort. That open ambition slapping up against them can translate into Helen's perception that girls today are overreaching, disrespectful, and even dangerous. Many older women do not feel as confident in their power as their younger counterparts might anticipate. Most did not enter the workplace with any assurance that the world was their oyster. They entered, as Helen did, "just happy to have a job." They have spent considerable time and energy battling prejudices and abuse. Young women may get tired of hearing it, but things were harder for them.

Though young women on the job today may have it easier, they do not necessarily have it easy. There are far more options, but there are also far more women competing for those options. What looks like youthful cockiness masks its own mountain of insecurities. Women entering the workplace today often arrive with romantic preconceptions in tow, expecting power, money, and independence without the drudgery and politics most real work entails. They can feel intense pressure to achieve everything and achieve it now, department head by thirty or you're slacking. Admitting to difficulties or asking for help may feel like failure. Research indicates that younger women tend to feel more competitive toward other women and to have lower self-esteem in the workplace than women who have had time to establish more solid professional identities.[2]

In my midthirties, I rest somewhere between these two compass points, slightly young of center but capable of seeing both sides. It is the ideal vantage from which to recognize that we all need to start looking a little more empathetically at the other point of view. If these cross-generational relationships are among the trickiest we will encounter, they are also some of the most crucial. Working women have finally reached a point from which we can transmit professional power and wisdom across generational lines. We can hire and fire and make raise and promotion decisions. Most important, we have lived through a period of workplace watershed, gleaning valuable lessons that will serve all of us to see passed on.

The Family Line

Cassie works as a flight attendant for a major international airline. She has logged five and a half years on the job and, at twenty-eight, has finally gained a modicum of security, including a guaranteed monthly flight schedule that includes trips to Tokyo and Hong Kong. She has a round freckled face, a well-perfected "pleased to meet you" smile, and voices instant enthusiasm about her profession. As we talk in the bar of a midtown Manhattan hotel—home during her forty-eight-hour layover— she tells me that most of her job conflict emerges from tension between the senior and junior flight attendants. I am surprised when she adds that she thinks airlines should enforce a mandatory retirement age, somewhere around fifty, to push veterans off the job.

"I don't think longevity should be rewarded," she explains. "Some of the women who've been around forever are wonderful, but most have gotten bitter. They constantly think the company is trying to take advantage of them. Some have worked thirty-five years and only have three flights a month, and they still do nothing but complain. If they're so miserable, why are they still flying? All they do is bring the rest of us down."

Cassie goes on to describe the strict seniority system under which flight attendants operate. Everything from monthly schedules to who does what once on board is determined by how long you have worked for the airline. In her opinion, most senior women have lost any appreciation for what it is like to start out with no regular schedule or regular paycheck, routinely having to fly off on a few hours' notice. When contract resolutions come up, the veterans belabor every tiny issue that remotely affects them, unwilling to give an inch. They had recently joined together to veto a provision that would have made scheduling more reliable for flight attendants with young children because they opposed junior women getting preferential treatment.

"On every issue, they create this us versus them feeling against the company. It's like they want to drag stuff up from the past and poison the younger generation with it," Cassie tells me. "To be honest, most of us would rather have a peaceful relationship. We don't want to spend our days off going to a rally, saying 'we deserve this, we deserve that.' Let's face it, the glamour days of the stewardess are over. Women now are doing it for one reason, the travel."

Though Cassie tries to steer clear of the rumor mill, she cedes that most of her peers deal with these cross-generational tensions by venting in airport lounges and plane galleys. A good deal of catty and damaging gossip makes the rounds. Cassie also admits that our sitting down to talk was the first time she had taken a long clear look at the senior women's perspective.

"I know there are reasons they feel this strong loyalty to the union that we don't feel," she says when I ask why the older flight attendants seem so rigid. We discuss how, in the 1970s, newly formed flight attendants' unions fought for privileges that transformed the profession, bringing it into the modern age. Previously, stewardesses often had to meet strict weight and bust-waist-hips-thigh measurement regulations— meaning they could be fired for coming in one pound too heavy.[3] Many airlines set age limits, requiring women to quit when they turned thirty-two or -three, and most forbade them to work once they married or had children. They flew long hours with few breaks and had little or no recourse from harassment from supervisors and passengers.

"I guess it makes sense that they fight tooth and nail for every perk," Cassie concedes. "I might, too, if I'd been on the job when none of these perks existed at all."

As with Cassie and the senior flight attendants, the rifts women encounter in their cross-generational relationships often stretch beyond individual conflicts. They reflect an ongoing struggle for equal opportunity in the workplace and a past laced with powerful waves of social change. Cassie's resentment does not stem so much from the fact that she is selfish or disrespectful, but rather from an overall disconnect— one I encountered repeatedly—between what happened to her older female colleagues and what is happening to her.

The pivotal seventies and eighties experience of banding together against the male establishment feels, if not entirely foreign, then certainly less clear-cut to most young women today. Some I spoke to claimed, however naïvely, that if there is an old-boy's network they have yet to experience it, not a sentiment echoed in anyone over the age of forty. Younger women are not always aware of the recent struggles for equal rights—one twenty-three-year-old college graduate was surprised to hear that affirmative action applied to women—or they view such concerns as inapplicable to their own lives. They expressed a far stronger sense that the workplace is ultimately fair and that if you perform well you will be respected and rewarded. As a twenty-six-year-old computer programmer put it, "If you're good at your job it doesn't matter if you're a man, a woman, or purple." Though some older women suggested that this was how things should and even could be, none saw it as the universal state of affairs.

Older women can perceive this distance between the generations as youthful smugness or a lack of investment in women's collective future, and feel as if all their hard work is being flushed down the drain. "I think young women today have gotten too accustomed to the idea of equality," a former congresswoman told me. "They see women's second-class status as ancient history and it's made them selfish. They're not willing to join a fight or stand behind an issue unless it affects them directly. They don't want to take the sorts of risks women in the sixties and seventies took, the kind where you might wind up losing or looking foolish. I suppose it's because women now really do have something to lose."

This distance both sides are feeling is also fueled by fears about how much things have not changed. One disturbing tendency I heard from a number of younger women, particularly those in highly demanding corporate professions, was a distancing from and even contempt for older women who had made considerable life sacrifices in order to succeed on the job. They assumed successful women in their forties and fifties who had forgone family life entirely were forced into that position by the rigors of their profession—rarely did they think high-powered women remained single or childless by choice—and considered them pathetic or sad. Many were unwilling to confront the possibility that they, too, could "turn out like that," though the possibility very much exists. For example, a 2001 survey of women on Wall Street—median age of forty-one—found that 67 percent of women were married compared to 86 percent of men, and that only half the women had children as opposed to three-quarters of the men.[4] A 2002 General Accounting Office report on women managers in ten key industries showed that only 40 percent had children as opposed to 60 percent of male managers.[5] Demanding hours and pressure to measure up as one of the guys continue to make it extremely difficult for many high-powered women to make room for family. Yet younger women often viewed this lack of personal life as the fault of the women themselves rather than of the organizational environment in which both of them operated.

"Generally, I find women to be in one of two situations: totally without ambition for a meaningful professional contribution, or totally without ambition for a meaningful personal life," Saskia, a technical engineer in her midtwenties, wrote about her inability to find a female mentor. "Most of the women in the positions I want have foregone a personal life, and I don't see them as models. I just have to trust that brute force and some measure of talent will allow me to do what they could not."

Like Saskia, these young women often felt that their best chance for achieving life balance was to defy the odds via the "brute force" method, rather than by working with those more powerful to try to better the odds for all concerned. They recoiled against seeing similarities between themselves and those women who had to make hard choices, whose lives did not appear full or happy. It is far pleasanter to believe the equality messages young women received growing up in the eighties and nineties, that women can "have it all," that the workplace is fair no matter what your gender, race, or background. Until experience teaches them otherwise, they want to retain hope that the old struggles really are ancient history.

In Cassie's case, she has little sense of herself as a link in an ongoing flight attendant chain. Though her older colleagues still battled all out to preserve job privileges, not one of them had ever pulled Cassie aside to explain, "look, this is what we're protecting and why." Such communication is critical to sustaining women's rights and our professional relationships. Not only would Cassie better appreciate her predecessors' vigilance, but she also might feel more invested in fighting for the privileges they so adamantly preserve. As things stand, the mandatory retirement age Cassie proposed sounds disturbingly similar to those strictures her veteran coworkers fought so hard to eradicate.

The Aprils and Cassies of the world bear equal responsibility in oiling the lines of communication. They owe it to previous generations to recognize the sacrifices they made—whether they chose to or not—toward opening professional doors. A brief glance at any modern society should be enough to tell us that without vigilance, rights won can easily be lost again.

There is another key step in this dynamic, and that involves letting go. Women of earlier generations need to recognize that wisdom and experience accrued decades ago often are not directly applicable today—the same way contemporary college students will not find success by imitating Katharine Hepburn. Those senior flight attendants carried their die-hard mentality into an environment in which it was safe, even beneficial, to relax it some. They were no longer in a position in which every issue boiled down to us versus them. In vetoing the provision to help women with young families, they turned the very privileges they had won against those female colleagues they had won them for.

Though older generations can and should take an active role in passing down the rights for which they fought, they then need to step back and entrust those rights to the next wave. Though at times Cassie and her peers may appear naïve or selfish, they are entitled to make their own choices and, when required, learn through their own mistakes. Women's struggle for professional equality is not a self-contained phenomenon with a beginning and an end. It is a living, breathing, ongoing legacy.

By the end of our conversation, Cassie has reversed herself on the idea of mandatory age restrictions. She figures there has to be some better way to recognize and reward younger women without squeezing out those who came before. "It's really not their age that causes the problems," she says. "It's what the job has been like for them. I can respect that. I just hope they can respect that I don't want that same antagonism to be part of the job for me."

Nothing Personal

Patrice is a slim, angular woman of Southeast Asian descent, with olive skin, sharp green eyes, and a reserved, slightly formal manner. Three years ago, after completing a graduate degree in environmental policy, she moved to Washington, D.C. One of her professors arranged an interview with Whitney, a successful environmental lobbyist who had been in the field for over twenty years. Whitney not only hired the twenty-nine-year-old Patrice as her assistant, but she also set about molding her for a lobbying career.

Since Patrice's father worked for the foreign service, she had grown up in Italy and Brazil. She spoke three languages and was an accomplished classical pianist.

"I stood out among the usual policy wonks," Patrice volunteers. "Whitney seemed drawn to my atypical background. Most lobbyists kept their assistants toiling in obscurity, but Whitney would always introduce me around, almost like she was showing me off."

Ostensibly, Patrice's job fell along the lines of answering the phone and sending faxes, but soon Whitney was bringing her along to meetings. She saw to it that Patrice got to travel and attend events, and she provided career advice and networking opportunities. Whitney's life revolved around her work, and she was good at it—quick-minded, street smart, fair, and personable. She also seemed very caught up in the high salary and prestige of her position, values that Patrice did not particularly share.

"I was interested in as broad a view of the profession as possible," Patrice explains. "I made friends with other lobbyists and with those working on the congressional side of things. Whitney was quick to discount most of their opinions, and I got the feeling she resented my forays into fields beyond her control."

After a year, Patrice began to sour on the business of politics. She had been drawn to environmental policy for intellectual reasons and Whitney had originally described the job as awash in debates and ideas. Instead, it was slow and laden with bureaucracy, not what Patrice was interested in pursuing at all. She decided to take some time off, work as a temp, and rethink her career options.

When Patrice told Whitney she was leaving, the two had a half-hour meeting in which they discussed her decision and the reasons behind it. Patrice explained her disillusionment and why she didn't think lobbying was the right spot for her. Though disappointed, Whitney seemed to understand. She wished Patrice well and even offered to write her a recommendation. They parted on what Patrice considered good terms.

Then a few months later, as Patrice began interviewing for jobs again, one of her interviewers called her and warned her she might want to stop using Whitney's recommendation.

"She told me that this person had written terrible things about me," Patrice recalls. "Then she read me a letter in which Whitney detailed my immaturity, lack of loyalty, and inability to follow through on my commitments."

Patrice was floored. "If Whitney decided she didn't like me that would've been one thing, but I would never have guessed she'd do something so duplicitous. Looking back, I guess she felt like I'd humiliated her by not valuing her world. It became about much more than me making a different career choice. It was a personal affront. My leaving—especially with no new job lined up—came across as a comment on her staying. Emotional boundaries got invaded, her feelings were hurt, and she struck back."

Mentoring relationships between women can be tremendously influential and rewarding. A female mentor can help a less experienced woman decipher internal politics and unwritten rules, smoothing the social integration process necessary to become part of the organizational whole. In a 2001 study of mentoring among women lawyers, sociologist Jean Wallace found that though male mentors helped young women in direct salary gains, female role models provided more emotional and social support, infusing their charges with greater career satisfaction and job commitment and less work-family conflict.[6]

Despite the proven benefits, our society places relatively little value on professional mentoring between women, especially compared to the cultural heft it has for men. Movies from *Wall Street* to *Men in Black* to *The Matrix* offer takes on the veteran schooling the young gun. When they are depicted at all, such stories about women tend to focus on dysfunctional versions of the relationship, à la *Working Girl*. In the workplace itself, cross-generational templates cover mainly father-son or even father-daughter dynamics. Women can feel confused about how to adopt these models for ourselves. Does a mentor act as a leader, protector, caregiver, or all of the above?

Whether or not we expressly set out to find a mother or daughter figure when we embark on a mentoring relationship, it can be difficult—especially given the lack of alternatives—to prevent that dynamic from rearing its head. When this happens, professional autonomy often suffers as one or both women wind up overinvested in the relationship. A "daughter" may become unhealthily dependent on a mother figure to play the fairy godmother, protecting her from any and all professional tribulations. Or, as happened with Whitney and Patrice, a "mother" can count too heavily upon a daughter figure to fulfill her own dreams and desires. Whitney wanted to groom a protégée to follow in her footsteps and wound up feeling personally rejected when it turned out Patrice did not want the same.

Adopting too intimate a relational model also risks creating an environment in which unprofessional behavior is more easily accepted. Melody, an assistant in a public relations firm, described to me how her boss and mentor went out of her way to create a convivial, maternal relationship with twenty-five-year-old Melody. She brought homemade muffins in for breakfast and freely dispensed boyfriend and apartment-hunting advice.

"She made me feel like I was special to her, not just as a worker but as a person," Melody explains. "We gossiped about other people in the office, I went over on weekends and helped her clean her apartment. I was on the inside." Melody's boss also managed to convince Melody that the bounced paychecks she issued every couple of months were forgivable, given that their relationship was "like family." Since she felt so eager to please and win the older woman's approval, Melody agreed to forgo the one essential tenet of being a professional—money provided for services rendered.

Women often feel most comfortable slipping into a maternal or daughterly role. Unlike the void of professional images, society thrusts this one upon us repeatedly, from Hallmark cards to telephone commercials to books and movies like *The Joy Luck Club* and *Terms of Endearment.* But mentoring is not a family dynamic. Establishing differentiation in such relationships is as important as establishing identification. A professional mentor bears certain responsibilities. She gives her mentee a safe place to float ideas, dissect challenges, and make mistakes, and helps her take advantage of career opportunities. A mentor's role does not include forcing her standards or vision of the future on an underling, however well intentioned. Trouble arises as soon as she allows her reputation or self-worth to get caught up in that of her charge. There is a key difference between helping a mentee to facilitate what you want for her and helping her to facilitate what she wants for herself.

"My relationship with my boss works because from day one she has been crystal clear about what she wants from me," says Alicia, an assistant at a film and television talent agency. "She only inserts herself in a situation when she feels it's absolutely necessary. Otherwise, she trusts me to handle things on her behalf. I feel the perfect balance of protected and respected. There is never any question that our relationship is all about the job."

A mentee shares responsibility for maintaining a healthy, and healthily autonomous, relationship. It rests equally on her shoulders to understand what she desires from her mentor and to ensure those desires are communicated. Patrice must have realized at some point that she and Whitney had veered down different roads. Clarifying things earlier may have eased some of the shock and hurt Whitney felt when Patrice seemingly abandoned her.

Perhaps the best way to minimize the kind of misunderstanding that unfolded between Patrice and Whitney is to outline our expectations for the mentoring relationship going in, to make sure such expectations seem realistic on both sides, and to keep communicating as the relationship progresses. If caught less off-guard when a mentor or mentee's ideas clash with our own, we will be less likely to take out our hurt and frustration in duplicitous or damaging ways.

Look Out Below

Darcy and I meet for drinks in a downtown Manhattan bar, near empty at 6:00 P.M. on a Tuesday night. She is Puerto Rican, raised in the Bronx, with spiky brown hair and a barely contained enthusiasm for just about everything. A fashion designer, she has worked with her boss and mentor, Lucinda, for twelve years. When she started as Lucinda's assistant, it was just the two of them. Darcy sewed, did the coffee run, opened the mail, and answered the phones. As the company expanded, so did her role, and for the past seven years she has held the title of chief design associate. Though Darcy now designs some of her own pieces, they still have to fit with Lucinda's creative vision. At thirty-six, she is itching to go out on her own.

"I feel held back with Lucinda," Darcy explains, launching a waterfall of pent-up frustrations. "She ignores my suggestions, then gives credit to someone else who has the same idea a week later. When one of my pieces appears in a magazine, she never posts it the way she does the other design associates. Basically, she still treats me like an assistant. It feels like the fact that we've been together so long makes her trust me less instead of more."

The pair have strikingly different personalities. Darcy, outspoken and sociable, adds an edgy, sexy slant to their clothing. She lives with her girlfriend in a hip section of Brooklyn and keeps up with the hottest new shops and clubs. Lucinda is more reserved and her designs tend toward the feminine and conservative. Their opposing styles used to complement each other. Now, more often than not, the two women just fail to connect.

Tensions between them have increased in the past year, as Darcy grows more inclined to test her own ideas and question some of Lucinda's. Darcy feels as if Lucinda's clothes are too old-fashioned to grab people in today's market, that her boss is coasting on what worked five years ago. "She's behind the times, and she knows it. I think that terrifies her."

About six months ago, Darcy proposed launching a younger line that she could run herself, but Lucinda instantly vetoed the idea on account of expense.

"She loved me as long as I looked up to her and did what she said," Darcy explains, "but she wants control of every aspect of the business. Her way of treating me well is taking me out to breakfast and telling me how fabulous I am instead of giving me bonuses or increasing my responsibilities. That's not enough anymore."

The tipping point came a few weeks ago, when Lucinda insisted upon ordering a cheaper fabric for a skirt Darcy had designed. Darcy objected, but Lucinda ignored her. When the fabric arrived, it was the wrong color, and they had to scrap the whole thing. Lucinda blamed the lost time and money on Darcy's design and refused to listen to objections.

Darcy has started secretly looking for studio space and hired a lawyer to help her explore the intricacies of small business ownership. When she does go, she will do it respectfully, without poaching any of Lucinda's staff. Even so, she admits to feeling extremely guilty at even thinking of cutting the cord.

"I feel like I'm screwing Lucinda over, even though a part of me knows it's time. I dread the day I have to tell her. She'll be really upset. And when those ties are cut, they're cut. This is a competitive business. Once I go, I become the competition, too."

Competition can pose a stumbling block in any mentoring relationship, especially as mentees begin to branch out and accumulate successes of their own. Mentors—male or female—can feel threatened by and resentful of an underling like Darcy who seems destined to equal or even outshine them. But because women so often emphasize the nurturing, maternal aspects of the mentor role, they can feel especially ashamed when they experience such "ungenerous" feelings toward their young charges. Unsure how to cope, they may react as Lucinda did with Darcy, discounting a mentee's contributions or limiting her responsibilities in an attempt to cow those frightening notes of independence. Given the rapidly shifting roles for women in the workplace, a female mentor is more likely than a man to provide her charge with opportunities she never received herself. Given the personal investment entailed, a mentee's urge to seize such opportunities and run can read like a betrayal.

Though feeling jealous or competitive toward a mentee can be uncomfortable, the emotions themselves are not the problem. The problems stem from how we choose to interpret and act upon such feelings. If aware of potential tensions from the start, a mentor can begin digesting the possibility that her mentee may eventually equal or even outperform her. Instead of waiting until the unpleasant emotions are full flower, she can ask herself early on how she will feel as the dynamic evolves and notes of rebellion are introduced.

A mentee can also be sensitive to how her increasing autonomy affects the relationship. A female mentor is rarely an übermother equipped to bestow infinite amounts of largesse. More often, like Lucinda, she is another professional woman carting her own share of qualms and doubts. Even if she appears successful on the outside, she may not experience herself as such. It may be asking too much to expect her to give indiscriminately when her own position feels so fragile. Lucinda invested a great deal of time and teaching in Darcy. Darcy could return that investment by making a point to validate and respect Lucinda's voice of experience, even if she did not always agree with what it had to say.

In their guide to corporate mentoring, the women's business group Catalyst cites four stages of a mentoring relationship, giving equal weight to the last two—separation and redefinition.[7] Relational dynamics will inevitably evolve as a mentee grows more independent. At some point, as with Darcy, she will probably want to break off and do her own thing, and at some point, both women will have to discuss how to either wrap up the relationship or shift into something more collaborative.

Separating oneself from such an influential bond can generate feelings of guilt, anxiety, and a deep sense of loss. Again, because relationships between women so often emphasize emotional connections, such awkward feelings can be sharper than they might be for men. As Darcy put it, "I feel like I'm telling my mother to go take a hike." If we avoid confronting such feelings, we risk generating the sort of simmering resentment that arose between Darcy and Lucinda. The end of a mentoring relationship might hinge upon formal guidelines—a set period of time or attainment of a certain career goal, like a raise or promotion—that signal the mentoring part of the relationship is over. More often, it will require readjusting on the fly.

One of the tougher aspects of dissolving a mentoring relationship is deciphering the role of gratitude. Younger women like Darcy can feel unclear about just what they owe their mentors in return for their efforts. There is a difference between being grateful and being beholden to those experienced women who have helped us along. At its best, mentorship is an act of generosity. The relationship fosters confidence and autonomy, not imitation and dependence, teaching the mentee to think, create, and innovate on her own. The goal is for her to flourish, not just in her current job but in the full scope of her career. Darcy's urge to assert her independence isn't "screwing Lucinda over." It is a sign the relationship has succeeded.

"Lucinda was great to me early on," Darcy tells me. "Working with her opened up a lot of opportunities. I'm extremely grateful to be able to call her my mentor, but I also realize, and hope she will, too, that I've grown. I'm not her assistant anymore. It's part of the natural cycle for me to want to let go and move on."

The Test of Time

In interviewing so many women, I heard about a number of cross-generational relationships that had run into problems, but I also came across many such relationships that had succeeded beautifully. Among these successes, a common theme reasserted itself. At some point, the women involved stopped searching for a perfect communion between young and old, and started recognizing the benefits even an imperfect bond could bestow.

Holly works as a critical-care nurse at a large midwestern teaching hospital. Three years ago, when word got out that she was going to be transferred to the ICU, she found herself inundated with rumors, gossip, and not a few warnings.

"Our ICU nurses have this intense reputation," she explains. "People call it the shark pool. Everyone kept telling me that being chewed up, bitched out, and left to drown was part of the experience. The week before I was supposed to start someone came up to me in the cafeteria and told me, 'Just pretend you know nothing. They will be very condescending, but you'll survive.' That was the most positive comment I'd heard. At least in her version there was a light at the end of the tunnel."

Though Holly had always wanted to work in critical care, and though she considered herself a pretty tough person, by the time the actual transfer came around she admits that she was terrified. "It felt a little like jumping off a cliff."

Hospital gossip had not been far off the mark. Holly's preceptor, the nurse responsible for breaking her in and evaluating her performance, was a twenty-year veteran named Tamika. She put Holly through the wringer in every possible way. Tamika regularly left Holly alone with patients, forcing her to think fast and figure out what to do. There was no babying or handholding. Instead, Tamika systematically broke down Holly's confidence, then, when Holly did not crack under the pressure, just as systematically built it up again.

"The more you seem like you're going to cave, the harder they push," Holly explains. "It took me awhile to figure out they aren't doing it to be mean. Learning not to take things personally is an important job skill. A lot of the things valued in women—being nice, stepping aside—won't get you anywhere in the ICU."

What the rumors had failed to mention was that Holly's time under Tamika and the other "sharks" would prove transformative. Holly emerged slightly battered but with a deep and lasting appreciation of what it meant to be a nurse. "Maybe 10 percent of the job really matters," she tells me. "Ninety percent anyone can do, but it's that 10 percent that proves you. This is not a team environment. You have to be able to handle things on your own."

She explains how years in the profession have taught the veterans what it takes to be a skilled and reliable ICU nurse and have also taught them the fastest, most down-and-dirty way to convey that message to the younger nurses. The preceptors tend to go easier on the few men under their charge, but Holly thinks that is because men are usually less enamored of the gentler aspects of the profession, arriving with a little more backbone so they don't need to be pushed quite so hard. The initiation process is neither gentle nor friendly but it prepares women to become nurses and that is why everyone is there.

"Once you prove yourself, you're part of an amazing group of professionals. This is an emotional job and it's impossible to totally split off from that. We support each other under remarkable circumstances. Not every woman makes it, but then again not every woman should."

Recently, Holly started helping to orient some new nurses herself and she tells me she considers it her job to be just as harsh with them as Tamika was with her.

"If I hadn't been through it myself, I wouldn't understand why the rough treatment is so necessary. Trust is pivotal in this job. You have to find any chinks in the armor right away."

She has come away with a great deal of respect and gratitude for the women under whom she works. They taught her when to be a cowboy and when to be politic, how to make independent decisions, and how to trust herself. She has also come to appreciate the difference between taking care of someone and teaching them the ropes.

"I'm proud to be part of this team. The women are opinionated, funny, and exceptionally skilled. I enjoy them as friends and coworkers, and trust them to let me know when I'm messing up and need to get a grip. I love the sharks. I can't wait until I'm considered one of them."

In the early 1990s, an anthropologist named Donald E. Brown set out to map the traits common to every culture that has left an ethnographic record. Among a long list of shared human experiences, he un-covered a universal emphasis on wisdom transmitted from old to young.[8] There is a basic human urge—one that crosses time and place, cultures and backgrounds—to pass knowledge down to the next generation.

Our contemporary work culture is no exception. Men have been mentoring one another for centuries through guilds, apprenticeships, clubs, and individual relationships, taking the time and the credit for nurturing new talent. I believe that women want to and can build equally powerful cross-generational ties. In interviewing, I spoke to a variety of women who expressed the desire for a female mentor, who had actively sought out other women and who, if one relationship did not material-ize, went in search of another. I spoke to women in male-dominated fields who regretted the fact that they had never found a woman they could consider a professional role model. I talked to women who had set up formal mentoring programs in their workplaces or made a point of more informally helping younger female colleagues with advice and op-portunities. One twenty-four-year-old woman just starting a career in the retail clothing industry told me that one of the primary reasons she joined a networking group was because she wanted the chance to thank those women who had paved the way. The stumbling blocks we en-counter lie not in our desire to connect but in the realities of the profes-sional world.

The contemporary workplace rarely facilitates smooth relationships between senior and junior women. Cassie admits to having heard ru-mors that her airline welcomed union demands that emphasized the gap between old and new, because they did not want the flight attendants to operate as a united body with the power that might entail. Those heavy personal sacrifices many women in authority have made can leave them more inclined to hoard achievements and rewards instead of spreading them around. As a result, in male-dominated or particularly cutthroat professional environments, it is especially difficult for young female employees to establish strong relationships with senior women or view them as role models.[9] Unfortunately, these are often the environments in which women need one another the most.

There is tremendous responsibility involved in being looked up to and setting behavioral examples. It puts older women in a position to convey critical messages to those younger and less experienced about what is desirable in a professional relationship and to provide positive models for how to hold power over other women. A multitude of female role models could preclude the need for a book like this one, by passing down skills for dealing with the woman-to-woman competition we encounter in the workplace every day. In order for such relationships to succeed, we need to be honest and realistic about our expectations. That includes getting clear on the differences between mothering and leading, and finding a balance between nurturing and making demands.

One of the most valuable things women can pass on to one another is perspective. Researchers have noted that as women reach their forties, they often become less frantically ambitious, competitive, and invested in career success.[10] In part this is due to the relatively small number of women who have actually attained conventional success by this age. In the mid-1990s, economist Claudia Goldin found that just one in six middle-aged, college-educated women with children earned more than the bottom 25 percent of college-educated men—the result of a glut of societal factors including glass ceilings, dead-end jobs, work-family stresses, pay inequities, and old-boy networks.[11] These women also represent a more universal human trend in which age prompts a desire to reevaluate our lives and reflect upon our experiences, values, and social contributions. It becomes less important to be successful in the eyes of the world and more important to foster an engaged and satisfying relationship with our work.[12] As one very successful entertainment executive put it, "What's the best way to smooth over relations between women? Have all the young executives work in nursing homes so their elders can tell them none of this matters all that much in the end."

Whether we are talking about specific mentoring situations or more general workplace relationships, healthy cross-generational bonds are critical to women's success on the job. These bonds foster a flow of information in both directions, reduce our sense of isolation, demystify the age gap, and allow both sides to feel more relaxed and confident in their positions. Mentoring relationships are also the first link in a chain, since those who have been mentored are far more likely to become mentors themselves.[13] We all have ties to the past and ties to the future that no amount of self-sufficiency can erase. None of us got where we are alone.

10

Women in Groups: Clicking or Cliquing?

If you can't say something good about someone, sit right here by me.
—ALICE ROOSEVELT LONGWORTH

Molly is in her late forties with wispy dark hair pinned at the nape of her neck, fair skin, and large square glasses. For the past four years, she has been head of the political science department at a small southern university. Recently, after reading statistics on the low number of influential women in politics, she and a group of twenty other female professors from surrounding universities decided they wanted to do something about it. Representing a variety of disciplines—economics, the humanities, the social sciences—they decided to form a group dedicated to educating women to be more effective leaders. Each agreed to pony up a set financial contribution and meet twice a month.

The group hired an outside woman, an economics professor, to serve as executive director of the organization. Molly was not crazy about the choice, since, albeit impressive academically, "she had zero experience in running anything." Beyond that, they opted to avoid any formal division of responsibilities. They liked the idea of a women-centered group remaining flexible, with each member organically taking on a role in her area of expertise.

"I'm embarrassed to admit that it didn't occur to us that we wouldn't agree on just who was most expert at what," Molly says. "Or that there would be less glamorous aspects of the group, the clerical-type stuff, that no one wanted to take on at all."

The group experienced some serious ego clashes from the start. A handful of women stepped up with strong opinions on how things should operate and a marked unwillingness to compromise. On the outside, the group behaved as if things were progressing swimmingly, but behind the scenes, the backbiting and gossip swelled.

"Someone would be warm and accepting toward an idea during a meeting, then secretly do everything she could to see to it that it didn't work," Molly recalls. "No one would openly contradict someone else, but they were constantly offering up a 'better' contact or idea in the guise of helping out. There was blaming, cutting people out, hoarding control and information. It was a nightmare."

The meetings were soon dominated by this unspoken competition. Two particularly strong personalities emerged, each backing a different approach for channeling funds. One woman wanted to go grassroots, with lectures and community meetings. The other favored targeting corporations and individuals with deep pockets who could fund select political candidates. Six months in, the group had split into two factions. No one could agree on anything.

"It was like a bunch of seventh-grade girls having a sleepover. I couldn't believe what was going on. We never sat down and talked about creating a united vision. I can't emphasize enough that this was a group of very successful and very influential women with no reason in the world to feel threatened. But all they seemed to care about was who had the most connections, and who would unofficially run this group that officially no one was supposed to run."

Eventually Molly volunteered to drop out and come back as a consultant to help facilitate a group dynamic that could actually achieve something. Her move to organize was universally rejected. A few members even accused her of trying to take over. Fed up and extremely disappointed, Molly quit the group entirely.

"The idea was wonderful," she insists, still sounding frustrated. "Theoretically we could've generated dynamite results. But the execution was a disaster area. A bunch of powerful women in a room, attempting to 'share' leadership responsibilities? I will never try that again. You can't put together a group based on sex and just assume they will work together well."

The Female Hierarchy

In recent years, the attention focused on group dynamics in the workplace—skills required to finesse everything from team projects to weekly department meetings—has snowballed. Groups have been tagged "the new functioning entities in organizations," the human touchpoints to its central nervous system.[1] Alongside this growing emphasis on group activity, organizational psychologists are examining the underlying architecture of group emotions. Studies indicate that though group settings offer considerable benefits, they can also exacerbate those problems coworkers encounter one on one. "Individuals experience substantial and continuing internal tensions as group members. . . . Participation in groups is usually stressful and only occasionally, for some, satisfying."[2] Researchers discovered what any basketball player could have told them in three seconds flat. Teamwork is hard.

No professional group, regardless of its gender makeup, is exempt from relational problems. However, one of the more striking themes to emerge among the women I interviewed involved the very different tensions described by those working in primarily female environments as opposed to environments inhabited and defined by men. In groups comprised of all women, members ran the danger of considering themselves exempt from the "teamwork is hard" rule. There is an illusion that women will naturally work well together, that we do not require structure or guidance just by virtue of our gender. We need to dismiss that illusion. Throw it out. There is an enormous difference between professional groups and those social or family groups in which women have typically grounded themselves. As long as we view conflict as an embarrassing and unwelcome interruption—something women should have advanced "beyond"—we risk conducting our professional groups in ways that force problems underground.

A common thread in groups formed within the women's movement of the sixties and seventies was the rejection of hierarchy. This distrust of leadership stemmed from an overall suspicion of power, viewed as a patriarchal tool used to dominate and exploit the female half of society. Instead of attempting to relax or reconstruct hierarchical systems to better suit their ideals, the women's movement tended to erase them altogether. Formal leadership gave way to communal groups in which all members were expected to contribute and benefit equally, in which no one person could stick out from the crowd.

Such utopian setups flourished in consciousness-raising groups and other noncompetitive situations in which women gathered to bond over shared emotional experiences. But on the political and professional fronts, things flowed less smoothly. As charismatic feminists began to speak out individually or were embraced by the mainstream media, they often found themselves punished by their less well-recognized colleagues. As the women's movement grew more powerful, encompassing women with a wider range of ethnic, economic, and sexual identities, the premise that all women could speak with a single voice grew increasingly strained.

In her memoir, *In Our Time,* writer and activist Susan Brownmiller details how "unhappy rumblings, internal grievances, theoretical disagreements, personality conflicts, and jealousies among the founders [of the women's movement] gnawed on the fragile concept of sisterhood."[3] Fissures developed as the movement worked up speed and groups ranging from the Chicago Women's Liberation Union to *Ms.* magazine split over issues relating to individual power, political ties, and public visibility. "We were all desperately ambitious, but people didn't want to recognize that there were enormous differences in individual talents, abilities, gifts," says early Chicago feminist Naomi Weisstein. "I spent years trying to appease other women in the movement, trying to be less powerful so they wouldn't hate me."[4] Even within groups designed to cater specifically to women's needs and communication styles, an absence of structure came far closer to creating chaos than a utopian ideal.

As both the women's liberation organizations and Molly's group experienced, it is extremely difficult to eliminate all traces of hierarchy within a professional group. The absence of formal structure creates a power vacuum that will be filled by those with stronger personalities, skills, and connections. The evolution of these unofficial hierarchies often generates resentment in those left out, especially when the group is operating under the guise of everyone participating equally. Uncertainty about our own responsibilities can exacerbate feelings of resentment toward those who take on more or less than their "fair share." In many cases, eradicating leadership can encourage negative competition. We begin comparing ourselves to one another, monitoring to ensure that no one person excels beyond anybody else, and the space for individual expression and talents dries up.

One reason these "everyone is responsible for everything" systems continue to appeal to women's groups like Molly's is that they offer a model in which nobody has to play the bad guy. If everyone is responsible for everything, then no one risks making a decision others will not like. Any blanket distrust of leadership echoes that outdated belief that women should not express too much autonomy or personal ambition, that the proper reaction in the face of disagreement is a docile nod and an ever-present willingness to give way. When this template is laid over the modern workplace, the lines do not match up. On the job, it does pay for an individual to stand out. Attaining power and position carry concrete professional rewards, and advancement is contingent on our contributions being recognized. Unlike in social and familial relationships, when we operate in professional groups we almost always have an individual concern—money, influence, reputation—at stake. Formal hierarchy or no formal hierarchy, a key way to raise our professional status is by taking on a leadership role.

In Molly's case, she was part of a group of successful women who had achieved within a university system that operated under a very clear hierarchy. All of them were used to having their ideas acted upon and probably assumed they would continue to experience the same.

"This was a group of women, each of whom had always taken the leadership position," Molly points out. "Understandably, we got into trouble trying to impose a traditionally feminine structure on an environment focused on money, influence, and power. Graciously stepping aside was one thing none of us had experience with at all."

While they need not have re-created the formal hierarchy of the universities they worked for, a more well-defined internal structure, with elected officers or preordained individual responsibilities, might have circumvented the massive angling for position that took place and allowed Molly's group to focus on accomplishing what they had gathered to accomplish. The clearer each member's role and area of expertise—be it president, secretary, or committee member—the less time and anxiety everyone will exert jockeying for individual status. Designating individual responsibilities does not automatically lead to those abuses of power the women's movement sought to avoid, as long as a forum remains for group members to voice their opinions and objections. Though problems will not disappear, there will be a system in place for dealing with them when they do arise.

By glorifying the leadership-free structure, professional women perpetuate the idea that authority and collaboration cannot coexist. We erase the entire middle ground between communal and autocratic. And we send a dangerous message: If we cannot trust other women to adopt a guiding role, it starts to look as if we do not believe women can handle power after all.

All in the Family

Sophia works as a program coordinator for a Texas family services agency operating under a series of state and federal grants. A petite, silver-haired, soft-spoken woman in her early fifties, she has been with the center twelve years, starting when the last of her five children reached elementary school. Though she has worked her entire life, she had no prior social work experience and the learning curve has been one long stretch of trial and error.

Since its inception, the center has expanded rapidly, and Sophia helped to design programs ranging from food banks to child-care services. For the first ten years, they operated with one director overseeing the heads of all the individual departments, which grew to include migrant worker aid and a federal nutrition program.

"It was always a very familylike atmosphere," Sophia explains of the all-female staff. "Since there was never enough money, we depended on each other to pitch in whenever possible. That could mean anything from sweeping floors to helping with grant applications."

Two years ago, a new director came on board. Justine had a great deal of experience in the financial and planning departments but, unlike her predecessor, she was not a particularly warm person and she discouraged much employee contact. One of her first acts was to reshuffle the office structure, creating an assistant director position just below her. Sophia and the other coordinators would report directly to this new hire, Marta. With Marta's arrival, the entire dynamic of the agency changed.

Marta held a master's degree in social work, an intimidating factor among the staff, a number of whom had not finished college. She did away with the weekly staff meetings, a time when coworkers typically checked in with each other, floated problems, or simply blew off steam. She changed fund allocation procedures without explanation. Though excellent with practical details, she seemed immune to the subtler emotional currents that kept the agency afloat.

The biggest feather in the agency's cap was the annual family services conference they had organized for the past three years. The first of its kind in the region, it drew representatives from charitable organizations all over Texas and a number of neighboring states. The conference had previously been a group effort, with one of the five program coordinators adopting the leadership role and everyone else contributing in her area of expertise. The year after she arrived, Marta took over all the responsibilities herself. Sophia and her colleagues—the women who actually dealt with the families on a daily basis—were not consulted at all. When introductory packets went out to that year's conference attendees, they contained a letter of welcome—not from the agency as a whole, but from Marta herself.

"I think we all felt threatened by that," Sophia explains, "like Marta shouldered her way in and immediately wanted to put her stamp on the most high profile part of the agency. In the process, she stepped on a lot of toes and hurt a lot of feelings."

Bitterness toward Justine and Marta grew, but there were few outlets for expressing such frustrations. The staff felt obliged to maintain a helpful, caring atmosphere at the center. The families they serviced came to them for practical and emotional guidance, and it was important that the clients not sense any discord among those working there. In lieu of public confrontation, plenty of bickering hatched behind the scenes. The staff felt they were being shut out of an agency in which they had invested far more time and energy than Justine or Marta ever would. They began to rebel in quiet ways, dishing out petty complaints and neglecting to cooperate with Justine or Marta. Finally, tensions grew so fierce that Justine brought in an independent mediation service to help flush out the lines of communication. The mediators, two women, held a series of meetings with the group.

"I'm sure they were well intentioned," Sophia says, "but in the end their interference only made things worse."

Sophia and the other coordinators found the mediation process cold and formal, an approach that clashed with the emotional sensitivity they valued so highly. No one wanted to be the one to speak up and make trouble, especially since it was hard to put into words exactly what had gone wrong. It felt silly to complain that Justine and Marta did not take time to sit around and chat with their coworkers, did not check in about little details, were not warm and fuzzy enough. But their ultra-businesslike approach had changed the entire atmosphere. It made the center an unpleasant place to be.

"When you're doing social work, it's important to preserve a sense of family," Sophia explains. "This isn't a corporate environment. There is a great deal of emotional involvement and a high burnout rate. The most important qualities are empathy and compassion, and there just isn't a lot of room for personal ambition. Unless everyone is a team player, the entire infrastructure falls apart."

The breech between new and old was never successfully resolved. Instead, the staff made it so unpleasant for Marta and Justine that six months later both women resigned.

"It was a very painful process," Sophia recounts. "One the center still hasn't recovered from. Looking back, I think there must have been a better way."

As Molly discovered, groups cannot operate if each individual's prevailing tenet is take, take, take, but it can be equally difficult to function under the auspices of give, give, give. Particularly in such caring or service professions as social work, teaching, or nursing—professions in which large numbers of woman tend to work together—there can be strong communal pressure to sacrifice our individual concerns in favor of the all-nurturing emotional grain of the group.

A number of the women to whom I spoke made a clear distinction between business-driven professions and nonprofit, service-sector work. They expressed particular disappointment and disillusionment when encountering problems within a group focused on women's issues, caretaking, or making a contribution to society. Women expected such groups—with missions firmly rooted in compassion and generosity—to be less vulnerable to rifts and personality differences. "It's flattering to feel as if what you do is morally impeccable," admitted an administrator at a foundation for breast cancer research. "You'll go to great lengths to sustain that belief."

Women who were employed in service professions tended to experience different stresses and relational tensions than those operating in more profit-oriented business atmospheres. When your job is so thoroughly geared around helping others, it can feel much harder to make demands. No one is supposed to covet power or resent others who possess it.

"Women approach nonprofit work with a sacrifice mentality," explained Lila, a marketing executive who has worked for a variety of arts organizations. "But it can be just as damaging to think everyone else's needs are more important than yours."

Though, as Sophia emphasized, there is often legitimate need for a less competitive, more generous professional environment, there are also pitfalls in focusing on selflessness to the exclusion of all else. Groups devoted to transcending personal concerns in order to please others often lack guidelines about how to deal with conflict, because conflict is not supposed to exist.

For Sophia and her colleagues, the initial difficulty was not an uncommon one. New leadership arrived and their style clashed with the old. The real troubles developed from the uncertainty over how to handle the situation. Groups often develop unspoken rules about what emotions can be appropriately expressed or even experienced in a particular professional setting.[5] In the name of preserving their familylike atmosphere, Sophia's group had such a rule against making waves. Even in the presence of outside mediators, the staff did not feel comfortable voicing their grievances. No one wanted to appear demanding or self-centered. Even two years later, Sophia is reluctant to discuss what happened and why.

"I felt leery about getting too involved," she explains. "The whole process of having outsiders come in was very intimidating. I wish there was a way Justine could've just quietly handled things herself."

That impulse against getting "too involved" presents a simple but enormous problem. If troubles are not voiced, they cannot be addressed. Organizational psychologists have discovered that conflict and competition are far more manageable in groups in which there is a structure for dealing with them—including clear reward systems, avenues for complaint, and a psychologically safe place where mistakes are allowed—as opposed to solely cooperative or "friendly" atmospheres that do not sanction competition at all.[6] Without an official outlet for disagreements, there is a danger of boundaries dissolving. Professional troubles become emotionally laden and can emerge couched in personal attacks.

Sophia and her colleagues had every right to speak up. They had valid issues to raise. Justine and Marta were behaving like bulls in the emotional china shop, and they could have benefited from an education in the agency's values. In addition, the staff may have benefited from the leadership and financial structure their new directors sought to impose. The fact that Justine brought in outside mediators indicated she was invested in making the compromises necessary for the center to function fluidly. She opened the door for Sophia and her coworkers to ask for a larger role in the conference or assert their need for weekly meetings with Marta. By venting their frustrations passive-aggressively—through petty complaints, grudges, and silent protests—they may have found a way to express their dissatisfaction without openly rocking the boat, but such tactics gave Justine and Marta little opportunity to respond. In censoring themselves, Sophia and the others wound up violating those very professional tenets they sought to protect—empathy, compassion, cooperation, and respect.

Standing Out from the Crowd

In environments where selflessness is overly prioritized, we also risk coming to resent those group members who go out of their way to develop individual reputations. Especially if we are not paid well or publicly recognized for our work, self-sacrifice can go a long way toward defining our professional worth. We can come to read the situation as an either-or proposition: Either we are personally ambitious or we are team players. Pressure mounts to suppress our own identities and abilities in the name of the greater good.

Marjorie spent eighteen years teaching fourth grade at a Catholic elementary school in Ohio. Over the years, she developed a reputation as one of the best teachers on staff. She worked well with children who had behavioral or learning problems, and they often made their first real educational strides in her classroom. Parents raved about their children's progress. Marjorie worked hard and felt proud of her reputation.

"It's a strange word for a teacher to use, but I would certainly call myself ambitious," she tells me. "My success mattered to me. I was happy to cooperate with the other teachers whenever needed, but I also wanted my students to have the highest test scores. I wanted the parents to respect me and, frankly, I wanted to be the best teacher in the school."

The women who taught the upper grades were less skilled and sensitive than Marjorie. On several occasions, parents pulled their children out of the school after Marjorie's class, figuring they had already benefited from the best the institution had to offer. As Marjorie's reputation grew, the other teachers turned notably frosty toward her, spreading rumors about her inflated ego. Though their behavior did not make her life any easier, it was a development Marjorie could understand. Before long, the principal, a woman in her early sixties, began to criticize Marjorie as well, accusing her of being too understanding, too tactful with the parents, and too easy on the kids in her class.

"She was under a lot of pressure from the parents and the church to run things seamlessly," Marjorie explains. "There weren't supposed to be any 'problems,' certainly not among the teachers. I think she figured it would be simpler to eliminate trouble by lowering the bar rather than raising it."

Marjorie wound up devoting—or, as she put it, "wasting"—considerable time to assuaging her principal's concerns, taking care not to point up her successes, and even manufacturing complaints so things did not appear to be going too well. She built close ties with those teachers who were supportive of her, and she paid particular attention to pleasing the parents and children in her classroom, figuring popularity with the clientele served as her best defense.

"Tackling the issues with those other teachers would've been very messy," Marjorie says when I ask why she thinks her high performance came in for criticism from the principal. "She didn't want to deal with that. She focused on things looking perfect rather than being well run, which meant burying any problems. It was an unfortunate stance, and I think the students suffered for it. Her priority wasn't to create the best educational atmosphere, it was to make the school look happy from the outside. I disrupted that by sticking out, even in a positive way."

In many ways, care and service professions provide soil rich for healthy group relations. Women working in such environments often have an especially keen appreciation for preserving the emotional integrity of the group as a whole. But it is critical to recognize that an emotionally healthy group is not one that consumes its individual members. Even in the most caring professions, autonomy has its place. The sense that individual members have a voice in decisions and outcomes goes a long way toward maintaining group solidarity. By creating space in which to express our opinions and abilities, we can build a collective identity that supercedes without erasing the identities of the individuals involved.

Closing Ranks

Alice is the definition of a pistol, with curly bleached blonde hair, hot-pink fingernails, and an act-first-ask-questions-later approach to life. We talk as we drive across the midsection of Kentucky tucked into her latest love, a spanking-new cherry-red sports car. She has worked all kinds of jobs over the course of her life, from tending bar to running a church day care. One of the first things she tells me is, "I'm not someone who likes to be pinned down."

Alice was forty with four kids and two ex-husbands when she applied for a position at an auto parts factory near her hometown. She started on the assembly line, molding plastic gearshifts for luxury cars. Her fellow line workers were all women, but the supervisors and management were exclusively male.

Though Alice had always considered herself a people person, someone who excelled at fitting into just about any group, the gearshift women were a tough, nearly impenetrable crowd. On the outside, they were perfectly pleasant, but from her first hour on the job, Alice was subject to heavy-duty messages about just who was in control.

Several times a day, somebody would booby-trap Alice's machine, once reversing a cutting blade so that she came centimeters from slicing open her hand. She would get word the supervisor wanted to see her immediately, drop everything, and run upstairs. When she arrived at his office, he would have no idea who she even was. Upon returning to the floor, she would get written up for delaying production and abandoning her station.

Everyone in Alice's section worked with flammable materials, and fire safety was a factory-wide concern. One day, several of the women dumped papers and a lit match in one of the trash cans. When Alice tore from the room yelling, "Fire! Fire!" the entire line collapsed into hysterics. From then on, everyone called her "fire girl." When she arrived in the mornings, she would find burned matches and cigarette butts littering her station.

"The idea was to make me as miserable as possible," she explains. "Just to see how much it'd take for me to crack. If you were sensitive at all, then forget about it. New girls who got their feelings hurt went home every day in tears."

The unofficial leader of the group was a large, quiet woman named Ivy who had been working at the factory for more than ten years. Most of the women were young, in their late teens and early twenties, and they readily took their cues from Ivy about whom to like and dislike, when to speak up, and when to keep their mouths shut.

Alice had always prided herself on being independent-minded, a quality Ivy did not necessarily admire. When Alice had been on the job a few months, the factory began getting complaints from the car company that the handles on the gearshifts were too rough. Blame traveled down the pipeline and landed squarely on the line workers, so Alice suggested to the other women that they try using a finer grade of sandpaper. They ignored her.

"They were all afraid of doing anything except exactly what they'd been told to do," Alice explains. "So I just pulled the finer paper and tried it out myself."

The solution worked like a charm, and Alice's supervisor saw that she was recognized. Her initiative earned her commendation from the management, and everyone else a new sanding system. For weeks afterward, the women on the line refused to acknowledge Alice even existed.

"The two girls on either side of me would sit there complaining about how badly they needed a cigarette," Alice recalls. "When I'd volunteer to cover for them, they acted like I was speaking Chinese."

Their silent treatment was far worse than the hazing that had preceded it. It was a job where the women needed each other—to vent, to provide human contact, to cover during cigarette and bathroom breaks—and those weeks of pointed silence brought Alice to the brink.

"After the sandpaper thing, I think the supervisor figured I was on his side. He started coming to me with questions about how the floor was running. Every time I saw him, I wanted to melt into the ground. The more attention I got, the worse the other women hated me. They didn't trust me for acting on my own."

Alice figured the group's antipathy stemmed from some combination of low morale and miserable working conditions. There was constant pressure from management to work faster and produce more, but the line workers received little in the way of compensation. Their section of the factory was a pit, with the toilets in the women's bathroom so clogged they often had to wade through inches of water to get to them. The tables in the lunchroom were covered with cigarette ash and old food, and the floor was crawling with ants.

"It was a shithole," Alice says. "There's no other way to describe it. With treatment like that, you'd think the women would want to join together even more."

Alice dedicated time and energy to softening up her coworkers. She liberally lent out cigarettes and offered to cover for people during breaks. She embraced her "fire girl" entity by bringing in her son's plastic firefighter hat and volunteering to become the safety inspector for the floor. Eventually, her efforts paid off. She made friends among the other line workers—most of whom proved kind and eager to engage—and came to enjoy her colleagues, if not the work itself. Though they never grew particularly close, Alice even forged a détente with Ivy by bonding over how badly they were treated. When Alice proposed they fix up the lunchroom, Ivy supported the idea and helped organize a group effort. Alice and a handful of others brought in rags and a can of Lysol, and stayed on after their twelve-hour shifts to scrub down the tables.

"By the time we came back twelve hours later, it would be a pit again," she recalls, "but the general idea got through. We had to take care of each other, because you can be damn sure no one else was going to do it for us."

We tend to think of hazing as exclusively male territory, something equated with military institutions and fraternity hijinks, but among the women I interviewed, I heard a number of such stories, especially when they involved a group bringing down someone too confident, too independent, too inclined to step out on her own. Such harassment within groups of women can transcend gentle prodding to become a powerful and threatening way of putting a newcomer in her place. This can prove especially true in situations in which women have few growth opportunities and little formal control, such jobs as sales clerks, secretaries, and certain low-level factory workers, jobs that are frequently female dominated. If Molly's problem with her university group revolved around women taking on positions of power, then Alice's troubles stemmed from just the opposite—the impact of having no power at all.

When a job offers little in the way of a future, workers often develop unofficial behavioral codes that protect them in the present. These might include orienting their peer group inward to provide support and reassurance; discouraging members from trying to move up the promotional ladder; forming stronger attachments to their local group than the larger organization; a general distrust of power; and a reluctance to seek change or engage in direct protest.[7] For those who do not have access to legitimate workplace authority, it is possible to acquire it by developing an unofficial hierarchy the way Ivy and the other line workers did. Such groups can create their own tests and conditions of acceptance, conditions that fall outside and even conflict with the formal structure of the workplace. By setting rules for our coworkers, we bestow an element of control on our surroundings. New members like Alice are forced to figure out this new language, make mistakes, and suffer the accompanying humiliation before they can become part of the whole. These group dynamics are not unique to women, but over time women have consistently found themselves in the sorts of jobs that give rise to such patterns.

The pressures on women to please those around them, older males in particular, coupled with their frequently low job status could have easily made them sitting ducks for dictatorial management. To the contrary, since entering the industrialized workforce in large numbers, women with limited professional power have acted to protest unfair treatment and retain a degree of influence, even when it required punishing other women who refused to fall in line. Female department store clerks in the early twentieth century rejected managerial authority by purposely slowing down customer sales to avoid exceeding company expectations, a process known as "the stint." Any woman who defied the stint and continued to sell wholeheartedly came in for condemnation from her coworkers, everything from messing up her section of the store to sending her warnings via the gossip column of an in-house newsletter.[8] Half a century later, sociologist Arlie Hochschild chronicled the strain generated by flight attendants who refused to join their colleagues in rebelling against the airline's "service with a smile" demands.

"Inevitably, a few workers will not close ranks and will insist on working even harder to serve passengers with genuinely sincere feeling. Some want to please in order to compensate for a 'flaw' . . . that they have been made to feel guilt about. Some want revenge on certain coworkers. Some are professional 'angels' to whom the company eagerly points as good examples. Under slowdown conditions, they become the 'rate-busters' who are resented by other workers."[9]

For Alice, the decision to go straight to her supervisor about the new sandpaper probably placed her in the rate-buster category, linking her with management before she had established trust with her peers. The introduction of a new person disrupts any group, requiring readjustment and compromise. Such readjustment means a threat to the system, and the less actual power we have, the more vital it can seem to keep that system in place. Though it may have made their lives easier to use a finer grade of sandpaper, when Alice stepped out on her own, she upset something far more precarious than gearshift quality control—she was toying with the control Ivy and the others exerted over their environment.

Ivy had good reason to assume that she could not count on Alice's loyalty just because they were all in the same professional boat. Studies show that group affiliation in workers of both sexes largely depends on whether membership bodes well for their personal goals and desires.[10] Being a line worker did not have many tangible job rewards, so Ivy and the others made following their rules beneficial in other ways—as a route toward inclusion and a sense of belonging. The threat of excommunication is a powerful social tool, one girls begin using against one another in childhood. Ivy's choice to shut Alice out not only sent unmistakable signals about the price of operating solo, but she also used Alice to draw the group closer together, allowing them to bond more tightly by cutting the newcomer out.

Upon entering a new situation, women need to be sensitive to the rules and power structures, both official and unofficial, already in place. Just because a group is made up of other women does not mean it will automatically take us in. As group members, it is also important to weigh the balance between risk and reward. Alice was probably correct in assuming that if the line workers did not help each other, no one else would. The very qualities that scared Ivy, Alice's initiative and independent streak, also made her a powerful ally for the group to have on their side.

As for most disenfranchised workers, Ivy and the other line workers' demand for obedience stemmed from serious factory-wide concerns: poor working conditions, high job stress, and a company insensitive to the needs of its employees, all resulting in a great deal of fear and frustration. On a large scale, resolution depended upon those who ran the factory making the workplace more humane. On a smaller scale, the bonds Alice formed with her coworkers could and did make a difference.

Though coming together to clean the lunchroom may seem insignificant in the face of issues like low wages and punishing hours, it lent Alice and her crew some small sense of independence from the system. Overcoming divisions within their core group enabled an initial step toward change.

Getting It Together

From early social reformers through the recent feminist movement, there are powerful precedents for groups of women gathering to advance a common goal. In circumstances in which our individual power remains limited, coming together can create a whole far stronger and more effective than its parts.

"I do what I do, because I got tired of seeing and reading about women as victims," says Gillian, a union organizer for health-care and educational workers. "I asked myself how women can have more power in their lives, and the answer seemed to be, by asserting themselves in a collective way. Most of the workplaces I go into are made up entirely of women. It's a profound experience for them to unite around a common cause, sit at a bargaining table, ask for something and get it. For many of them, it's the first time they've ever had a voice."

As women's roles in the workplace continue to shift and grow, it is important that we keep asking ourselves what we mean when we say we want to create women-friendly or women-positive environments. Our definition cannot be so delicate and protective that it will not withstand the rigors of the professional world. A common theme to all the stories in this chapter—the stumbling block for Molly, for Sophia, for Marjorie, for Alice—involved pressure to hide their true feelings in order to fit into a group of other women. Instead of making space for a range of voices, these groups were so eager to appear outwardly cohesive that they discouraged the expression of individual needs and concerns.

In the course of my interviews, I spoke to a number of women who were involved in professional women's organizations, and I attended some of their meetings. Networking groups have become a popular forum for working women to brainstorm problems, pool resources, and build contacts. But members of such groups expressed frustrations as well. At a meeting of a New York coalition of female executives—following a presentation about how women still fall far behind men when it comes to job-related accomplishments—a longtime member ventured her opinion on why the group was not as effective as it might be. Her thoughts seemed to crystallize much of what I had heard from other women in similar positions. She cautioned members against focusing exclusively on what they could get out of the group to help them on their professional way.

"We need to concentrate on both give and take," she said. "Each member should come to these meetings with a clear idea of how she wants to benefit and an equally clear sense about how she can contribute. What am I here for? How can I help myself and help you at the same time?"

Her comment touches upon questions critical to groups of women in all professional situations. How can we work as a unit without losing our autonomy? How do we negotiate teamwork without demanding self-sacrifice? How do we maintain solidarity while still allowing for conflicts and differences? A healthy group is not one from which competition and conflict have been banished entirely. Research has shown women are more likely to work together successfully in environments in which they are allowed to compete openly and legitimately for promotions, raises, and other rewards.[11]

In group situations, as with our individual relationships, there is a difference between the personal and the professional. A professional group is united by a common goal rather than by the social constructs that join us as peers. Members do not have to share identical personal or political values in order to cohere. If we are to maximize our collective potential, women working together need to focus on enhancing our self-confidence and initiative, not squashing it, learning how to distinguish between eradicating our differences and incorporating them. We must determine how to combine our various strengths, talents, desires, and flaws without negating what we want or who we are.

HAPPILY EVER AFTER?

11

Instructions from the Playing Field

To compete, you must acknowledge your desires, declare your intentions, and trust that you can handle the outcome, as well as the process, with some degree of grace. It's scary. It takes courage.
—MARIAH BURTON NELSON, AUTHOR AND
PROFESSIONAL BASKETBALL PLAYER[1]

When I interviewed Toni King, a black and women's studies professor at Dennison College, she told me, "If you study one thing, it will lead you to the opposite." In the course of my research and interviews for this book, her words grew increasingly significant. By exploring conflict and competition among women in the workplace, I also came across numerous stories about women who had figured out how to work together successfully. Word from the front lines is that healthy, conflicting, competitive relationships among women on the job can and do unfold all the time.

Nearly every woman with whom I spoke truly cared about the problems that rise up among women in the workplace. They did not want to write off these problems as trivial. They wanted to do the exploration, have the difficult conversations, debate, compromise, challenge, and change. In part, this process will require redefining competition and conflict so that they are not emotional panic zones but factors we can recognize and absorb into our working relationships. The presence of open, healthy competition should signal that things are healthy rather than that things are falling apart. One of the first places those old definitions are crumbling is the world of women in sports.

I have been an athlete my entire life. Not necessarily a good one, but enough of one that it has taught me what fair competition does and does not mean. It has taught me about teamwork and facing fears. But I think the most useful lesson arrived by way of Carey Saulter on track-and-field day at Epiphany School when I was in the fifth grade. We were running the 220, a quarter-mile sprint around the Montlake track. I—soccer player and swim team member—felt fairly confident about my prospects. The whistle sounded and I popped forward, lungs heaving, legs charging. Before I had reached the first curve of the track, I heard the whip and crunch of footsteps, then Carey smoked past me as if I were standing still. More like I was moving backward. While part of my competitive eleven-year-old self felt humiliated, another part of that same self was steeped in admiration. Carey was fast. Leave-me-in-the-dust fast. Fast in a way I could only dream to be.

The message took a while to sink in, and you can bet I saw to it that I never raced head to head against Carey again. In the end, getting annihilated by her did teach me something crucial about competition. There is always someone faster, stronger, better than you are. The best you can do—in fact all you can do—is run your race.

In interviewing other women, I was curious about how a grounding in athletic competition might play into their feelings about conflict and competition in other areas of their lives. I asked them about their game-playing histories, about any correlation they saw between sports and how they dealt with competition in the workplace. I spoke to a handful of premier-level athletes and quite a few weekend ones. One key point surfaced repeatedly.

In the world of female friendships, competitive often equals harmful, manifesting itself in a desire to take the other person down. In the professional rubric, healthy competition can be highly desirable. It generates new ideas, talents, and resources. Sports—an arena in which there are clear winners, losers, and rules of the game, where competition does not have to be hidden or downplayed—provides a logical way to help bridge that gap.

It's Not Whether You Win or Lose

Becky, now in her early thirties, is a world champion downhill skier and three-time Olympian, who spent ten years as a member of the U.S. Ski Team. When in active training, she and her teammates spent eight months a year together. They lived together, ate together, traveled together, rode the lift together. They shared coaches and training facilities. They also competed against one another in nearly every race they entered, which could mean a race a week during the height of the season. Every four years, the top seven skiers also contended for four coveted spots on the U.S. Olympic team.

All the women with whom Becky skied were ambitious and competitive, herself included. The work ethic and sacrifices entailed were too intense to shoot for anything less than number one. They were also very much a team.

"Yes it's an individual sport," Becky says, "but you still need the support of those around you. You need to share information about slope conditions or tackling a particularly difficult section of the mountain. You need someone to talk you up when you aren't skiing well. You're never so good that there isn't a great deal you can learn from your team."

On their best days, any of the top flight of women skiers might have beaten any other and rankings among them shifted as people got injured, went through slumps, or found their groove. They all had different approaches. Becky was extremely disciplined, "bordering on obsessive," while others were more instinctual and laid back. Over time, she figured out how to stop comparing herself to her teammates and find a style and rhythm that worked for her, but she admits such lessons took awhile to settle in. When she initially joined the team in her early twenties, she was miserable.

"In my first five years of training, I put so much pressure on myself to win," she recalls. "It really battered my self-confidence. I felt like I had to prove myself every time I got out on the slope. And my skiing suffered for it. Because I was so anxious about falling or messing up, I wound up tense and fearful and overly cautious on the mountain."

Such self-doubt not only affected her own performance, it also spilled over into her relationships with her teammates.

"There were some people you just didn't get along with," she volunteers, "who you wouldn't have chosen as friends. One woman in particular always tried to beat me whenever we were on the hill. I grew very self-conscious around her. I felt like she cheered when I fell. Early on she always out-skied me in competitions, even though I wasn't all that impressed with her ability. She also had a very different personality than I did. She always needed to be at the center of everything. Usually I'm very independent and happy to take care of myself, but I was jealous of her. I hated that she won and that she got so much attention."

Looking back, Becky admits that her reaction stemmed less from her teammate's behavior than from the cracks in her own self-confidence. When she joined the U.S. team at twenty-one, Becky's entire focus, and much of her self-worth, centered around one goal—winning a gold medal at the 1998 Olympics. Though she did make the Olympic team, the rest of her dream didn't come to pass.

"I was devastated," she acknowledges, "but in retrospect, I think it was a blessing. When the gold medal didn't happen, I had a sort of mini breakdown. I really considered quitting. And I realized I could only go on if I found other reasons to be there. I had to do it for the skiing and not for the winning. As an athlete, you compete all the time. You have to find a way to make that relaxed and livable for yourself. If it's do or die every single time you get on the mountain, you'll burn out. Once I relaxed, my performance, not to mention my enjoyment level, improved enormously. When I stopped focusing on winning, that's when I became the most competitive."

Working with so many premier athletes, Becky also came to realize that she did not have to reside at the top of the heap in order to be important. When she managed to ease off and allow her skills on the mountain to speak for themselves, she became more willing to listen to and learn from her coaches and teammates, and to laud their victories without it bruising her ego.

"At first I equated losing with being a failure," she explains. "I thought I'd have no friends, no life. It took winning a world championship and not winning that gold medal to realize that wins and losses didn't define me. It was a question of maturity. Over the years, I learned not to constantly compare myself to my teammates, but to focus on besting my previous performance. I began reframing each run as an opportunity to perform rather than an opportunity to fail."

Two years ago, after a decade on the racing circuit, Becky decided to retire and make the shift to coaching. So far, the transition has been smooth.

"I consider myself lucky. I've seen plenty of people who couldn't let go, and who resented the young talent coming up the pipeline. But I'd done my stint as an athlete. My body was worn out, and I wanted to start a family. I think because my friends and colleagues were so supportive and because I'd achieved what I wanted to achieve as a skier—not everything, but the important things—I was able to move on."

As a coach working with young skiers, Becky says she does her best to emphasize technique, camaraderie, and pleasure over who collects the most points and medals.

"I think it's too much pressure, especially for a young athlete, to feel like you're only worthwhile if you win. They have to learn what I did. It is possible to be competitive without laying your entire identity on the line."

As a society, we are growing increasingly familiar with seeing women in competitive, even adversarial, situations. This is due in a large degree to the burgeoning relationship between women and sports. A record 40.6 percent of the Olympic athletes in the 2004 Athens summer games were women.[2] High-profile women's tennis, golf, basketball, and soccer players—the Williams sisters, Annika Sorenstam, Lisa Leslie, Mia Hamm—and movies like *Million Dollar Baby* and *A League of Their Own* have all helped to counter the stereotype of women as perennially sweet and nonconfrontational. Sports offer up rare public examples not only of the competitive woman herself but also how that competition factors into her relationships with other women.

When the Women's Tennis Association decided to set up a program to help players deal with the stresses of the pro tour, they held hearings with the coaches and players to discover the most pressing concerns. The pressure of competition ranked far down the list, behind parents and coaches, behind travel, the media, the loneliness of life on the tour. For women who had grown up schooled in and surrounded by it, competition simply was not an issue. Provided time and exposure, competition was something with which they had come to feel entirely at home.[3]

"I don't think that female athletes have more problems being outright competitive than men do," agrees Jenny Susser, a sports psychologist and former All-American college swimmer. "If you're a high-level athlete, you've probably found a way to come to terms with or even thrive on the competitive aspects of the job."[4]

According to Susser, top-tier female athletes tend to report the most pressure in two areas. First off, premier women athletes can encounter considerable envy and resentment in the face of their excellence. Many feel they have to go out of their way to diffuse their performance level by being extra gracious and humble toward fans, team members, and opponents. When they do not, they risk suffering the fate of Venus and Serena

Williams who—despite the athletic brilliance that propelled them to face one another in an unprecedented four consecutive Grand Slam finals—wound up reviled by much of the women's tennis circuit for displaying an overabundance of attitude. Their aloof demeanor and such straightforward comments as Venus saying, "I don't come to make friends, I come to win matches," made them targets for their fellow players and the media. The criticism reached its ironic height when one of tennis's most notorious bad boys, John McEnroe, accused the sisters of "lacking respect and humility" for the sport.[5] The Williams sisters agitated people on a number of levels, upsetting convention because they were black, because they trained together, because they rarely interacted with the other women on the tour. Still, it is difficult to imagine such a fuss being generated around a pair of extremely gifted male players, however cocky they came across in person.

"The message young female athletes get today is that it's okay to be competitive, but do it in a ladylike way," says Carol Otis, a member of the Women's Tennis Council and for eight years chief medical adviser for the WTA women's professional tennis tour. "They compete on the court and it's about ability and mental toughness, but they're also competing on the level of looks and beauty and manners. There's pressure to succeed in both."

Society presents female athletes with the same contradictions encountered by many professionally ambitious women, the tug of war between what it means to be competitive and what it means to be a woman. "There can be a real struggle," admits Otis. "As athletes, these women are in a field where being aggressive is valued. As women, they're still socialized to please people and fit in."

The second set of problems Susser mentions is confidence related. "Competitive sports create an opening for some difficult questions," she says. "Questions like: Am I good enough? Will putting myself in a competitive situation reveal this? Do I really want to know the answer?"

Female athletes, perhaps due to the particular cultural pressures women undergo to measure up to others' expectations, can fear that failing in a professional context will make them failures all around. Though men experience such anxieties, too, Susser suspects women athletes are more inclined to get their entire self-worth tangled up in how they perform. "It's not lack of talent or dedication so much as a fear of desire. What would it be like to want something that badly and have it taken away?"

Questions of confidence and uncertainty about how to blend aggression with femininity are problems that resonate with many professional women. Since competition is a given for athletes, some of the dilemmas that might remain underground in other contexts are readily apparent in a professional sports environment. In the workplace, we can dodge our worries about excelling, but performance anxiety shows up immediately on the court or playing field. Sports bring us face to face with the fact that female competition—like male competition—is not necessarily pretty, nor does it necessarily bring out the best in all its players. Sports present women in openly competitive situations that provide opportunities to work through our internal and external conflicts and to acknowledge our generous and our more aggressive sides.

When I interviewed Fiona, a former professional basketball player who now works in marketing at a high-tech firm, she compared the competition she has witnessed among women on the job to her sports experience with a note of longing.

"I always felt like basketball was as close as you could get to an even playing field. Merit was rewarded. If you played well, you played more; if you didn't, you didn't. You could be friends with someone but still get out on the court and want to kill them, and no one took it personally. Even as a woman, it was safe and accepted to push as hard as you could. I miss that sort of clean, impersonal competition. We give men such a hard time for all their sports talk but, in a way, I suspect they're on to something. I think our professional relationships would be stronger if we could treat the office a little more like the basketball court."

Stepping Out of the Comfort Zone

Sports—even the beginner level, weekend kind—may be one of the most powerful mediums women have for adapting ourselves and our relationships with one another to the professional arena. They supply a blend of camaraderie and competition that easily lends itself to the workplace and that can help orchestrate the balance between self and others so many women find difficult to strike.

There is a strong connection between game playing and the workplace. Sports talk and sports metaphors have a traditional role among men on the job. In the past, women have tended to write this off as testosterone-filled and exclusionary. As more and more women enter the workplace with experience in competitive athletics, that perception may be shifting, too. According to a 2002 survey commissioned by Oppenheimer Funds, more than four out of five executive businesswomen, 82 percent, played organized sports growing up, and the majority say lessons learned on the playing field have contributed to their success in business.[6] In a 1988 study, University of Virginia psychology professor Linda Bunker found that 80 percent of women recognized as holding key positions in Fortune 500 companies participated in sports during childhood and identified themselves as having been "tomboys" in their youth.[7]

It can be tricky for a woman to pursue power or excellence in a world where she wants to impress men and befriend other women. Sports provide a training ground upon which competition is sanctioned, where participants have the freedom to be as ambitious and as driven as they please. A grounding in competitive games can help wash away the habit of imposing standards of modesty or false humility on ourselves and other women. In a broader sense, women with athletic experience may be more likely to take purely professional competition in stride and plunge in despite the uncertainties.

"Competition pushes you outside your comfort zone in a direction it's often too scary to go on your own," says Jess, a surgeon and former

NCAA college soccer player. "Once you hit that shaky ground, you really start to learn and grow."

The beautiful thing is that such lessons are not physical but mental and emotional. You do not need excessive doses of athletic ability in order to absorb them. One of the more powerful components of athletic competition is that it encourages players not only to embrace their strengths but also to come to terms with their limitations. Just as in the workplace, athletics is a field in which participants are rewarded for pushing themselves while simultaneously learning from those who excel beyond them, in which they discover how to use their community to support them, how to work with coaches and leaders and ask them for help. Athletes gain experience in competing against friends without taking the outcome personally, and they hone the art of collaborating with people with whom they do not necessarily get along or even like.

"Sports taught me that I could hip-check my best friend," a former college lacrosse player, now an accessories designer in the fashion business, told me. "Within the confines of the game, it was okay to let loose. I learned it was possible to push myself and still love and respect my team."

According to researchers from University of California at Berkeley, female athletes in particular tend to view competition and cooperation as interdependent rather than opposing concepts.[8] They do not see being competitive framed as a choice between helping a friend, colleague, or teammate and helping themselves. In fact, a strictly adversarial definition of competition can repel female athletes. Rather than swearing off competition altogether, they tend to develop alternative options. Sports psychologist Susser notes that instead of embracing the dominant, cutthroat, and typically "male" sports culture, women athletes often choose to treat their opponents more respectfully.

"It isn't that women are less intense," Susser explains. "It's just that they give that intensity a different focus. It's more about pulling themselves up than slamming other people down. It's an approach that I think translates more gracefully to the world at large."

This gentler definition of competition, figuring out how to succeed but not at another's expense, echoed a style that most appealed to the women I interviewed. They often described themselves as being competitive "with myself" or wanting to succeed but not when it meant seeing another person fail. They made a clear distinction about where the line crossed into "too competitive," making a point to let me know that they considered it just as important to play fair as to win. A grounding in sports can help us realize that there is more than one way to compete.

Alongside such lessons in gracious victory, athletic competition also teaches participants how to fail. Eventually, by way of every lost race, missed basket, and squandered point, an athlete discovers that setbacks—large and small—can be sifted over, learned from, and then transcended. They realize that it is possible to compete without destroying their rivals, and without being destroyed themselves.

Of course, women are hardly immune to the darker side of competition. Pursue any athletic endeavor long enough and you will discover that results are not always fair. Opponents will cheat, fight dirty, and even get away with it, and sometimes talent and connections win out over hard work—all lessons highly applicable to the workplace. If we have experienced the lengths some people—male and female—will go to in order to win, we arrive on the job less naïve and more prepared for how to react when we do come across the inevitable low blow.

Sports is not a magic formula. Lessons in one area of life do not automatically transfer to another. In the workplace, rules can be hazier, competition less openly sanctioned, winners and losers less clearly cut. But in talking to so many women, I did find basic principles of athletic competition—communication, fortitude, teamwork, trust—consistently echoed in the stories of those who had successfully worked out their differences on the job.

There Are No Superstars

When Caroline and her partner launched their Southern California women's sports medicine clinic ten years ago, it was the first of its kind in the country. Caroline was an athlete from way back; a competitive cyclist, runner, hiker, and tennis player. She had always been an achiever, with a strong personality and impressive professional credentials. Now in her early forties, she is tall and tanned with short dark hair and a definite air of command.

Throughout her early career, most of Caroline's colleagues and a good portion of her patients were male. While working at several university hospitals, she began to consider focusing on the problems of female athletes instead. When she and her husband moved from Denver to Los Angeles, Caroline met a colleague, another female sports medicine doctor, who shared a similar vision and together they convinced their hospital to give the idea a chance. The two women started small, with minimal staff and even less office space. As the patients flocked, the center gradually expanded. Today the group consists of four doctors and a support team of nutritionists, nurses, a sports psychologist, an exercise physiologist, assistants, and receptionists, all of whom share that initial vision. With the exception of two office workers, the entire staff is female.

"We didn't set out to be women only," Caroline says, "but most of us come from a sports background, and we feel strongly about creating a place where female athletes, from beginners to professionals, will be taken seriously. It just made sense that everyone drawn by that mission would be a woman."

From the start, Caroline and her partner selected their staff carefully, weighing accomplishments and personalities. They were not afraid to bring on doctors capable in areas in which they were not. The idea, always, was to build a whole stronger than its parts. This focus has kept unhealthy competition to a minimum.

"Among the doctors, we're all equally well educated and secure in our jobs," Caroline says. "There are no superstars and that discourages the sort of 'who has more patients' or 'who gets more attention' contests I've seen among other doctors. We're all still very driven, but I don't see why that has to preclude being supportive. I think that's a lesson most of us got from playing sports. You're only as strong as your weakest player."

Though there is some overlap, each staff member has her own area of expertise. The doctors often refer patients to one another or call on each other for second opinions. Caroline and her partner have done their best to build racial and ethnic diversity into their hiring, so that a wide variety of patients might feel comfortable. The entire staff meets and communicates regularly, and they plot out every major decision together.

"There's very little sense that when one staff member succeeds it's at another's expense," Caroline explains. "We've tried to set it up so there's room for everyone to do well. The doctors here work on research projects, sometimes independently, sometimes together. We also make a point of helping more junior staff in areas where women can be less comfortable, like negotiating hospital contracts. We don't want them stuck in a situation where they feel they have no control. In a professional environment, I think that can happen more easily with women."

Caroline asserts that the center has a very strong work ethic, standards to which everyone from the top down is expected to adhere.

"We don't yell or throw things, but we're not entirely warm and fuzzy either. Everyone who works here is a part of what we've created. If they leave a negative impression, that rubs off on us. We've had several nurses who chose not to join us because they'd heard we were too difficult. I think women doctors are often expected to be pushovers in a way that male doctors aren't. If people feel that way, I'm okay with it. They probably didn't belong here after all."

Caroline and her cofounder have split the leadership duties, with a third woman taking on much of the administrative work. Everyone is respected, but there is also a clear structure in place. Caroline tends to play the primary conflict resolver, and she credits much of their office harmony to the ability to confront problems immediately and directly.

"My philosophy is that as soon as something comes up, we sit down and talk about it. Nothing gets swept under the rug."

She stresses that it is not that the staff does not experience differences, but that they have a system in place for dealing with them. She is also quick to make the distinction between liking conflict and being willing to deal with it. "I think a lot of women see themselves as nonconfrontational just because they don't enjoy taking people on. I don't like conflict either, but I'm not afraid of it. With practice, you develop skills and strategies. I know from experience that if issues hang around they only get worse."

The center's administrator, Susannah, handles the mechanics of day-to-day operations. She is the repository for any organizational or personality glitches and her problem-solving techniques lean heavily on the notion of give and take. When a conflict arises, she tries to get input from both sides, figuring that those who are most involved will best know how to solve it. "Whatever solutions we come up with are framed as compromises," she explains. "My big phrase is: It may not be what you wanted, but can you live with it?"

The clinic operates on the trickle-down leadership theory: Strong, well-adjusted people at the top create a healthy office atmosphere by listening, fostering a sense of trust, not feeling threatened by excellence, and striking a personal-professional balance. Research has shown that organizational leaders build cooperation just as Caroline and her partner have—by giving those under them a voice in proceedings, ensuring that they feel they belong to the whole, and indicating a willingness to make sacrifices for the group if they are asking others to do the same.[9]

The clinic is not organized along the traditional corporate model, and it has not succeeded because those involved "act like men." Caroline agrees that working entirely with women sometimes requires special adjustments, like taking increased emotional attachments into account.

"It can be frustrating when nonwork issues invade the job, but the fact is that a lot of our staff are dealing with family responsibilities. There will be times when those stresses show up in the workplace."

Nor have they attempted any version of an easygoing, collaborative utopia. Caroline and her colleagues can be demanding, a requirement when facing a hospital administration that at times thinks it can take advantage of a group of women, not to mention a bureaucracy in which they are battling against influential men for dollars and space.

"It's not easy being the tough one," Caroline concedes. "Of course, I want people to think I'm a nice person. Who doesn't want to be liked? But I also know that the most beloved boss is not necessarily the best one. I may not win a popularity contest, but I think my colleagues respect me and I respect them. I see my role as part of something bigger, something that's clearly working."

Caroline and her coworkers have succeeded by pulling together a group of people who share the values they share, who are passionate, ethical, and sincere. And they have managed to expand and reshape the traditional workplace model to suit their own needs.

"I think our success comes from a collection of strong, talented people," Susannah tells me, "but also from our ability to strike the right balance between collaboration and individual achievement."

All in all, it is a fairly accurate definition of teamwork.

12

Coming to Our Own Rescue

The truth itself is ambiguity, abyss, mystery: once stated,
it must be thoughtfully reconsidered, re-created.
—SIMONE DE BEAUVOIR, *THE SECOND SEX*

What's good for the goose can also be good for the gander . . .
or, in this more complicated case, what's good for the goose
can also be good for the other goose.
—LYNDA OBST, HOLLYWOOD PRODUCER[1]

When I described this project to people early on, I would occasionally get the response, "Oh, God, how depressing." In fact, just the opposite has proved true. The stories told here are very much tales of optimism, movement, and hope. The outcomes always have the potential to go both ways. These stories are unfolding because women are charging into territory in which our old relational rules—those centered around nicety, modesty, and restraint—no longer apply.

"People have become more aware of conflicts among women precisely because women are trying to act in new ways and to enter new places in society," wrote feminist psychologist Jean Baker Miller in 1986. "The seeds of these conflicts always existed, but the conflicts did not always surface. Conflict becomes more obvious when people try to do new things."[2] Professional women are at a point where all of us can be innovators. Wherever we reside on the food chain, we are in a position to foster growth and change. That's not a bad place to be.

Our professional problems do matter tremendously. There are larger

ramifications, enormous ones, to women failing to forge productive relationships with one another. Women are still playing some serious catch-
up in the workplace. Women hold only 13.6 percent of board seats at
Fortune 500 companies, and women of color hold just 3 percent.[3] In
seven out of ten industries examined in a General Accounting Office report on the glass ceiling—industries representing 73 percent of women
managers in the United States—the earnings gap between full-time female and male managers had actually widened between 1995 and 2000.[4]
In 2002, just 3.79 percent of venture capital dollars went to companies
with female CEOs, a drop from 5.06 percent in 1999.[5] These disparities
are not caused by problems among women, nor will they be resolved by
tackling our internal tensions alone. But if women cannot successfully
build relationships that allow for both competition and cooperation, we
risk sacrificing our voices to the decision-making power of the men
above us. The perception that women cannot work together is not only
false, it is dangerous to us all.

Women owe it to other women to be supportive, to treat relationships
with their female colleagues seriously and respectfully, to do their best to
create opportunities for other women. We also need to understand that
support is not the same as suspension of conflict, competition or criticism. Addressing our workplace problems requires that we act in spite of
fears, doubts, and reservations raised by competitive situations. We do
not have control over how others behave. Sometimes when we do everything right, when all the proper ingredients seem to be in place, things
will go swimmingly. Sometimes they will fall apart. As Fiona, the former
professional basketball player, told me, "The outcome doesn't matter
nearly so much as the effort. You just have to walk out on that tightrope.
Even if you feel insecure, even if you feel shy, someone has to take that
first step."

I have interviewed more than a hundred women and talked informally to countless others. I have listened to positive tales, negative tales,
and everything in between, but not one of the stories I heard was a fairy

tale. Not one began with "once upon a time" or ended with "happily ever after." Working out our differences entails more than just the occasional gesture or good intention. Resolving conflicts requires ongoing, sustained commitment. Change occurs by means of small steps and subtle shifts. It takes time. The issues we are facing are packed with rich, messy, ambiguous, and often contradictory impulses. There is no universal cure-all to fix every fractured relationship, but there are some general truths we can keep in mind as we continue to move forward.

Turning the Mirror

One of the questions included in the survey I sent to the women I interviewed was whether the participant had ever behaved toward a female colleague in a way she was not proud of or satisfied with. A telling number of women simply replied no. The pressure to see ourselves as perennial good girls can overshadow our ability to admit how our own behavior contributes to our professional relationships. If we are to break into troublesome areas, it is imperative that we begin to turn the mirror on ourselves. As a health-care lawyer in her early thirties responded, "At some point I've behaved toward just about everyone in my work life in a way that I was not proud of or satisfied with. I think most people have. I've tried to learn from those situations and make my future relationships stronger for it."

As in any relationship, when troubles develop on the job rarely, if ever, is one person totally at fault. We can start to address any uncomfortable situation with a female colleague by asking, What am I contributing? What can I do to change? Writing this book has made me examine my own role in the tensions I have experienced, not only with coworkers but with all the women in my life. It has made me look closely at my feelings about competition, my fears of failure or not being liked, and how that affects my behavior toward other women. I have emerged more compassionate, more constructive, and more likely to speak up for myself.

A key tool in effectively resolving interpersonal conflict entails the ability to separate what is actually going on from our perception of what's going on. "We inevitably make assumptions about other people's desires and motivations," says Dr. Beth Fisher Yoshida, of Columbia University's International Center for Cooperation and Conflict Resolution, "many of which may be accurate, but which can be damaging when they are wrong."[6] As individuals and as a culture, we need to beware of falling into generalized gender-specific expectations, the kind that frame women as more relational and maternal and less confrontational and driven than men. Just because historically women's personal duties have eclipsed professional ones does not mean this will hold true in the workplace today. There are countless women who straddle traditional gender molds or break them altogether. I spoke to women of all ages and backgrounds who aspired to CEO titles, to opening their own businesses, to assuming college presidencies. They were not scaling back their desires to seem sweeter or less intimidating to those around them. I spoke to women who considered themselves extremely direct and others who avoided conflict at all costs. Professional women's personalities and flaws are as varied as their positions and their dreams.

Women also need to learn to separate our individual relationships from our more overarching frustrations with the workplace itself. Organizational culture is a frequent source of alienation and disillusionment, and behaving "unprofessionally" toward our female colleagues can be a way of acting out against unfair pressures and practices on the job. But there are more productive avenues of protest. Experts have posited that the recent upsurge in women-owned businesses—48 percent of privately held firms are at least 50 percent women-owned, and the growth rate in the number of such businesses from 1997 to 2004 was nearly twice that of all firms[7]—is in some part due to women fleeing the macho environment of big businesses.[8] On a smaller scale, I spoke to women who had formed informal groups within larger companies or institutions, groups dedicated to infusing some degree of humanity and social responsibility back into the job.

"I think we should be shamefully biased toward the success of other women, assuming they merit support," Rita, the museum worker with the new baby, told me. "I also think we need to be extremely open-minded about what success means to each individual. It's not always about getting the corner office."

Of course, all the understanding in the world is not useful until we act upon it. Many of the women to whom I spoke had strong feelings and stronger opinions about how they had behaved when things broke down on the job and what they wished they had done differently. Some involved individual behaviors. Some entailed deeper organizational and societal shifts. All indicated a genuine commitment to facilitating change.

What We Can Do as a Society

SOCIAL POLICY: There are a number of social policy issues that affect women's experiences and relationships on the job. As the reigning industrial country, America makes a decidedly weak showing in this department. In Sweden, women get ninety-six weeks of paid maternity leave; in Italy, forty-seven weeks; in Great Britain, twenty-six weeks. In the United States, women receive just twelve weeks[9] of federally subsidized child care. Family- and flexible-leave policies, reliable hours, schedules, and benefits would all help weave a safety net to reduce women's professional stresses. When our jobs seem more secure, when we feel less desperate and compromised by the system, we will feel that much more generous about helping others.

Such policies benefit all of us. To women at the age of twenty-two, government-funded child care might seem a minor concern. If those women look at the coworker who is never available in the afternoons because she has to pick up her children, or at themselves ten years down the line, the issue becomes critical. During periods of economic downturn and higher jobless rates, government and businesses often feel less motivation to maintain women- and family-friendly policies. Pressure from female customers, employees, and voters is necessary to keep such issues front and center.

MEDIA: The media is a strong indicator of what we value as a society. For better or worse, people frequently take their cues about what is important from what they read in a magazine or see on screen. Such workplace-based reality TV shows as *The Apprentice* have revealed that women can be just as professionally ambitious and ruthless as their male counterparts. Now we are ready to dig deeper. Popular and critically acclaimed TV series set in the working world—from *The West Wing* to *CSI* to *The Sopranos*—might feature story lines about women's professional relationships. Though a few small independent films have looked at women's workplace dynamics, like 2001's *The Business of Strangers* and 1997's *Clockwatchers,* such cinematic tales remain rare. As we know, the subject can provide for plenty of explosive narrative drama.

Conflict and competition among working women is also a natural topic for talk shows, women's magazines, or other public forums for women's issues. We need to overcome our embarrassment, our sense of awkwardness and political incorrectness concerning the problems we encounter with one another. Until we create a context and vocabulary with which to discuss such issues, they will remain what they are now—a professional dirty little secret. This subject is provocative because it matters. Our workplace relationships have great influence on our lives.

ORGANIZATIONS: The idea that companies do not have the time or financial wherewithal to deal with problems among female workers is shamefully shortsighted. In downplaying or dismissing such problems, they are losing employee time and energy that should be extended to the job itself. And they are losing employees. A number of the women with whom I spoke had either left or were planning to leave their jobs because a relationship with a female coworker had grown unbearable and they did not know what else to do.

Organizations and individual employers can be sensitive to the problems that manifest among women just as they are to discrimination, sexual harassment, and other male-female conflicts. They can have a referral system in place to deal with such problems so that female employees have outlets beyond just their superiors. They can sponsor talks and workshops that call attention to the issues surrounding women and competition. Finally, they can actively incentivize mentoring and other women's support groups.

One woman I interviewed, Alexandra, had spent nine years as a partner in a large education and health-care law firm in Arizona. During that time, she played a primary role in developing a mentoring program that paid particular attention to women's concerns. The firm paired its first-year associates, both male and female, with peer, department, and firm mentors. At least one of those relationships continued throughout the associate's first three years on the job. In addition, each year a different female partner was designated as a mentor to deal specifically with women's gender-related concerns—discrimination, work-family tensions, troubles with another female colleague. Mentors made it clear that no problem would be considered too small or stupid. The program has been in place for nearly a decade, and the partners continue to expand and modify it to suit the firm's needs.

"I think it's extremely important to acknowledge that individuals can get lost in the shuffle of a large firm," Alexandra explains. "Many women do have a different experience in the workplace than men do, and we owe it to each other to recognize that. The bigger the firm, the harder it becomes to value people on a human level. When that happens, both the workers and the work start to suffer."

GROUPS: In some cases, women may already be operating within an ideal framework for exploring conflict and competition issues. Independent women's networking and professional associations have blossomed in the last decades, gathering women of a common age, location, or profession, ranging from the Financial Women's Association to Women in Film to reams of others. Many of these groups already run mentoring and support programs. Since they exist separately from the workplace, they can also provide a safe environment in which to broach questions about the conflict and competition we experience on the job.

We should also take advantage of other venues in which professional women gather outside the formal workplace—for example, leadership conferences and management workshops—to begin addressing our problematic dynamics. Relational patterns cannot be stripped and replaced in the course of an afternoon like hanging new wallpaper, but we can use such forums to recognize competition issues and thus lend them legitimacy. If we begin transmitting the message that these issues are important, individual women will be that much more likely to return to the workplace prepared to address their conflicts head on.

What We Can Do as Individuals

Effective change certainly is not limited to a group, governmental, or policy scale. The smallest of positive steps can engender others, building gradually like beads on a string. Subtle shifts in individual behaviors have the power to elicit major shifts in our overall relationships.

Women on the job can begin by acknowledging conflicts, even small ones. By doing so, we will allow colleagues to come out from under that intense pressure to always look clean, and we can begin learning to accept both victory and defeat gracefully. We can be sensitive to, without making ourselves martyrs to, our female coworkers' personal lives and emotional landscapes. Above all, we can make a point of behaving ethically and showing respect.

"Lying is done with words, and also with silence," writes poet Adrienne Rich.[10] Women need to begin speaking up. Though it may seem easier and safer to keep quiet about a conflict or to complain behind a colleague's back, such safety is largely an illusion. "I often feel that I lack the confidence to stick up for myself, defend a position, right a wrong, etc.," wrote a university administrator in her early thirties, "even if it's clearly the right thing to do. I've been trained by my home life to be nice, polite, and courteous and just let things be, even when it's clearly not an appropriate option for me in my professional life. Being too polite and nonconfrontational, wishing that a problem will go away, is probably the worst stance you can take. I've had to retrain myself to recognize potential problems and act upon them as soon as I can."

Once I had opened the door, I found the women I interviewed eager to communicate. They wanted to know if other women had related similar experiences. They wanted reassurance that they weren't inept or unlikable or crazy. Above all, they wanted to know they were not alone. Initially, it may be awkward to raise this topic in a professional group, requiring all involved to suspend judgment and resist rushing to dwell on hurt feelings. Until someone summons the courage to take the first step, nothing will change.

Be sensitive. Many of the managers and supervisors with whom I spoke felt that women often needed an extra dose of attention or validation on the job. Criticism did not always roll off their backs as easily as it might off a man's, and they usually responded better when conflicts were soothed instead of steamrollered. "In my experience, women tend to be people pleasers, and they also tend not to feel as confident about their performance," said one human resources manager. "They operate more effectively when their worth is regularly acknowledged." This does not mean that criticism should not be offered but that, as we tackle problems, we can pay attention to doling out praise and rewards as well.

Beware of reputations. It is unwise to thrust ourselves into a conflict-ridden situation assuming that if the other player or players are women we will automatically get along. There are plenty of difficult, temperamental, and unhappy women on the job, just as there are plenty of difficult, temperamental, and unhappy men. A number of the women I interviewed had been warned about a problematic female colleague or employer before they began working together. Of course reputations, especially those of strong-minded and driven women, can be unreliable and should not be the only criterion for evaluating a job prospect. But if you fear your personality may clash with that of a potential employer, it is acceptable and advisable to weigh the risks and research further before accepting the job.

Upon looking back, many women were amazed at how long they had withstood a miserable situation. Contrary to popular belief, there are no rewards for those who suffer the most. There are always other options: head-on confrontation, complaining to a superior, or just plain leaving. Women should not be afraid to depart a dynamic that is damaging. You did not fail or betray the women with whom you work, nor do you owe them anything more than they owe you. Of course economic realities weigh heavily, but even if you cannot leave immediately, you can allay some of the misery by stepping back and considering other options.

Sometimes the conflicts we have with our female colleagues are so unexpected and so traumatic that we react emotionally, forgetting all about practical concerns. In extreme circumstances, employees may have legal recourse if they have been subject to unsafe conditions, denied benefits, or have been fired without cause. These regulations, enforced by the Department of Labor, exist for a reason—workers can and do suffer abuse. If you feel you have been legally mistreated, it is within your rights to respond.[11]

As professionals, we can emphasize forming networks and strategic alliances with our female colleagues as an alternative to more intimate personal bonds. We can foster workplace relationships in which professional and private agendas are not inextricably tangled and move past the sense that the narrower focus of a business affiliation is somehow manipulative or shallow. Networking is not self-serving. It requires considerable give and take, figuring out how to balance our own job needs with extending support and advice to others.

Networking relationships take practice, and they comprise one relational arena in which women frequently enter at a disadvantage. Many of us arrive in the workplace equipped with few networking skills. We are either terrified of overstepping our bounds by soliciting advice or contacts, or we shove a résumé right in someone's face and ask for a job. There is a middle ground. A business connection is akin to a friendship. It is not something you use and discard in the same afternoon, but a valuable, investment-worthy, long-term relationship.

"Networking was really scary to me," says Mercedes, a recent college graduate who served as president of a campus "Women in Business" group, an organization through which she landed her first full-time job. "But I knew it was a skill I needed to have if I was going to succeed in the corporate world. At first I felt very awkward. I just stood back and shadowed an older woman to see what she did. With practice, I learned that it's okay to focus on what you want and who has it. Networking is all about how, in a professional context, you can help others while they are helping you."

Above all, we can fuel the belief that each individual has something to offer the world, that one woman's gain is not necessarily another's loss. Competition ceases to feel life threatening when we realize that there will always be further openings and opportunities. We will move through the awkward moments, the tensions, the anger, and the hurt. All the women whose stories appear in this book and the many others to whom I have spoken, provide evidence that, whatever may unfold in our professional universe, life can and does go on.

Women on Top

> For unto whomsoever much is given, of him shall be much required: and to whom men have committed much, of him they will ask the more.[12]

This biblical quote, shortened to "to whom much is given, much is expected," has long served as an aphorism in African American communities. With the shift of a few pronouns, it also speaks of and to every influential woman in the workplace today. For decades women have posited how the world would change when we attained positions of power. Just reaching those positions is not enough. What matters is what each woman does when she gets there.

"When successive levels from top to bottom of an organization are analyzed, the effect is very much like a set of Russian dolls, one stacked inside the other, with the leader containing all the rest," writes Daniel Goleman.[13] For all those women working under them, and even those watching from the sidelines, female bosses, managers, and corporate officers are in a unique position to shape what we value and how we behave.

At forty-seven, Octavia is the president of financial services for a major international banking firm, overseeing twenty-seven thousand employees and responsible for delivering $1.5 billion after taxes. She is the highest-ranking woman in the history of the bank. Though men dominate the executive suites, the company itself is made up of 70 percent women. Octavia realizes that she serves as a figurehead and a role model, and she takes the responsibility seriously.

"Our company has a very strong value system," she tells me. "I feel like it's particularly important that I embody those values in how I conduct myself day to day on the job. I want other female employees to see me as proof that, with hard work and integrity, a woman can rise to a high level."

Octavia's sense of responsibility extends beyond simply doing her job well. She has had two children since joining the bank and during her second maternity leave she became, for a time, the company's first remote worker. She has pushed the bank to develop flexible policies on maternity leave and job sharing and she initiated programs that actively recruit female interns. She is also open with colleagues about how highly she values her family life and that maintaining each side of this equation has required personal and professional sacrifices.

"It's a continual challenge staying involved in my children's lives, especially as they get older," Octavia admits. "You have to be creative to integrate work and family, but for me the benefits have far outweighed the difficulties. I want other women to see me and realize that it can be done successfully, if not always gracefully."

Again and again, I heard from women—on all levels—that a charismatic, well-adjusted woman at the top goes a long way toward creating a healthy office atmosphere. When powerful and highly visible women like Octavia are seen helping other women by becoming members of boards or committees, by pushing for women-friendly corporate policies, by mentoring young women, or by simply honoring their word, they set a standard for everyone else. When they acknowledge and address problems among women on the job just as they would any other problems, conflicts are far less likely to travel underground.

Women on top can establish an atmosphere of trust in which those under them feel free to take risks and still be supported, in which they do not fear punishment for honest feedback, and in which they are confident that troubles raised will be addressed. If women in positions of authority do not treat conflict and competition among women as serious enough to deal with officially, chances are nobody else will either.

Though many of us may not tag ourselves as powerful, almost every woman is in a position to share with and support other women in her organization or her field. By doing what we can to pull up and look out for those with fewer opportunities, we begin to counter the notion that there are not enough resources to go around.

We are all in a position of power in another sense as well. We can pass it down. Women who had built productive relationships with their female coworkers often cited childhood role models as a source of the necessary skills. They came from families of strong women or found sustenance in their schools and their communities. They had known grandmothers, mothers, aunts, sisters, teachers, and coaches early on who imbedded in them a sense of agency and confidence that they carried with them onto the job.

Where Do We Go from Here?

I wrote this book because I wanted to provoke discussion on a subject that I believe many women think about but few have felt comfortable enough to raise. Ideally, the book can serve as a launching pad for further research and debate. The variety of women I interviewed confirmed that conflict and competition occur and do damage across a wide spectrum of professions. Detailed examination of the various permutations would be too much to cover in a single volume, but I hope I have left the door open for others. Women from various industries, from different generations, from diverse racial and economic backgrounds all have specific relational tensions to navigate and stories to tell.

There is no recipe for the perfect mix of competition and collaboration that will always result in a healthy relationship. As professional women, we will have to experiment with the ingredients constantly as our roles shift and expand. I do believe that a balance can be reached. The issues raised in this book can encourage women to seriously consider how to help each other succeed and just what such support entails. Addressing these issues can help us reach a point at which we understand conflict as a natural part of daily life and from which we can approach problematic situations with a commitment to professionalism and respect.

While there may not be a foolproof formula for mending our professional relationships, there are a number of questions all of us can begin carrying with us into the workplace and into the world:

- How do we cope with ambition, wealth, and success in other women and in ourselves?
- How do we forge relationships with our female colleagues based on honesty without cruelty, empathy without dependence, generosity without self-sacrifice?
- What shapes our self-confidence and sense of entitlement?
- How realistic are the expectations we have for our female bosses and employees?
- How do we openly address our fear of other women's disapproval?
- How might we redefine such terms as competition, conflict, power, and influence to suit women's roles in the workplace today?

The problems that erupt between women on the job are complicated. They rattle our deepest insecurities about what it means to be a successful woman in the twenty-first century. Until we confront those fears, we cannot create the rich, healthy, and productive relationships we want and deserve to experience with one another on the job. I hope this book offers insight and ideas regarding potential paths toward change. Most of all, I hope that it gets women—and men—talking, arguing, and innovating. I hope that it compels us to redefine the roles conflict and competition play in our interactions, to recognize opportunities for growth, and to act upon those opportunities together.

Interview Statistics

100 WOMEN

AGE

UNDER 25	25-30	31-35	36-40	40-45	46-50	51-55	OVER 56
4	19	25	15	9	7	11	10

RACE

WHITE	AFRICAN-AMERICAN	ASIAN	HISPANIC
75	12	6	7

MARITAL STATUS

SINGLE	MARRIED	DIVORCED	DOMESTIC PARTNERSHIP	WIDOWED
35	47	10	5	3

KIDS

YES	NO	STEPCHILDREN
48	49	3

EDUCATION

HIGH SCHOOL OR SOME COLLEGE	COLLEGE DEGREE	GRADUATE DEGREE
13	51	36

PARTICIPATED IN SPORTS GROWING UP

YES	NO	N/A
53	22	25

"I Can't Believe She Did That!" Questionnaire

SECTION ONE

1. WHAT IS YOUR NAME?

2. CONTACT INFORMATION:
   E-MAIL:
   PHONE:
   ADDRESS:

3. AGE?

4. RACE?

5. PLACE OF RESIDENCE?

6. EDUCATION?

7. WHAT IS YOUR MARITAL STATUS?

8. DO YOU HAVE CHILDREN? HOW MANY? HOW OLD ARE THEY?

9. WHAT ARE YOUR JOB AND TITLE? HOW LONG HAVE YOU HELD THE POSITION? WHAT IS YOUR PROFESSIONAL BACK-GROUND? (IF YOU HAVE A RÉSUMÉ, PLEASE ATTACH)

SECTION TWO

1. HOW OFTEN DO YOU WORK DIRECTLY WITH OTHER WOMEN? IN WHAT CAPACITY?

2. DO YOU CONSIDER YOURSELF AN AMBITIOUS PERSON? WHY OR WHY NOT? WHAT ARE YOUR CAREER GOALS?

3. DO YOU CONSIDER YOURSELF A COMPETITIVE PERSON? WHY OR WHY NOT?

4. WHAT ARE YOUR PERSONAL STRENGTHS AT YOUR JOB? DO

YOU THINK THE WOMEN YOU WORK WITH VIEW THESE AS STRENGTHS?

5. HAVE YOU EXPERIENCED COMPETITION WITH ANOTHER WOMAN IN THE WORKPLACE? WHAT HAPPENED? (EXPLAIN) DO YOU WISH THINGS HAD PLAYED OUT DIFFERENTLY? IF SO, HOW?

6. HAVE YOU EXPERIENCED CONFLICT WITH ANOTHER WOMAN IN THE WORKPLACE? HOW WAS IT RESOLVED, IF AT ALL? IF NOT, WHY NOT? (EXPLAIN) DO YOU WISH THINGS HAD PLAYED OUT DIFFERENTLY? IF SO, HOW?

7. HAVE YOU EVER HAD A PROBLEM WITH A FEMALE COLLEAGUE YOU COULDN'T RESOLVE TO YOUR SATISFACTION? (DESCRIBE)

8. HAVE YOU EVER BEHAVED TOWARD A FEMALE COLLEAGUE IN A WAY THAT YOU WEREN'T PROUD OF OR SATISFIED WITH? (EXPLAIN) WHY DO YOU THINK THIS HAPPENED?

SECTION THREE

1. HAVE YOU EVER HAD A FEMALE BOSS? HOW WOULD YOU DESCRIBE YOUR RELATIONSHIP? HOW DID YOU DEAL WITH CONFLICTS?

2. HAVE YOU EVER BEEN A BOSS? HOW WOULD YOU DESCRIBE YOUR RELATIONSHIPS TO YOUR FEMALE EMPLOYEES? HOW DID YOU DEAL WITH CONFLICTS?

3. HAVE YOU HAD ANY FEMALE MENTORS OR ROLE MODELS IN THE WORKPLACE? WHAT WAS THE RELATIONSHIP LIKE? WERE THERE ANY PROBLEMS? (DESCRIBE)

4. HAVE YOU EVER EXPERIENCED RACISM OR DISCRIMINATION FROM ANOTHER WOMAN IN THE WORKPLACE? (DESCRIBE)

5. HOW MUCH OF A RESPONSIBILITY DO YOU THINK WOMEN HAVE TO SUPPORT OTHER WOMEN PROFESSIONALLY? WHY OR WHY NOT? HOW OFTEN DO YOU THINK THIS OCCURS?

6. WHAT DO YOU CONSIDER TO BE THE MAIN CAUSE OF PROBLEMS AMONG WOMEN IN THE WORKPLACE? WHAT, IF ANYTHING, CAN WE DO ABOUT IT?

SECTION FOUR

1. DID YOU PARTICIPATE IN COMPETITIVE SPORTS OR GAMES WITH OTHER GIRLS GROWING UP? DO YOU DO SO NOW? HOW DOES WHAT YOU LEARNED ON THE "PLAYING FIELD" TRANSFER TO THE WORKPLACE, IF AT ALL?

2. WHILE GROWING UP, WHAT MESSAGES DID YOU ABSORB ABOUT COMPETITION AND CONFLICT WITH OTHER GIRLS OR WOMEN? HOW DO YOU THINK THIS TRANSFERS TO THE WORKPLACE, IF AT ALL?

Notes

Introduction: Not the Same Old Story

1. U.S. Department of Labor, Bureau of Labor Statistics, "(Unadj) Civilian Labor Force—Women (1971 to Present)."
2. U.S. Census Bureau, "Income, Poverty, and Health Insurance in the United States: 2003."
3. Catalyst, "Fact Sheet: Women CEOs."
4. Susan Antilla, *Tales from the Boom-Boom Room*, p. 297.

1: Lessons We Learned in Childhood

1. See: Kaj Bjorkqvist and Pirkko Niemela, eds. *Of Mice and Women: Aspects of Female Aggression*; Lyn Mikel Brown and Carol Gilligan, *Meeting at the Crossroads: Women's Psychology and Girls' Development*; Nancy J. Chodorow, *The Reproduction of Mothering: Psychoanalysis and the Sociology of Gender*; Carol Gilligan, Nona P. Lyons, and Trudy J. Hanmer, eds. *Making Connections: The Relational Worlds of Adolescent Girls at Emma Willard School*; Peggy Orenstein, *Schoolgirls: Young Women, Self-Esteem, and the Confidence Gap*; Mary Pipher, *Reviving Ophelia: Saving the Selves of Adolescent Girls*; Rachel Simmons, *Odd Girl Out: The Hidden Culture of Aggression in Girls*.
2. Nancy J. Chodorow, *The Reproduction of Mothering: Psychoanalysis and the Sociology of Gender*, pp. 108–10.
3. Judith Rich Harris, *The Nurture Assumption: Why Children Turn Out the Way They Do*, p. 226.
4. Natalie Angier, *Woman: An Intimate Geography*, p. 264.
5. Eleanor Emmons Maccoby and Carol Nagy Jacklin, *The Psychology of Sex Differences*.
6. Kaj Bjorkqvist and Pirkko Niemela, "New Trends in the Study of Female Aggression" in *Of Mice and Women: Aspects of Female Aggression*.

7. Rachel Simmons, *Odd Girl Out: The Hidden Culture of Aggression in Girls*, p. 21.

8. Kaj Bjorkqvist, Kirsti M. J. Lagerspetz, and Ari Kaukiainen, "Do Girls Manipulate and Boys Fight? Developmental Trends in Regard to Direct and Indirect Aggression," pp. 117–27.

9. Ibid.

10. Carol Gilligan, *In a Different Voice: Psychological Theory and Women's Development*, p. 10.

11. Ibid., p. 9.

12. The Women's Sports Foundation, "Women's Sports Foundation 2002 Annual Report."

13. Peggy Orenstein, *Schoolgirls: Young Women, Self-Esteem, and the Confidence Gap*, pp. xv–xviii.

14. Mary Pipher, *Reviving Ophelia: Saving the Selves of Adolescent Girls*, p. 22.

15. Kaj Bjorkqvist, Kirsti M. J. Lagerspetz, and Ari Kaukiainen, "Do Girls Manipulate and Boys Fight? Developmental Trends in Regard to Direct and Indirect Aggression," p. 124.

16. Rachel Simmons, *Odd Girl Out: The Hidden Culture of Aggression in Girls*, p. 21.

17. See: Peggy Orenstein, *Schoolgirls: Young Women, Self-Esteem, and the Confidence Gap*; Rachel Simmons, *Odd Girl Out: The Hidden Culture of Aggression in Girls*.

18. Kaj Bjorkqvist, "Sex Differences in Physical, Verbal, and Indirect Aggression: A Review of Recent Research."

2: AMBITION, COMPETITION, AND OTHER FOUR-LETTER WORDS

1. Alice Kessler-Harris, *Out to Work: A History of Wage-Earning Women in the United States*, p. 257.

2. Susan Brownmiller, *Femininity*, p. 207; cite Inge K. Broverman, Donald M. Broverman, et al. "Sex-Role Stereotypes and Clinical Judgments of Mental Health," *Journal of Consulting and Clinical Psychology*, Vol. 34, No. 1.

3. U.S. Department of Labor, Bureau of Labor Statistics, "Employment Status of the Civilian Population 16 Years and Over by Sex 1971 to Date."

4. See: Nancy J. Chodorow, *The Reproduction of Mothering: Psychoanalysis and the Sociology of Gender*; Carol Gilligan, *In a Different Voice: Psychological Theory and Women's Development*; Jean Baker Miller, *Toward a New Psychology of Women, Second Edition*.

5. Susan Faludi, *Backlash: The Undeclared War Against Women*, pp. 325–32; Katha Pollit, "Marooned on Gilligan's Island: Are Women Morally Superior to Men?" in *Reasonable Creatures: Essays on Women and Feminism*.

6. Jean Baker Miller, *Toward a New Psychology of Women, Second Edition*.

7. Letty Cottin Pogrebin, "Competing with Women," *Ms.*, 1, July 1972; reprinted by Valerie Miner and Helen E. Longino, eds., *Competition: A Feminist Taboo?*

8. Carol Gilligan, *In a Different Voice: Psychological Theory and Women's Development*, p. 14.

9. Ibid., p. 40.

10. Lisa Belkin, "The Opt-Out Revolution."

11. Linda Tischler, "Where Are the Women?"

12. Peggy Orenstein, *Flux: Women on Sex, Work, Love, Kids, & Life in a Half-Changed World*; cite Jean Lipmen-Blumen, Todd Fryling, Michael C. Henderson, Christine Webster Moore, and Rachel Vecchiotti, "Women in Corporate Leadership: Reviewing a Decade's Research." Special Report, Wellesley, Mass: Center for Research on Women, 1996.

13. Susan Estrich, *Sex & Power*, pp. 235–39.

14. Peggy Orenstein, *Flux: Women on Sex, Work, Love, Kids, & Life in a Half-Changed World*, p. 218; Deborah Tannen, *Talking From 9 to 5: Women and Men at Work*.

15. Internet Movie Database Web site.

16. "Women Who Hate Women," *Dr. Phil*, April 17, 2003.

3: When the Professional Gets Personal

1. Helen Fisher, *The First Sex: The Natural Talents of Women and How They Are Changing the World*, p. 149.

2. Angel Kwolek-Folland, *Incorporating Women: A History of Women and Business in the United States*, pp. 108–9.

3. Arlie Russell Hochschild, *The Time Bind: When Work Becomes Home and Home Becomes Work,* p. xxii.

4. Daniel Goleman, *Emotional Intelligence.*

5. Sigal Barsade, associate professor of management, Wharton School, University of Pennsylvania, personal interview, April 2003.

6. Luise Eichenbaum and Susie Orbach, *Between Women: Love, Envy, and Competition in Women's Friendships,* pp. 94–95.

7. Pepper Schwartz, professor of sociology, University of Washington, personal correspondence, May 2003.

4: Looking Clean, Dealing Dirty

1. Natalie Angier, *Woman: An Intimate Geography,* p. 267.

2. Nancer H. Ballard, "Equal Engagement: Observations on Career Success and Meaning in the Lives of Women Lawyers," p. 26.

3. Sigal Barsade, associate professor of management, Wharton School, University of Pennsylvania, personal interview, April 2003.

4. Dana Crowley Jack, *Behind the Mask: Destruction and Creativity in Women's Aggression,* p. 282.

5. Deborah Tannen, *Talking from 9 to 5: Women and Men at Work,* p. 202.

6. Ibid., p. 179.

7. Pepper Schwartz, professor of sociology, University of Washington, personal correspondence, May 2003.

5: Sex and Beauty on the Job

1. Elaine Carey, "Women Aren't So Nice After All?"

2. Nancy Friday, *Our Looks, Our Lives: Sex, Beauty, Power, and the Need to Be Seen,* p. 519.

3. Robin Morgan, "A Ms. Conversation: Robin Morgan and Madeleine Albright."

4. U.S. Department of Labor, Bureau of Labor Statistics, "Table 11. Employed Persons by Detailed Occupation and Sex, 2002 Annual Averages"; Erika Falk and Erin Grizzard, "The Glass Ceiling Persists: The Third Annual APPC Report on Women Leaders in Communications Companies."

5. Pepper Schwartz, professor of sociology, University of Washington, personal correspondence, May 2003.

6. Alison Overholt, "How to Make Love in the Office."

7. Patricia A. McBroom, *The Third Sex: The New Professional Woman*, p. 237.

6: THE WORK-FAMILY DIVIDE

1. U.S. Department of Labor, Bureau of Labor Statistics, "Employment Status of the Population by Sex, Marital Status, and Presence and Age of Children Under 18, 2002–2003."

2. Families and Work Institute, "The 2002 National Study of the Changing Workforce: Executive Summary."

3. U.S. Department of Labor, Bureau of Labor Statistics, "Employment Status of the Population by Sex, Marital Status, and Presence and Age of Children Under 18, 2002–2003."

4. U.S. General Accounting Office, "Women's Earnings: Work Patterns Partially Explain Difference between Men's and Women's Earnings."

5. Arlie Russell Hochschild, *The Second Shift*, p. 3.

6. Barbara Ehrenreich, "A Grubby Business."

7. U.S. Department of Labor, Bureau of Labor Statistics, "American Time Use Survey."

8. Peggy Orenstein, *Flux: Women on Sex, Work, Love, Kids, & Life in a Half-Changed World*, p. 215.

9. Families and Work Institute, "The 1997 National Study of the Changing Workforce: Executive Summary."

10. Heather Boushey, economist, Center for Economic and Policy Research, personal interview, March 2003.

11. Catherine Kirchmeyer, "Change and Stability in Managers' Gender Roles," p. 937.

12. Families and Work Institute, "The 1997 National Study of the Changing Workforce: Executive Summary."

13. Kate Lorenz, "Are Married People More Successful?"

14. Jean E. Wallace, "The Benefits of Mentoring for Female Lawyers," p. 385.

7: The New Tokenism

1. Alice Kessler-Harris, *Out to Work: A History of Wage-Earning Women in the United States*, p. 314–15.
2. Rosabeth Moss Kanter, *Men and Women of the Corporation*.
3. National Center for Women and Policing, "Equality Denied: The Status of Women in Policing: 2001."
4. U.S. Department of Labor, Bureau of Labor Statistics, "Table 11. Employed Persons by Detailed Occupation and Sex, 2002 Annual Averages."
5. Catalyst, "Quick Takes: Women in Law."
6. Erika Falk and Erin Grizzard, "The Glass Ceiling Persists: The Third Annual APPC Report on Women Leaders in Communications Companies."
7. Rosabeth Moss Kanter, *Men and Women of the Corporation*, p. 316.
8. Kathleen Hall Jamieson, *Beyond the Double Bind: Women and Leadership*, p. 141.
9. Robin Ely, "The Effects of Organizational Demographics and Social Identity on Relationships among Professional Women," p. 203.
10. Rosabeth Moss Kanter, *Men and Women of the Corporation*, p. 201.
11. Catalyst, "Fact Sheet: Women in Financial Services: The Word on the Street."
12. Catherine Kirchmeyer, "Change and Stability in Managers' Gender Roles," p. 929.
13. Catalyst, "Fact Sheet: Women in Financial Services: The Word on the Street."
14. Susan Antilla, *Tales from the Boom-Boom Room*.
15. Linda Tischler, "Where Are the Women?"
16. Gretchen Cook, "Gender-Bias Victories Pay More than Money."
17. Jean E. Wallace, "The Benefits of Mentoring for Female Lawyers," p. 366.
18. Kathleen Hall Jamieson, *Beyond the Double Bind: Women and Leadership*, p. 141.
19. Rosabeth Moss Kanter, *Men and Women of the Corporation*, p. 241–42.

8: Negotiating Race and Class

1. U.S. Department of Labor, Bureau of Labor Statistics, "Household Data Annual Averages: Median Weekly Earnings of Full-time Wage and Salary Workers by Selected Characteristics," 2005.

2. Catalyst, "Fact Sheet: Women of Color in Corporate Management: A Statistical Picture."

3. Jane Prather, professor of sociology, California State University Northridge, personal interview, December 2003.

4. Marita Golden, "White Women at Work," p. 192.

5. Julianne Malveaux, "What You Said About Race," pp. 24–30.

6. Tim Wise, "Is Sisterhood Conditional: White Women and the Rollback of Affirmative Action," pp. 4–5.

7. Ibid., p. 18.

8. Veronica Chambers, *Having it All? Black Women and Success*, p. 112.

9. Ella L. J. Edmondson Bell and Stella M. Nkomo, *Our Separate Ways: Black and White Women and the Struggle for Professional Identity*, p. 246.

10. Toni King, associate professor of black studies and women's studies, Denison University, personal interview, June 2003.

11. Patricia Hill Collins, *Black Feminist Thought: Knowledge, Consciousness, and the Politics of Power*, p. 7.

12. U.S. Department of Labor, Bureau of Labor Statistics, "Table 11. Employed Persons by Detailed Occupation and Sex, 2002 Annual Averages."

13. Barbara Ehrenreich, "A Grubby Business."

14. Elaine Bell Kaplan, "I Don't Do No Windows: Competition Between the Domestic Worker and the Housewife," in *Competition: A Feminist Taboo?*, p. 104.

15. Judith Rollins, *Between Women: Domestics and Their Employers*, pp. 101–4.

16. U.S. Department of Labor, Bureau of Labor Statistics, "Table 11. Employed Persons by Detailed Occupation and Sex, 2002 Annual Averages."

17. Sigal G. Barsade, Andrew J. Ward, Jean D. F. Turner, and Jeffrey A. Sonnenfeld, "To Your Heart's Content: A Model of Affective Diversity in Top Management Teams," p. 808.

18. Teresa Wiltz, "When Sista Ain't Nothin' but a Word," pp. 119–20, 192–96; Taigi Smith, "Girl Fight," pp. 100–4; Toni C. King and S. Alease Ferguson,

"Charting Ourselves: Leadership Development with Black Professional Women," pp. 123–41.

9: BRIDGING THE GENERATION GAP

1. Robin Morgan "A Ms. Conversation: Robin Morgan and Madeleine Albright," p. 44.
2. Gloria Cowan, Charlene Neighbors, Jann DeLaMoreaux, and Catherine Behnke, "Women's Hostility Toward Women," p. 281.
3. Arlie Russell Hochschild, *The Managed Heart: Commercialization of Human Feeling*, pp. 102–3.
4. Catalyst, "Fact Sheet: Women in Financial Services: The Word on the Street."
5. U.S. General Accounting Office, "A New Look at the Glass Ceiling: Where Are the Women?" p. 11.
6. Jean E. Wallace, "The Benefits of Mentoring for Female Lawyers," *Journal of Vocational Behavior*, p. 366.
7. Catalyst, *Mentoring: A Guide to Corporate Programs and Practices*, p. 21; cite Kathy Kram "Phases of a Mentor Relationship," *Academy of Management Journal* 26, No. 4, 1983, pp. 608–25.
8. Steven Pinker, *The Language Instinct*, pp. 413–15.
9. Robin Ely, "The Effects of Organizational Demographics and Social Identity on Relationships Among Professional Women," pp. 222–23.
10. Daniel J. Levinson, *The Seasons of a Woman's Life*, pp. 373–74.
11. Peggy Orenstein, *Flux: Women on Sex, Work, Love, Kids, & Life in a Half-Changed World*, p. 215.
12. Daniel J. Levinson, *The Seasons of a Woman's Life*, pp. 373–74.
13. Catalyst, *Mentoring: A Guide to Corporate Programs and Practices*, p. 10.

10: WOMEN IN GROUPS: CLICKING OR CLIQUING?

1. Daniel Goleman, *Emotional Intelligence*, p. 160.
2. Sigal G. Barsade and Donald E. Gibson, "Group Emotion: A View from Top and Bottom," p. 86; cite A. Sinclair, "The Tyranny of a Team Ideology," *Organizational Studies*, No. 13, 1992, pp. 611–26.
3. Susan Brownmiller, *In Our Time: Memoir of a Revolution*, p. 41.
4. Ibid., p. 62.

5. Janice R. Kelly and Sigal G. Barsade, "Moods and Emotions in Small Groups and Work Teams," pp. 114–15.

6. Sigal Barsade, associate professor of management, Wharton School, University of Pennsylvania, personal interview, April 2003.

7. Rosabeth Moss Kanter, *Men and Women of the Corporation*, pp. 246–48.

8. Susan Porter Benson, *Counter Cultures: Saleswomen, Managers, and Customers in American Department Stores, 1890–1940*, p. 249.

9. Arlie Russell Hochschild, *The Managed Heart: Commercialization of Human Feeling*, p. 130.

10. Robin Ely, "The Effects of Organizational Demographics and Social Identity on Relationships among Professional Women," p. 206.

11. Ibid., p. 230.

11: INSTRUCTIONS FROM THE PLAYING FIELD

1. Mariah Burton Nelson, *Embracing Victory: How Women Can Compete Joyously, Compassionately, and Successfully in the Workplace and on the Playing Field*, p. 10.

2. International Olympic Commission on Women and Sport, "New Record Participation of Women at the Olympic Games."

3. Dr. Carol Otis, Women's Tennis Council, personal interview, July 2003.

4. Jenny R. Susser, sports psychologist, personal interview, March 2003.

5. L. Jon Wertheim, *Venus Envy: Power Games, Teenage Vixens, and Million-Dollar Egos on the Women's Tennis Tour*.

6. "From the Locker Room to the Boardroom: A Nationwide Survey on Sports in the Lives of Women Business Executives."

7. Mariah Burton Nelson, *Embracing Victory: How Women Can Compete Joyously, Compassionately, and Successfully in the Workplace and on the Playing Field*, p. 89.

8. Ibid., p. 179.

9. David de Cremer, "How Do Leaders Promote Cooperation? The Effects of Charisma and Procedural Fairness," pp. 858–66.

12: Coming to Our Own Rescue

1. Lynda Obst, *Hello, He Lied & Other Truths from the Hollywood Trenches*, p. 150.
2. Jean Baker Miller, *Toward a New Psychology of Women, Second Edition*, p. 133.
3. Catalyst, "2003 Catalyst Census of Women Board Directors of the Fortune 500."
4. U.S. General Accounting Office, "A New Look at the Glass Ceiling: Where are the Women?" p. 3.
5. Andrea Coombes, "Nothing Ventured: Women, Like Men, Finding Venture Capital Hard to Come By."
6. Dr. Beth Fisher Yoshida, Associate Director, International Center for Cooperation and Conflict Resolution, Columbia University, personal interview, September 2004.
7. Center for Women's Business Research, "Top Facts About Women-Owned Businesses."
8. Heffernan, Margaret, "The Female CEO ca. 2002," p. 58.
9. Mercer Human Resources, "Worldwide Benefit and Employment Guidelines 2002/2003."
10. Adrienne Rich, "Women and Honor: Some Notes on Lying," in *On Lies, Secrets, and Silence: Selected Prose 1966–78*, p. 186.
11. For more information, see the Department of Labor Web site at http://www.dol.gov/.
12. *King James Bible*, Luke 12:48.
13. Daniel Goleman, *Working with Emotional Intelligence*, p. 189.

Bibliography

Angier, Natalie. *Woman: An Intimate Geography.* New York: Houghton Mifflin, 1999.

Antilla, Susan. *Tales from the Boom-Boom Room.* New York: HarperBusiness, 2003.

Ballard, Nancer H. "Equal Engagement: Observations on Career Success and Meaning in the Lives of Women Lawyers." Wellesley Center for Research on Women Working Paper Series, no. 292, 1998.

Barsade, Sigal G., and Donald E. Gibson. "Group Emotion: A View from Top and Bottom." In *Research on Managing Teams,* vol. 1, JAI Press Inc., 1998, pp. 81–102.

Barsade, Sigal G., Andrew J. Ward, Jean D. F. Turner, and Jeffrey A. Sonnenfeld. "To Your Heart's Content: A Model of Affective Diversity in Top Management Teams." *Administrative Science Quarterly,* (45) 2000: pp. 802–836.

Belkin, Lisa. "The Opt-Out Revolution." *The New York Times Magazine,* October 26, 2003.

Bell, Ella L. J. Edmondson, and Stella M. Nkomo. *Our Separate Ways: Black and White Women and the Struggle for Professional Identity.* Boston: Harvard Business School Press, 2001.

Benson, Susan Porter. *Counter Cultures: Saleswomen, Managers, and Customers in American Department Stores, 1890–1940.* Urbana, Ill.: University of Illinois Press, 1986.

Bjorkqvist, Kaj. "Sex Differences in Physical, Verbal, and Indirect Aggression: A Review of Recent Research." *Sex Roles,* vol. 30, no. 3/4, 1994: pp. 177–87.

Bjorkqvist, Kaj, Kirsti M. J. Lagerspetz, and Ari Kaukiainen. "Do Girls Manipulate and Boys Fight? Developmental Trends in Regard to Direct and Indirect Aggression." *Aggressive Behavior,* (18) 1992: pp. 117–27.

Bjorkqvist, Kaj, and Pirkko Niemela, ed. *Of Mice and Women: Aspects of Female Aggression.* San Diego: Academic Press, 1992.

Brown, Lyn Mikel, and Carol Gilligan. *Meeting at the Crossroads: Women's Psychology and Girls' Development.* Cambridge, Mass.: Harvard University Press, 1992.

Brownmiller, Susan. *Femininity.* New York: Linden Press/Simon & Schuster, 1984.

———. *In Our Time: Memoir of a Revolution.* New York: Dell, 1999.

Carey, Elaine. "Women Aren't So Nice After All?" *The Toronto Star,* online edition at www.thestar.com, February 18, 2004.

Catalyst. *Mentoring: A Guide to Corporate Programs and Practices.* New York: Catalyst, 1993.

———. "Fact Sheet: Women CEOs." New York: Catalyst, October 2003.

———. "Fact Sheet: Women in Financial Services: The Word on the Street." New York: Catalyst, 2001.

———. "Fact Sheet: Women of Color in Corporate Management: A Statistical Picture." New York: Catalyst, 1999.

———. "Quick Takes: Women in Law." Catalyst, March 2004.

———. "2003 Catalyst Census of Women Board Directors of the Fortune 500." New York: Catalyst, 2003.

Center for Women's Business Research. "Top Facts About Women-Owned Businesses." Washington, D.C.: Center for Women's Business Research, 2003.

Chambers, Veronica. *Having it All? Black Women and Success.* New York: Doubleday, 2002.

Chodorow, Nancy J. *The Reproduction of Mothering: Psychoanalysis and the Sociology of Gender.* Berkeley: University of California Press, 1978.

Collins, Patricia Hill. *Black Feminist Thought: Knowledge, Consciousness, and the Politics of Power.* London: HarperCollinsAcademic, 1990.

Cook, Gretchen. "Gender-Bias Victories Pay More than Money." Women's eNews, www.womensenews.org, December 20, 2004.

Coombes, Andrea. "Nothing Ventured: Women, Like Men, Finding Venture Capital Hard to Come By." *CBS Marketwatch,* June 18, 2003.

Cowan, Gloria, Charlene Neighbors, Jann DeLaMoreaux, and Catherine Behnke. "Women's Hostility Toward Women." *Psychology of Women Quarterly,* no. 22, 1998: pp. 267–84.

De Beauvoir, Simone. *The Second Sex*. New York: Alfred A. Knopf, 1952.

de Cremer, David. "How Do Leaders Promote Cooperation? The Effects of Charisma and Procedural Fairness." *Journal of Applied Psychology*, vol. 87, no. 5, 2002: pp. 858–66.

Ehrenreich, Barbara. "A Grubby Business." *The Guardian*, July 12, 2003.

Eichenbaum, Luise, and Susie Orbach. *Between Women: Love, Envy, and Competition in Women's Friendships*. New York: Penguin Books, 1987.

Ely, Robin. "The Effects of Organizational Demographics and Social Identity on Relationships among Professional Women." *Administrative Science Quarterly*, no. 39, 1994: pp. 203–238.

Estrich, Susan. *Sex & Power*. New York: Riverhead Books, 2000.

Evans, Gail. *She Wins, You Win: The Most Important Rule Every Businesswoman Needs to Know*. New York: Gotham Books, 2003.

Falk, Erika, and Erin Grizzard. "The Glass Ceiling Persists: The Third Annual APPC Report on Women Leaders in Communications Companies." The Annenberg Public Policy Center of the University of Pennsylvania, December 22, 2003.

Faludi, Susan. *Backlash: The Undeclared War Against Women*. New York: Crown, 1991.

Families and Work Institute. "The 1997 National Study of the Changing Workforce: Executive Summary." New York: 1997.

———. "The 2002 National Study of the Changing Workforce: Executive Summary." New York: 2002.

Fillion, Kate. *Lip Service: The Truth About Women's Darker Side in Love, Sex, and Friendship*. New York: HarperCollins, 1996.

Fisher, Helen. *The First Sex: The Natural Talents of Women and How They Are Changing the World*. New York: Random House, 1999.

Friday, Nancy. *Our Looks, Our Lives: Sex, Beauty, Power, and the Need to Be Seen*. New York: HarperCollins, 1996.

"From the Locker Room to the Boardroom: A Nationwide Survey on Sports in the Lives of Women Business Executives." OppenheimerFunds, February 2002.

Gilligan, Carol. *In a Different Voice: Psychological Theory and Women's Development*. Cambridge, Mass.: Harvard University Press, 1993.

Gilligan, Carol, Nona P. Lyons, and Trudy J. Hanmer, ed. *Making Connections: The Relational Worlds of Adolescent Girls at Emma Willard School.* Cambridge, Mass.: Harvard University Press, 1990.

Golden, Marita. "White Women at Work," *Essence*, October 2002, pp. 190–98.

Goleman, Daniel. *Emotional Intelligence: Why It Can Matter More Than IQ.* New York: Bantam Books, 1995.

———. *Working with Emotional Intelligence.* New York: Bantam Books, 1998.

Harris, Judith Rich. *The Nurture Assumption: Why Children Turn Out the Way They Do.* New York: Touchstone, 1998.

Heffernan, Margaret. "The Female CEO ca. 2002." *Fast Company*, issue 61, August 2002: p. 58.

Heim, Pat, and Susan Murphy, with Susan K. Golant. *In the Company of Women: Turning Workplace Conflict into Powerful Alliances.* New York: Tarcher/Putnam, 2001.

Hochschild, Arlie Russell. *The Managed Heart: Commercialization of Human Feeling.* Berkeley: University of California Press, 1983.

———. *The Second Shift.* New York: Avon Books, 1989.

———. *The Time Bind: When Work Becomes Home and Home Becomes Work.* 2nd ed. New York: Henry Holt, 2000.

International Olympic Commission on Women and Sport, "New Record Participation of Women at the Olympic Games." August 19, 2004, available online at http://www.olympic.org/uk/organisation/commissions/women/full_story_uk.asp?id=1017/.

Internet Movie Database, available online at http://www.imdb.com/.

Jack, Dana Crowley. *Behind the Mask: Destruction and Creativity in Women's Aggression.* Cambridge, Mass.: Harvard University Press, 1999.

Jamieson, Kathleen Hall. *Beyond the Double Bind: Women and Leadership.* New York: Oxford University Press, 1995.

Kanter, Rosabeth Moss. *Men and Women of the Corporation.* New York: Basic Books, 1993.

Kelly, Janice R., and Sigal G. Barsade. "Moods and Emotions in Small Groups and Work Teams." *Organizational Behavior and Human Decision Processes*, vol. 86, no. 1, September 2001: pp. 99–130.

Kessler-Harris, Alice. *Out to Work: A History of Wage-Earning Women in the United States*. 20th ed. New York: Oxford University Press, 2003.

King, Toni C., and S. Alease Ferguson. "Charting Ourselves: Leadership Development with Black Professional Women." *National Women's Studies Association Journal*, vol. 13, no. 2, Summer 2001: pp. 123–41.

King James Bible.

Kirchmeyer, Catherine. "Change and Stability in Managers' Gender Roles." *Journal of Applied Psychology*, vol. 87, no. 5, 2002: pp. 929–39.

Kwolek-Folland, Angel. *Incorporating Women: A History of Women and Business in the United States*. New York: Twayne Publishers/Simon & Schuster Macmillan, 1998.

Levinson, Daniel J. *The Seasons of a Woman's Life*. New York: Knopf, 1996.

Lorenz, Kate. "Are Married People More Successful?" CareerBuilder.com, 2004. Available online at: http://msn.careerbuilder.com/Custom/MSN/CareerAd vice/413.htm/.

Maccoby, Eleanor Emmons, and Carol Nagy Jacklin. *The Psychology of Sex Differences*. Stanford: Stanford University Press, 1974.

Malveaux, Julianne. "What You Said About Race." *Ms.*, May/June 1992: pp. 24–30.

McBroom, Patricia A. *The Third Sex: The New Professional Woman*. New York: William Morrow and Company, 1986.

Mercer Human Resources. "Worldwide Benefit and Employment Guidelines 2002/2003." Mercer Human Resources Consulting: Melbourne, Australia, 2003.

Miller, Jean Baker. *Toward a New Psychology of Women: Second Edition*. Boston: Beacon Press, 1986.

Miner, Valerie, and Helen E. Longino, ed. *Competition: A Feminist Taboo?* New York: The Feminist Press, 1987.

Morgan, Robin. "A Ms. Conversation: Robin Morgan and Madeleine Albright." *Ms.*, Spring 2004: pp. 43–46.

National Center for Women and Policing. "Equality Denied: The Status of Women in Policing: 2001." National Center for Women and Policing, a division of the Feminist Majority Foundation, 2002.

Nelson, Mariah Burton. *Embracing Victory: How Women Can Compete Joyously,*

Compassionately, and Successfully in the Workplace and on the Playing Field. New York: William Morrow and Company, 1998.

Obst, Lynda. *Hello, He Lied & Other Truths from the Hollywood Trenches.* New York: Little Brown, 1996.

Orenstein, Peggy. *Flux: Women on Sex, Work, Love, Kids, & Life in a Half-Changed World.* New York: Doubleday, 2000.

———. *Schoolgirls: Young Women, Self-Esteem, and the Confidence Gap.* New York: Doubleday, 1994.

Overholt, Alison. "How to Make Love in the Office." *Fast Company,* issue 65, December 2002: p. 60.

Pinker, Steven. *The Language Instinct.* New York: William Morrow and Company, 1994.

Pipher, Mary. *Reviving Ophelia: Saving the Selves of Adolescent Girls.* New York: Ballantine, 1995.

Pollit, Katha. *Reasonable Creatures: Essays on Women and Feminism.* New York: Vintage Books, 1995.

Rich, Adrienne. *On Lies, Secrets, and Silence: Selected Prose 1966–78.* New York: W. W. Norton & Company, 1979.

Rollins, Judith. *Between Women: Domestics and Their Employers.* Philadelphia: Temple University Press, 1985.

Simmons, Rachel. *Odd Girl Out: The Hidden Culture of Aggression in Girls.* New York: Harcourt, 2002.

Small, Linda Lee. "What White Women Are Really Saying About Us!" *Essence,* March 2003: pp. 152–55, 198.

Smith, Taigi. "Girl Fight." *Honey,* June/July 2003: pp. 100–104.

Tanenbaum, Leora. *Catfight: Rivalries Among Women—from Diets to Dating, from the Boardroom to the Delivery Room.* New York: Seven Stories Press, 2002.

Tannen, Deborah. *Talking From 9 to 5: Women and Men at Work.* New York: Avon Books, 1994.

———. *You Just Don't Understand: Women and Men in Conversation.* New York: Ballantine Books, 1990.

Tischler, Linda. "Where Are the Women?" *Fast Company,* issue 79, February 2004: p. 52.

U.S. Census Bureau. "Income, Poverty, and Health Insurance in the United States: 2003." August 2004.

U.S. Department of Labor, Bureau of Labor Statistics. "American Time Use Survey." 2003.

———. "Employment Status of the Civilian Population 16 Years and Over by Sex 1971 to Date." 2002.

———. "Employment Status of the Population by Sex, Marital Status, and Presence and Age of Children Under 18, 2002–2003." April 2004.

———. "Household Data Annual Averages: Median Weekly Earnings of Full-time Wage and Salary Workers by Selected Characteristics." 2005.

———. "Table 11. Employed Persons by Detailed Occupation and Sex, 2002 Annual Averages." 2002.

———. "(Unadj) Civilian Labor Force—Women (1971 to Present)." Series ID: LNU01000002, 2005.

U.S. General Accounting Office. "A New Look at the Glass Ceiling: Where are the Women," January 2002.

———. "Women's Earnings: Work Patterns Partially Explain Difference between Men's and Women's Earnings." October 2003.

Wallace, Jean E. "The Benefits of Mentoring for Female Lawyers." *Journal of Vocational Behavior,* no. 58, 2001: pp. 366–91.

Wertheim, L. Jon. *Venus Envy: Power Games, Teenage Vixens, and Million-Dollar Egos on the Women's Tennis Tour.* New York: HarperCollins, 2001.

Wiltz, Teresa. "When Sista Ain't Nothin' but a Word." *Essence,* May 1999: pp. 119–20, 192–26.

Wise, Tim. "Is Sisterhood Conditional: White Women and the Rollback of Affirmative Action." *National Women's Studies Association Journal,* vol. 10, no. 3, Fall 1998: pp. 1–26.

The Women's Sports Foundation. "Women's Sports Foundation 2002 Annual Report." 2002.

"Women Who Hate Women." *Dr. Phil,* Harpo Inc., April 17, 2003.